Friendship, Descent and Alliance in Africa

Integration and Conflict Studies
Max Planck Institute for Social Anthropology, Halle/Saale

Series Editor: Günther Schlee, Director at the Max Planck Institute for Social Anthropology

Editorial Board: Brian Donahoe (Max Planck Institute for Social Anthropology), John Eidson (Max Planck Institute for Social Anthropology), Peter Finke (University of Zurich), Joachim Görlich (Max Planck Institute for Social Anthropology), Jacqueline Knörr (Max Planck Institute for Social Anthropology), Bettina Mann (Max Planck Institute for Social Anthropology), Stephen Reyna (University of Manchester)

Assisted by: Cornelia Schnepel and Viktoria Zeng (Max Planck Institute for Social Anthropology)

Volume 1
How Enemies are Made – Towards a Theory of Ethnic and Religious Conflicts
Günther Schlee

Volume 2
Changing Identifications and Alliances in North-East Africa
Vol.I: Ethiopia and Kenya
Edited by Günther Schlee and Elizabeth E. Watson

Volume 3
Changing Identifications and Alliances in North-East Africa
Vol.II: Sudan, Uganda and the Ethiopia-Sudan Borderlands
Edited by Günther Schlee and Elizabeth E. Watson

Volume 4
Playing Different Games: The Paradox of Anywaa and Nuer Identification Strategies in the Gambella Region, Ethiopia
Dereje Feyissa

Volume 5
Who Owns the Stock? Collective and Multiple Forms of Property in Animals
Edited by Anatoly M. Khazanov and Günther Schlee

Volume 6
Irish/ness is All Around Us: Language Revivalism and the Culture of Ethnic Identity in Northern Ireland
Olaf Zenker

Volume 7
Variations on Uzbek Identity: Strategic Choices, Cognitive Schemas and Political Constraints in Identification Processes
Peter Finke

Volume 8
Domesticating Youth: The Youth Bulge and its Socio-Political Implications in Tajikstan
Sophie Roche

Volume 9
Creole Identity in Postcolonial Indonesia
Jacqueline Knörr

Volume 10
Friendship, Descent and Alliance in Africa: Anthropological Perspectives
Edited by Martine Guichard, Tilo Grätz and Youssouf Diallo

Friendship, Descent and Alliance in Africa

Anthropological Perspectives

Edited by
Martine Guichard, Tilo Grätz and Youssouf Diallo

berghahn
NEW YORK · OXFORD
www.berghahnbooks.com

Published in 2014 by
Berghahn Books
www.berghahnbooks.com

© 2014 Martine Guichard, Tilo Grätz and Youssouf Diallo

All rights reserved. Except for the quotation of short passages for the purposes of criticism and review, no part of this book may be reproduced in any form or by any means, electronic or mechanical, including photocopying, recording, or any information storage and retrieval system now known or to be invented, without written permission of the publisher.

Library of Congress Cataloging-in-Publication Data
Friendship, descent, and alliance in Africa : anthropological perspectives / edited by Martine Guichard, Tilo Grätz and Youssouf Diallo.
　pages cm. — (Integration and conflict studies ; volume 10)
Includes bibliographical references and index.
ISBN 978-1-78238-286-7 (hardback : alk. paper) —
ISBN 978-1-78238-287-4 (ebook)
　1. Friendship—Africa, Sub-Saharan. 2. Kinship—Africa, Sub-Saharan. 3. Africa, Sub-Saharan—Social life and customs. I. Guichard, Martine. II. Grätz, Tilo. III. Diallo, Youssouf. IV. Series: Integration and conflict studies ; v. 10.
BF575.F66F745 2014
302.340967—dc23

2013029907

British Library Cataloguing in Publication Data
A catalogue record for this book is available from the British Library

Printed on acid-free paper

ISBN: 978-1-78238-286-7 hardback
ISBN: 978-1-78238-287-4 ebook

Contents

Foreword   vii
    Günther Schlee

Acknowledgements   viii

Introduction   1
    Martine Guichard

Part I. Friendship, Kinship and Age

Chapter 1. Where Are Other People's Friends Hiding? Reflections on Anthropological Studies of Friendship   19
    Martine Guichard

Chapter 2. Comradeship and the Transformation of Alliance Theory among the Maasai: Shifting the Focus from Descent to Peer-Group Loyalty   42
    Paul Spencer

Part II. Friendship and Ethnicity

Chapter 3. Friendship Networks in Southwestern Ethiopia   57
    Wolde Gossa Tadesse and Martine Guichard

Chapter 4. Friendship and Spiritual Parenthood among the Moose and the Fulbe in Burkina Faso   74
    Mark Breusers

Chapter 5. Labour Migration and Moral Dimensions of Interethnic Friendships: The Case of Young Gold Miners in Benin (West Africa)   97
    Tilo Grätz

Part III. Friendship, Politics and Urbanity

Chapter 6. Friendship and Kinship among Merchants and Veterans in Mali   119
    Richard L. Warms

Chapter 7. 'Down-to-Earth': Friendship and a National Elite Circle in Botswana   133
    Richard Werbner

Chapter 8. Negotiating Friendship and Kinship in a Context of
　　Violence: The Case of the Tuareg during the Upheaval in Mali from
　　1990 to 1996　　　　　　　　　　　　　　　　　　　　　　　145
　　　Georg Klute

Afterword. Friendship in a World of Force and Power　　　　　　161
　　　Stephen P. Reyna

Bibliography　　　　　　　　　　　　　　　　　　　　　　　　180

Notes on Contributors　　　　　　　　　　　　　　　　　　　200

Index　　　　　　　　　　　　　　　　　　　　　　　　　　　202

Foreword

This book is about interactions among different types of relationship in a comparative setting – a rather complex topic. Because the English concepts for the types of relationship at issue –friendship, descent and alliance – cannot be assumed to be universally valid and precisely translatable, another difficult task arises: seeking rough equivalents of such terms in other languages and exploring their meaning in different cultural settings.

Social cohesion is what makes a society out of a mere collection of people. But there is no social cohesion as such. It comes in different shapes. A closer look reveals that there are several binding forces of different kinds at work. Yet, although social cohesion should be at the core of what sociology, social anthropology or any social science is about, the differentiation and interpenetration of these binding forces has rarely been studied in a systematic way. Different scholars have specialized in the study either of kinship or of friendship, possibly because the former was associated with 'traditional, kinship-based societies' and the latter with modern ones – a dichotomy which hardly stands scrutiny.

I congratulate the editors for addressing a core issue in research on 'Integration and Conflict' (the title of this series and the name of the department of which I am the director), and I feel proud to be associated with this book in ways that reflect some of the binding forces discussed in the various chapters. With the editors and many of the authors, I am linked through ties of friendship and alliance, often as a result of my being a (former) supervisor, a (former) employer or an occasional host. To this volume, our common descendant, our many-mothered and many-fathered brainchild, I wish a vigorous life on the book market.

Günther Schlee
Max Planck Institute for Social Anthropology

Acknowledgements

We would like to thank the contributors to this book for sharing their expertise on friendship with us and for supplying material showing that friendship deserves to be explored and theorized seriously, as has been the case with kinship. We greatly appreciate the spirit of amity that has accompanied our exchanges with the authors who joined forces with us in providing evidence that friendship, a still neglected topic in anthropological research, is best understood in conjunction with kinship, its much more favoured counterpart.

We are also grateful to the members of the editorial board of the series 'Integration and Conflict Studies' at the Max Planck Institute for Social Anthropology, and to the anonymous reviewer for Berghahn Books, for their helpful suggestions regarding the contributions compiled in this volume.

Last but not least, we are particularly thankful to Günther Schlee, the director of the Department 'Integration and Conflict' at the above-mentioned Max Planck Institute in Halle/Saale, Germany, for his support, his generosity in sharing ideas and his unwavering encouragement.

Martine Guichard
Tilo Grätz
Youssouf Diallo
June 2013

Introduction

Martine Guichard

Friendship, descent and alliance are basic forms of relatedness that have received unequal attention in social anthropology. To this day, friendship still remains understudied, even if the subject has become more fashionable over the last three decades.[1] Recent research has been mainly conducted in Western countries,[2] probably paying less heed to other parts of the world because of the premise that the room left for friendship to flourish as an extra-kin relationship is inversely proportional to the importance of kinship as a factor structuring community. This premise is variously discussed in the present volume which shows that the relationship between friendship and kinship is more complex than commonly assumed in the literature, while offering new insights into the ways in which friendship is conceptualized, realized and used in diverse sub-Saharan African settings.

In these settings, as elsewhere, the development of friendships follows certain rules and is constrained by broader relationships over which individual actors have little control (e.g., Allan 1979; Adams and Allan 1998b). Among the sets of broader relationships regularly taken into account in recent studies are those based on social class, gender, age and occupation. This is not to say that ethnicity, religion or, even more basically, formal features of kinship organization are not recognized to play a role in patterning friendship; they all are. Nonetheless, it is ironical that the last set of factors belongs to those particularly neglected by research. Given that the worlds of kinship and friendship are already premised to be closely interrelated at a higher level, the inverse situation could have been expected. By including analyses focusing on how friendship patterns are influenced by formal features of kinship organization, this book attempts to fill a gap in the existing literature.

The very fact that friendships never occur completely randomly, but are also structured by external factors certainly contributes to make them an interesting field of study. Indeed, there is no denying that both friendship practices and friendship discourses convey messages about the society in which they are generated. Taken together, the most remarkable thing about these practices and discourses is thus that they contain information about principles of social organization, modes of production and economic, political, belief and value systems. Given this, it is clear that friendship is a phenomenon which merits being explored and theorized with the same seriousness as that of kinship. As reflected in the first part of the title of this book, this awareness is widely shared by the contributors to the present volume which enlarges the basis for comparative studies of friendship and itself comprises several of such studies.

Despite a wide diversity of local contexts and regardless of the forms of friendship they are more specifically referring to, the chapters that follow – and which will not systematically be presented below according to their order of appearance in this book – largely allow for cross-references.[3] As suggested above, they all demonstrate that friendships point beyond themselves and are much more than an extra sweetening everyday life. Second, they recurrently deal with issues of change while attempting, each in their own way, to reassess the relationship between friendship and kinship. As a whole, they aim to provide an incentive for reconsidering friendship in sub-Saharan societies and to contribute to the current debate on new paths for future research.

Friendship and Structures

Friendship is a socially constructed form of relationship governed by norms serving as cultural scripts specifying from among whom to choose friends, how to act toward them and what is appropriate to expect from them. These scripts may vary across historical periods and societies. As increasingly stressed in the literature (e.g., Silver 1989; Adams and Allan 1998b), friendships are the product of the times and the spaces in which they occur. However, the contemporary call for contextualization of friendship is a return to placing these relationships within a system of structures. To be sure, the structures which are now increasingly elaborated upon are of a somewhat different nature than those dealt with in friendship research up to the 1960s. But the approach in itself is largely analogous to that privileged in early accounts of non-Western friendships and in early attempts to discuss these friendships comparatively.

One of these early attempts was that made by Eisenstadt (1956) with a focus on highly formalized or institutionalized forms of friendship – including phenomena such as 'best friendship', 'blood-brotherhood', trading partnership and godparenthood. Eisenstadt, whose main objective is to identify social conditions conducive to the development of institutionalized friendships, hypothesizes that the latter mostly arise in predominantly particularistic societies, i.e., 'kinship-' and 'caste-based' societies. Such societies are notably associated with social groups putting a great emphasis on the principle of diffuse solidarity. By virtue of this emphasis, ample latitude is left within these groups for the manipulation of the principle of diffuse solidarity which can easily be referred to by certain people to make claims that may go beyond what others consider to be their legitimate rights. Since the groups constituent of particularistic societies (clans, lineages, castes, etc.) are supposed to exhibit a very strong degree of internal solidarity, they also appear especially prone to see their own obligations of internal solidarity come into conflict with various exigencies of co-operation with one another.

In this situation, intergroup friendships can be expected to be largely fraught with ambivalence and caution. An important means to minimize this tendency is indeed to strongly set such friendships within a framework of diffuse solidarity and thus to endow them with a kinship-like character. This point is stressed by Eisenstadt who posits that the social function of institutionalized friendships is to 'mitigate some of the tensions and strains of predominantly particularistic societies' (Eisenstadt 1956: 92) and consequently to alleviate some of the problems of integration inherent to those societies.[4]

Another early attempt to analyse non-Western friendships from a comparative point of view was that of Cohen (1961) who proposes a typology of both friendships and societies. Besides classifying the latter along a continuum of four degrees of solidarity, Cohen distinguishes between four types of friendships associated with differing degrees of commitment and emotional propinquity between friends. In addition, he seeks to correlate particular types of friendships with particular kinds of societies. Inalienable friendships are expected to be found in 'maximally solidary' societies where descent groups are largely localized and the component families of these groups are 'socially, physically and emotionally inbred within their respective societal nuclei *vis-à-vis* other groupings' (Cohen 1961: 315). Close friendships are inferred to be characteristic of 'solidary-fissile' societies where 'ties and alignments of kinship are not solidified into corporate groups' (1961: 315), and where solidarity is split between kinship group and locality. Casual friendships are supposed to prevail in 'non-nucleated' societies, where isolated, solidary nuclear families are bounded loosely together. Finally, expedient friendships are presumed to predominate in individuated social structures where there is an emphasis on competitive individuated wealth and relatively little solidarity even in the nuclear family.

Furthermore, Cohen is particularly interested in demonstrating how specific cultures of community solidarity help to shape differing emotional predispositions of individuals to share, give and trust within friendship. Despite some weaknesses,[5] Cohen's study remains relevant because it stresses that the institutionalization of friendships does not necessarily represent a mechanism having a strain-mitigating effect. In contrast to Eisenstadt (1956), he notes that it can generate conflicts of loyalties which many societies strive to minimize by narrowing down the range and extent of institutionalized friendships their members can have both within and outside their own kinship social groupings.[6] As pointed out by Cohen (1961: 376), in order not to pose a threat for the society in which they occur, such friendships, especially those which ideally cannot be withdrawn, need to be rather strictly limited in number.

In certain respects, Cohen's analysis of friendship entails assumptions reminiscent of those formulated by Tönnies (1968 [1887]) with regard to Western societies. Tönnies does not just associate industrialization and urbanization with a decline of *Gemeinschaft,* i.e., communities based on kinship, friendship and neighbourhood. He also postulates that the capacity to form strong emotional bonds with friends is at the highest in settings where kinship constitutes an important principle of social and economic organization. His corollary view that the Industrial Revolution, with its emphasis on efficiency and task-oriented behaviour, led to a weakening of the importance of friendship has notably been challenged by Silver (1989, 1990, 1997). Building on writings of A. Smith (2002 [1759]) and other social theorists of the Enlightenment period, Silver stresses that the rise of commercial society in the eighteenth century already promoted the flourishing of friendships founded on mutual sympathy and affection as well as a dissociation of friendship from calculations of interest and instrumentality. According to him, the development of impersonal markets in products and services was of paramount significance for the emergence of the modern ideal of friendship as a relationship 'grounded in the irreplaceable qualities of partners – their "true" or "real" selves, defined and valued independently of their place in public systems of power, utility and esteem' (1989: 274). In this ideal, friendship is a freely chosen relationship which is relegated to the personal/private sector of social life and 'diminished in moral quality if friends consciously monitor the balance of exchange between them' (1990: 4777).[7]

However, it is important to recall that instrumentality and affectivity are not mutually exclusive categories. Not only can they be seen as poles of a continuum, but also as basic aspects of friendship. Indeed, even friendships based on mutual liking have their instrumentalities. The provision of emotional support is just one of them and a form of exchange that is not less useful or functional than economic support. Taking into account the potentiality of interactions with friends to increase one's ability to acquire new resources, it can be stressed that friendship ties constitute a 'social capital' (Bourdieu 1986 [1983]). In practice, they help to solve a variety of problems and can be serviced by mobilizing diverse sectors of one's personal network (bonds of kinship, acquaintanceship,[8] etc.). Such servicing strategies are certainly widespread within friendships that are multistranded in content. As shown by some proponents of social network analysis, they also seem to be particularly pronounced among actors with dense personal networks and whose separate networks show a high degree of cross-linkages (e.g., Boissevain 1974). This kind of network is well known for having both advantages and disadvantages. On the one hand, its structural features make it possible to get more help through the intermediation of friends than those of low-density networks. On the other hand, they may compel one to do more for a friend than one would actually like to do.

In the literature it is often noted that friendship networks are largely composed of individuals who are socially similar. To begin with, it is regularly emphasized that friends tend to share the same socioeconomic status. Taking this tendency into consideration, it can be supposed that in many cases the informal exchanges of services occurring within friendships reinforce rather than weaken class differences in resources (e.g., Eve 2002: 407). This issue is discussed in the last chapter of this volume by Stephen Reyna who presents a 'string being theory' concerning the relationship between friendship and power. Within this theory, it is both stressed that friendship enhances actors' power by increasing the force or resources (people, tools, knowledge) available to them and that the resources obtained through friendship themselves, when exercised, allow actors to accumulate powers. In his analysis of empirical data from various contributions to this book and from external sources dealing with African societies and the United States, Reyna points out that among affluent people friendships provide access to additional force resources allowing them 'to continue the power of acquiring wealth' and of maintaining an elevated class position. Among the poor, in contrast, friendships help to acquire the power of having *enough* to survive and for households to get by (see also Liebow 1967; Stack 1974).

But let us return briefly to the dimensions that are seen as important with regard to status similarity in friendship. As frequently mentioned in research, these dimensions are culturally and socially constructed and much revealing about the wider structures in which friendships are actually embedded. Thus, in class-stratified societies there is a strong social pressure to avert friendships between individuals of differing class backgrounds. In age-stratified societies, friendships will be particularly likely to be homogenous in terms of age. In societies with strong gender hierarchies and/or sex-segregated social spheres, friendships between men and women will be highly discouraged. However, it is well recognized that, in a 'gender-differentiated' world, friendship practices and friendship discourses convey messages about power relations between the sexes, normative gender roles and ideologies of masculinity and femininity (e.g., Uhl 1991; Nardi 1992; Walker 1994; Dyson 2010). In this volume, this issue is addressed by Martine Guichard (Chapter 1) who also touches on gender differentials in the sociocultural availability of friendships. These differentials seem to have been especially overestimated until the 1980s due to the long tendency to focus simply on male friendships in research. Meanwhile, male friendships are increasingly described as being more activity orientated and less person orientated or less centred on self-disclosure than female friendships.[9] However, and as stressed by Wright (1982), the associated portrayal of male friendships as being primarily 'side by side' relationships and that of female friendships as rather being 'face to face' relationships should be treated with caution. One reason for this is of methodological nature. Indeed, such a contrast is often emphasized by scholars having actually paid unequal attention to one of these two forms of same-sex friendships in the course of their empirical research. In practice, differences between male and female friendships frequently decrease as the strength and duration of the friendships increase (Wright 1982: 19).

The question of differences between male and female friendships will be further dealt with in the next section which is especially concerned with the relationship between friendship and kinship. Before reexamining this relationship, it may be worth to recall that interethnic friendships are often a sensitive topic in contexts in which ethnicity is an important axis of self-identification and of social construction of otherness. In these contexts, interethnic friendships are frequently described as being principally inferior to intraethnic ones. Such a characterization does not necessarily account for the fact that members of different ethnic groups have different concepts of friendship. In many instances, it points both to similarities in friendship concepts and to shared ideas about the relevance of issues of exogamy and endogamy for doing friendship.

Friendship and Kinship

As a particular type of social relationship, friendship is often differentiated from kinship along the lines of achievement versus ascription and terminability versus permanence. First, the status of being a friend is rarely assigned at birth; it is usually acquired later in life and is more easily revocable, once allocated, than that of kin. Second, friendship is frequently stressed to be an elective relationship predicated on a positive evaluation of the other and a shared sense of compatibility, the maintenance of which requires a greater amount of relational 'work' than that of kinship ties. The future of friendship bonds remains all the more uncertain since the feelings, on the basis of which the relationships are established, have to be more regularly experienced, demonstrated and renewed in order for these relationships to endure.

In practice, however, the understanding that friendship and kinship can be contrasted with each other in certain respects regularly goes hand in hand with the understanding that they nevertheless should not be simply treated as polar opposites. These two kinds of relationships are largely premised to have overlapping dimensions and it is widely recognized that some of the attributes of friendship, such as affection, trust and loyalty, should also be part and parcel of kin relationships. These points are taken up in this volume by Guichard (Chapter 1) who adopts a cross-cultural perspective and shows how a theory of size is possible with regard to degrees of overlapping between kinship and friendship. While dealing with the question of which kin are more likely to become 'friends', she attempts to do justice to the fact that the probability that personal relationships between relatives will qualitatively take on attributes of friendship is both structurally determined and dependent on the distinctive personal traits of individuals. The matching of these traits can even be a precondition for becoming aware of genealogical interconnections. Indeed, people do not always know that they are related by kinship. In many cases, it is because they are bound by friendship that they come to realize that they are also genealogically linked. Whether this kind of dynamic can be empirically retraced during fieldwork or not, it should not be taken for granted that all relationships phrased in the language of kinship are primarily ones of kinship. On numerous occasions, this language is metaphorically used and extended to friends, a practice supported by the widespread ideal that kinship bonds should share certain of the properties associated with friendships.

Yet, the spectre of kinship haunts friendship in multiple ways. To begin with, it is clear that institutions associated with kinship such as rules of inheritance and rules of postnuptial residence have consequences for friendship ties all over the world (Chapter 1). The same holds true for incest taboos which, given their importance in the constitution of kinship, can be assumed to play an important role in conceptualizations of friendship as another form of social relationship. As emphasized by Paul Spencer (Chapter 2), changes occurring in the domain of clanship and descent also have repercussions for friendships. Among the Kenyan and Tanzanian Maasai, friendships between men often grow out of experiences made after having become initiated as junior warriors and during the time they live apart from their families with their own age mates. During the years they spend together in villages separated from their kin, the junior warriors get the opportunity to bond with each other at the interpersonal level. They also increasingly become committed to an ethos of collective comradeship. This ethos, which condemns overt displays of intense, dyadic friendships, gained significance with the decline of clanship in the second half of the nineteenth century. The decreasing emphasis on clan and descent ties led to a transformation of the role of age-set membership with regard to the application of incest and exogamy rules. This role increased and by now incest and marriage avoidance among the Maasai concerns age-set 'daughters' more than clan 'sisters'. As pointed out by Spencer, such a configurational type involving the exchange of women as a binding force between different generations rather than between different descent groups was neglected by Lévi-Strauss in his alliance theory (1969 [1949]).

Nonetheless, for Lévi-Strauss, alliance is fundamentally an exchange of women between groups. More basically, however, it is an exchange of women between men and through men. The latter view has been repeatedly criticized and since the 1980s a number of scholars have shown that women are more actively involved in the negotiation of arranged marriages than was acknowledged by Lévi-Strauss (e.g., Strathern 1984; De Sousberghe 1986: 36 ff.; Carsten 1997; Boddy 2007, 2009). Further illustrations of this involvement can certainly be found in connection with cases of the transformation of friendship into kinship.

The marriages through which friendship is transformed into kinship encompass different constellations. Among the marriage constellations discussed in the following chapters is that involving children of friends. As indicated in the present volume, an ideal of friendship in diverse local settings is that it culminates in matrimonial unions between the offspring of the parties involved. How far such an ideal can be realized in practice is a question partly connected to the issue of milk kinship in various societies.[10] This form of kinship, which is created through the ingestion of breast milk from the same woman, is well known for conceptually generating a sibling bond between the children of the nurse and the other women's children having been co-suckled by her. It is also reputed for implying a prohibition of marriage between all these children. Taking into account the logic of the transmission of milk kinship and the gender-specific ability of female friends to suckle each other's children, it can assumed that – in societies cultivating such an institution – friendships between women are less likely to be cemented by matrimonial alliances in the next generation than friendships between men. But there are other grounds for stressing the role of gender in the realization of the above-mentioned ideal. Especially in patrilineal societies, women have a weaker power position than men. Hence they have greater reasons to fear that their own friendships would be negatively affected by dissensions between their children in case that these were to be linked by marriage. Drawing on her empirical findings from northern Cameroon, Guichard is inclined to believe that in a large number of patrilineal societies one difference between female and male friendships indeed lies in the capacity of these friendships to actually engender matrimonial alliances and thus to produce affinal and consanguineal relationships (see also Guichard 2007a).

The possibility for friendships to create kinship ties is dependent on degrees of preference for either group exogamy or group endogamy. In societies with extended exogamy rules and semicomplex systems of marriage alliances, matrimonial unions between children of intraethnic friends tend to be discouraged.[11] The inverse is the case in societies displaying a firmer preference for in-group marriages. However, the probability that friendships will result in matrimonial alliances in the next generation also varies according to the extent to which friendships can principally give rise to bonds of godparenthood. As long stressed in the literature, such bonds resemble those of milk kinship in the sense that they generally entail a marriage prohibition in the children generation. This kind of prohibition tends to be of lesser significance for forms of spiritual kinship related to religious representations which are still often discussed under the heading of ancestor worship. One of these forms of spiritual kinship is described by Mark Breusers (Chapter 4) in his comparative study of friendship among Moose (Mossi) agriculturalists and Fulbe agro-pastoralists in Burkina Faso. Both groups view friendship as implying symmetry and reciprocity. Furthermore, they both stress that the exchange of women constitutes the apex of good friendships. But only the Moose possess an institution of spiritual kinship stressing the participative role of deceased ancestors in the process of procreation and giving life. The relationships falling into this field of pseudo-kinship which involve Fulbe go hand in hand with the attribution of a sort of in-laws' status. The Fulbe who attain this status are those who have successfully provided help in solving fecundity problems among Moose. The latter form of interaction also plays an important role in the formation and consolidation of interethnic friendships. The same holds true for cattle entrustment and host-guest relations.

Another field of interactions which merits attention in this context is that involving institutionalized joking. Joking relationships are, indeed, not just common among specific categories of relatives – such as grandparents and grandchildren, maternal uncle and uterine nephew, cross-cousins – who are customarily allowed to transgress normal rules of good behaviour, teasing and 'insulting' one another in all impunity. They also often exist between groups and are then a form of alliance which can be additionally formalized through pacts sealed by ritualized exchanges of bodily substances (mainly blood).[12] In most cases, the general patterns of reciprocal joking between groups are fixed, even though they can be slightly adapted to fit the circumstances. Joking relationships do not represent institutions of friendship per se, but they are important bridges to friendship, especially between members of different ethnic groups or subgroups. Even in environments where joking relationships are no longer existent, their memory can still constitute a reference model for interethnic friendships (e.g., Pelican 2004).

Joking relationships between groups appear more widespread in West Africa than in East Africa, a region where, in turn, there is more contracting of institutionalized forms of friendship. In this volume, these regional differences are best illustrated by Wolde Gossa Tadesse and Guichard (Chapter 3) whose joint contribution largely deals with interethnic bond-friendships as practised and experienced by the Hor (also known as Arbore) of southwestern Ethiopia. Such friendship variants are well known for building on economic complementarities between neighbouring groups and for constituting significant pathways for exchanging and trading goods across ethnic boundaries. In practice, however, bond-friendships with out-group members involve a wider of range of exchanges than those described in classic studies on the subject (e.g., Almagor 1978; Sobania 1991). This point is made by Tadesse and Guichard who thus emphasize that interethnic bond-friendships are very meaningful networks of solidarity. According to them, such relationships are at least as crucial for the survival of individuals and the perpetuation of groups as those of kinship among politically marginalized populations living at the fringes of the state and displaying a low level of integration in the monetized market economy. In rural southwestern Ethiopia, bond-friendships forged across ethnic boundaries certainly continue to play an important role in alleviating suffering caused, for example, by adverse climatic events and violent conflicts between groups. Nevertheless, it cannot be denied that their life-saving function has become increasingly threatened since nongovernmental organizations (NGOs) have set foot in the region and expanded attempts to render assistance in times of hardship. Over the last decade, the growing presence of NGOs providing emergency relief has indeed begun to weaken relations of economic interdependence on which interethnic bond-friendships are largely based (see also Girke 2010). As exemplified by Tadesse and Guichard, the study of friendship can be used as a means to reassess some of the ways in which societies are interconnected. In their joint chapter, they hint at the fact that locally observable shifts in friendship practices cannot be adequately understood without reference to external, including global, forces.[13] While stressing that bond-friendships represent an institution which is itself closely interwoven with other institutions, Tadesse and Guichard provide further evidence of the plausibility of the idea that highly institutionalized forms of friendship are surrounded with less suspicion in 'kinship-based societies' than weakly institutionalized forms of friendship (e.g., Eisenstadt 1956).

Friendship, Migration, Urbanity and Politics

Kinship and friendship certainly often play a significant role in the decision to migrate and in the choice of migration destinations. Many moves are planned and undertaken together with individuals exhibiting such social ties. This point is emphasized by Tilo Grätz (Chapter 5) who explores the economic and social logics underlying friendship bonds within gold-mining communities in northern Benin. In these communities, friendship is both largely a result of working relations and a condition of their functioning. Migrant gold miners share the profits of their common labour as well as an experience of liminality which itself seems to favour the development of a specific ethos of sharing. This situation in certain ways resembles that described by Spencer concerning Maasai young men (Chapter 2). Furthermore, Grätz's data seem to lend support to the axiom equating 'less kinship' with 'more friendship: among gold miners' communities, friendship indeed emerges as a particularly important category in an environment where the degree of local concentration of own relatives remains rather low, compared to that of their home villages or home towns.

As newcomers, the gold miners often associate themselves with local household heads who become their personal hosts and are expected to ensure that their guests behave according to the communal norms. These hosts, who are ordinarily entitled to act as mediators when it comes to conflicts with members of the local population and problems with village authorities, can simultaneously be the heads of working teams in the mines and thus be doubly linked to the gold miners through patron-based ties. To be sure, the personal relationships between such hosts and their guests can vary considerably in terms of actual content. In northern Benin, as in many other West African settings, it is nevertheless not uncommon for these contractual relationships to evolve into friendships. In practice, however, there is frequently a more intimate bond between the younger migrants and the sons of the hosts, developing out of common work activities in the mines and jointly spent leisure time in the surrounding villages. Even when this is not the case, it is not unusual for host-guest relations to be quasi-inherited by following generations. Yet, this requires systems of permanent and equitable exchange to ensure mutuality, trust and intimacy in these relations over time or from generation to generation.

The question of the overlap of patronage and friendship is also addressed by Richard Warms (Chapter 6) in his comparative account on friendship bonds among merchants and army veterans in two southern Malian urban settings (Sikasso and Bougouni). Both the merchants and the veterans are ethnically heterogeneous groups which either emerged or changed in their composition as a result of political and economic changes. However, it is possible to identify differences between these two groups. Among merchants, bonds of friendship suffused with caring and interpersonal trust often supplement patron-client ties. In practice, the superposition of friendship bonds on patron-client ties is an important condition for the latter kind of ties to properly function. Yet, friendships between merchants tend to be more instrumental and more often lead to kinship than those among army veterans. These veterans of the French forces (*Tirailleurs sénégalais* or *anciens combattants*) notably refrain from converting friendship into kinship through marriages because they strongly wish to escape the demands made in the name of the kinship. At the same time, there is a sense of alienation among veterans who more clearly link their tendency to cultivate friendships among themselves with the feeling that other people, including their relatives, do not understand them. These differences in the valuation and evolution of friendships among merchants and veterans are, in some respects, not as great as it appears at first glance: they all can partly be explained with reference to the state. Of special relevance in the case of the merchants are the weakness of economic institutions and the inability of certain groups to get access to business capital through credit from state-run banks. Critical for the veterans is that they receive pensions from the state and are thus put in a financial position which in itself makes it easier for them to choose friendship over kinship.

In African countries, however, business exerts a great influence over the public sector and top public servants recurrently act as allies of commercial elites. This alliance is certainly supported by the fact that many public servants carry out business activities in addition to their official jobs and pursue postadministrative careers in business. It also accounts for the fact that high schools and universities represent an important 'breeding ground' for friendship circles that straddle ethnic lines. Richard Werbner (Chapter 7; see also Jacobson 1973; Bako-Arifari 2002) discusses these questions in his analysis of friendships among contemporary African elites in Gaborone, the capital of Botswana, where business and politics are two faces of the same coin. Werbner concentrates on circles of friends encompassing leading agents of the state and commercial elites who are very close to each other and whom he calls 'boon-companions'. Characteristic of these bonds of boon-companionship is that they are largely marked by conviviality and shared leisure time in both private and public spaces. Another common feature is that they are not reinforced by marriages in the next generation. Here, friendships are broadly dissociated from kinship and each generation of elites has, so to speak, to contract class endogamous marriages on its own.

Werbner's study undoubtedly reminds us of the structural importance of social class in both the selection of friends and in the designing of shared friendship activities. Furthermore, it demonstrates that friendship can be a change-inducing factor at the political level. By the same token, it implicitly hints at the potential of friendship to subvert authorities and hierarchies. This potential is well acknowledged all over the world, including by totalitarian and authoritarian political regimes. Under such regimes, friendship bonds are largely condemned to have a subterraneous existence. However, it cannot be denied that the concealing of friendships from public view is also a widespread strategy under more democratic conditions (see also Chapter 1). There too, it is often found a correlation between the need to veil friendships and the propensity of people's own 'emotional economy' to actually be in contradiction with certain norms governing the performances of formal roles. But underlying this correlation is also the basic awareness that friendships are a source of power.

Another context in which friendship is closely connected to politics is that of civil wars. Georg Klute (Chapter 8) examines this in his essay focusing on the Tuareg rebellion of 1990–1996 in northern Mali. As he indicates, this rebellion had been prepared, beginning in the 1980s, by clandestine organizations of Tuareg migrants whose sense of common and supratribal identity had been enhanced during the time they had spent in exile before returning home. In the first years of the armed upheaval, many of these former migrants privileged the idiom of friendship in addressing each other. They valued friendships that crosscut subethnic and social strata and drew on shared experiences in foreign countries and on shared longing for the autonomy or independence of their region of origin from the Malian state. These friendship networks, however, largely disintegrated as political divisions between two Tuareg rebel movements deepened and their relationship became so hostile that they engaged in a 'fratricidal' war in 1994. At the end of this war, friendship ceased to be an important concept in the project of building a Tuareg 'nation' and was replaced with that of kinship. The latter tendency found its expression in two strategies which aimed at overcoming divisions between members of different social strata and at reintegrating the members of the defeated vassal movement into the local society. The first strategy drew on the symbolic and political significance of intergroup marriages for marking a new era of relations between social groups having taken different sides in violent conflicts. The second strategy involved a rewriting of local history and a readjusting of local genealogies, so as to prove that Tuareg of vassal status were actually descending from the same forefathers as Malian Tuareg of noble origin. This claim of common ancestry, which was indeed coupled with the assertion that all Tuareg were interrelated, was especially made by the nobles, i.e., the winning party of the war of 1994. As Klute points out, the nobles did not just redefine the status of vassals by moving them into the class of 'relatives'. They also reasserted their power over the vassals by defining them as relatives in need of protection, a protection which the nobles were, they claimed, both willing and able to provide given their supposed commitment to moral ideals of extended kinship solidarity and their indisputable military superiority. By presenting themselves as protectors of the weak, the nobles sought to embody 'good leadership' and to further the legitimacy of their rule. This kind of moral reframing of leadership, in which the victorious group seeks to strengthen its position by stressing obligations towards the weak and portraying its members as eager to assume caretaking roles analogous to those of fathers or older brothers of the defeated, is certainly often part of attempts to rebuild social cohesion after war. Such a reframing may have the advantage of 'denaturalizing' some of the social divisions that need to be transcended in order to negotiate a relatively peaceful modus vivendi with former enemies. On the other hand, it is not unproblematic, since its existence also reminds the latter that have been vanquished. This point is implicitly acknowledged by Klute whose contribution suggests that the strategic use of kinship by the nobles as a bridge for reconciliation with former adversaries may have already been ambivalently viewed by the vassals years before the outbreak of the so-called 'rebellion' of 2007–2009, i.e., before it became obvious that efforts to restore lasting peace in northern Mali had failed.

Constructing a Research Agenda

As should have become clear, one overarching theme of this book is the relationship between friendship and kinship, a theme that certainly allows for different approaches and for discussing different dimensions of both friendship and kinship. Among the dimensions of friendship meriting closer attention in future research are certainly those linked to issues of power. Another aspect needing greater consideration is that concerning the plural character of friendship and how coexisting concepts and practices of friendship actually relate to each other in a given society or area of investigation. This would notably facilitate cross-cultural comparisons. We also need more longitudinal studies in order to better understand how broader social, economic and political transformations occurring in the societies under investigation impact friendship as an inherently social relationship. Furthermore, but partly for the same reason, we would welcome studies taking an intergenerational perspective. These would as well add much to our knowledge of the relationship between friendship and kinship.

Discussions of this relationship usually take as their starting point that there is a trade-off between kinship and friendship in contexts of social change. As is well known, this thesis has been especially elaborated with regard to Western societies which are thus largely considered to leave more space for friendship, as a special form of social relationship contracted outside kinship, than non-Western societies. Without denying the value of the latter thesis, it can be stressed that most of their proponents have tended to ignore many of the complex interactions between kinship and friendship. While dealing with such interactions in various African settings, this book suggests that our picture of friendship in other societies, too, would be enriched by research expanding efforts in the direction of a multidimensional analysis of the relationship between kinship and friendship. Given this, we have little problem to position ourselves within the current debate on the foundation of a new subdiscipline of anthropology called 'anthropology of friendship'. As the preceding sections and the following chapters indicate, neither can friendship and kinship be easily put into neatly separate boxes nor can friendship be aptly studied in isolation from kinship (see also Reed-Danahay 1999; Killick and Desai 2010; Obeid 2010; Rodgers 2010; Santos 2010; Aguilar 2011). Since the elevation of friendship studies to a subdiscipline could bear the danger of exploring friendship in greater separation from kinship than is already the case, we are – in some regards like Bell and Coleman (1999b: 16) – rather cautious towards such an endeavour.

Acknowledgements

I am very grateful to Patrick Heady, Bettina Mann, Stephen P. Reyna and Gonçalo D. Santos for their comments and suggestions on this introductory chapter. I would also like to thank Tilo Grätz and Youssouf Diallo for their stimulating effect on the present paper.

Notes

1. This resurgence of interest in friendship is notably reflected in books such as those by Bell and Coleman (1999a), Ravis-Giordani (1999a), Schmidt et al. (2007), Desai and Killick (2010), Hruschka (2010) and Descharmes et al. (2011). An overview on the kind of empirical data gathered on the phenomenon called 'friendship' between the 1930s and the 1950s can be found in Eisenstadt (1956) and Cohen (1961). As will be stressed below, these two scholars are among the first to have discussed friendship cross-culturally (see also Du Bois 1974; Eisenstadt 1974; Brain 1976).
2. As a matter of fact there was no edited book with special focus on friendship in non-Western contexts until 2010 (Desai and Killick 2010).
3. Parts of the following description of the individual chapters have been included in one of Grätz's earlier publications (Grätz 2011a).
4. See also Eisenstadt and Roniger (1999: 8–11).
5. For critical assessments of Cohen's analysis of friendship, see Ramsøy (1968), Paine (1974) and Ravis-Giordani (1999b).
6. In contrast to Eisenstadt (1956), Cohen identifies institutionalized friendships as existing at *both* the intra- and intergroup level.

7. For a critical assessment of Silver's interpretation of Smith's approach to friendship, see Hill and McCarthy (2004).
8. For the importance of acquaintances or 'weak ties' in finding employment, see Granovetter (1973, 1983). For the significance of friendships for achieving such a goal, see Morris (1984).
9. This view is especially put forward in studies dealing with Western contexts, as notably exemplified in *Ueno a*nd *Adams* (2007).
10. The literature on milk kinship is still sparse (e.g., Khatib-Chahidi 1993; Héritier-Augé 1994; Parkes 2004, 2005; Vernier 2006) and ignorant of the significance of this institution for the realization of the widespread ideal of friendship as culminating in matrimonial alliances in the next generation.
11. For studies dealing with semicomplex systems of marriage alliances, see, for instance, Lévi-Strauss (1969 [1949]) and Héritier-Augé and Copet-Rougier (1990).
12. For classic studies on joking relations, see Mauss (1969 [1928]), Labouret (1929), Paulme (1939), Radcliffe-Brown (1940, 1949) and Griaule (1948). For more recent contributions, see Diallo (2006), Hagberg (2006) and Tamari (2006).
13. See also Ogembo (2002) and Pritchett (2007).

Part I
Friendship, Kinship and Age

Chapter 1

Where Are Other People's Friends Hiding?

Reflections on Anthropological Studies of Friendship

Martine Guichard

Introduction

As Allan observed, it is far easier to discover who a person's kin are than who his or her friends are (1979: 30). One reason for this does indeed seem to be that the recognition of kinship is based on principles that are more firmly agreed on and more broadly socially acknowledged than those underlying friendship (Allan 1979: 30). Another reason is that in everyday speech, the term 'friend' tends to be 'a residual label, a description [first] applied to associates for whom no more specific title is available' (Fischer 1982: 305). Given that friends who are simultaneously neighbours and co-workers are rarely called 'friends' immediately, the friendships that bind them to one another can be easily overlooked by researchers. The same is true for interpersonal relationships that are locally conceived of as friendships even though they are superimposed on kinship ties. These friendships are likely to be neglected by researchers because of the widely shared assumption that friendship is a voluntary relationship of interdependence that can be ended freely at any time. There is certainly nothing wrong in emphasizing that friendship and kinship can be sociologically contrasted along the lines of achievement versus ascription, and terminality versus permanence. Such a contrast in structural features, however, should not always be taken up simply as justification for confining friendship strictly to extra-kin relationships. One problem here is that doing so may amount to imposing one's own definition on people, who, in practice, may themselves use different criteria for deciding what the boundaries of 'real' friendship are, and how far friendship can or cannot be added to the ascribed roles and formal ties associated with kinship. The limits and other attributes of friendship should be, further, a matter for inquiry and not one of prejudgment; otherwise, it is particularly difficult to make generalizations across studies. Moreover, given that friendship also refers to 'a quality of the personal relationship existing between individuals whereas kinship is [rather] based on criteria external to that relationship' (Allan 1979: 41), it is reasonable to accept that 'kin' and 'friend' are not *necessarily* mutually exclusive terms.

Now that it is clear why it is legitimate to operate with a broader concept of friendship than that used in many sociological works – namely, one that includes certain kin as I do in this contribution – it should be stressed that even though the overlapping of kinship and friendship has long been noted, its significance is still difficult to evaluate. In the literature on Africa, too, it seems to be either over- or underemphasized. This state of affairs is, without doubt, connected to methodological difficulties in the study of friendship. However, the fact that it is also related to ethnocentric conceptions of friendship, reflected in actors' descriptions and interpretations or in theoretical assumptions, makes it even more problematic.

In this contribution, I review literature on kinship and friendship and focus first on the interpenetration of both kinds of relationship, using classic texts on the subject like those of Gulliver (1971) and Campbell (1964). Besides showing how a theory of size is possible with regard to degrees of overlap between kinship and friendship,[1] I deal with the question of which kin are more likely to become friends. In the second section of this chapter, I emphasize further that many friendships have a veiled aspect and address partly the issues of ethnicity and gender. In both sections of this chapter, I draw attention to methodological problems linked with the analysis of friendship, and critically examine accounts that document how anthropologists themselves contribute to the concealing of the existence of such relationships.[2]

Friendship in the Shadow of Kinship

A quick look at the literature still reveals a great readiness to divide the world into 'friendship-oriented' versus 'kinship-oriented' societies.[3] This readiness finds expression notably in the fact that most of the empirical research on friendship is currently being conducted in Europe and in the United States. Such a regional bias, in turn, accounts for the popularity of the view that friendship is a product of 'modernity'. This view, which is widely shared by social scientists, is well formulated by Silver, who states that friendship is a relationship, the expansion of which 'requires the very impersonality of administration, contractualism and monetarized exchange over against which it is culturally distinguished' (Silver 1989: 293). Of course, the kind of friendship primarily discussed here is one of a personal, private and clearly recognized voluntary nature.

This kind of friendship may be a 'luxury' (Paine 1969: 508) that seems to be unaffordable in non-Western societies. However, it can be presumed that many members of these societies have a greater number of friends than is commonly recognized in the literature. This assumption will be substantiated later in this chapter. For now, I would like to reflect on the possibility that kinship may be suffused with friendship,[4] bearing in mind not only that affection, trust and loyalty are largely recognized to be defining attributes of friendship, but also that relatives, through their interactions, are actively engaged in shaping their relationships, even though they may not have entered into them on their own volition. In practice, they *do* kinship in various ways and not necessarily in one that is in close accord with the norms of amity[5] which are ideally to be realized within this realm of social ties. In this normative sense, relatives should make friendship a qualitative component of their actual interpersonal relationships.

As we all know, kinship does not consist solely of sets of rules governing descent, marriage, roles and expectations; it also has informal aspects and embraces interpersonal relationships experienced as evolving internally over time, both in terms of actual content and felt emotions. Such a point has been particularly stressed in some of the 'new' studies on kinship which provide an incentive for rethinking the nature of the relationship between kinship and friendship (e.g., Weston 1991; Carsten 2000). This relationship is at the core of this section. Here, one of my aims is to show how different forms of kinship tend to lead to different constellations of friendship. Accordingly, I concentrate on a phenomenon which has already been acknowledged in the anthropological literature (e.g., Campbell 1964; Wolf 1966), but not explored systematically. In addition to outlining that modes of descent, systems of inheritance and socially prescribed patterns of interaction between affines are important contextual factors influencing friendship, I take into account how formal attribution of genealogical closeness and distance affects the development of friendship within kinship. In the main, I attempt to extract general principles impacting friendship which have cross-cultural relevance.

It has been stressed in many studies, but rarely demonstrated numerically, that the proportion of kin-friends seems to be particularly high in non-Western societies. However, there is possibly a correlation between the type of kinship system and the degree of overlap of kinship with friendship. Cognatic systems may, in theory, allow people to have more kin as friends than unilineal ones, because they are more inclusive in the way in which they reckon descent. This is because they conceptualize descent links as being traceable through both males and females (instead of through one sex only). People who are related by descent, as opposed to a weaker kin tie, are considered more socially significant kin. Thus, in cognatic systems, an individual has more socially significant relatives and may subsequently have greater opportunity to have friends among kin. This hypothesis remains to be tested empirically.

One reason why this hypothesis remains untested is again partly related to the precedence given to the belief that 'real' friendship is a non-kin relationship, and subsequently, to the tendency to study it in isolation from kinship. As a result, there are very few works containing quantitative data on the significance of kin-friends in local communities or among groups already studied. Moreover, since no anthropologist seems to have yet made estimates of kin-friends for unilineally organized societies, data that could be compared to that available on cognatic societies still appears to be lacking.

Before discussing some of the data collected in cognatic societies, it is important to define further what 'cognatic' means in the present context. Here, I will employ the term in a broader sense than Stone (1997) does. Stone reserves it for societies that 'actually use descent to form corporate groups' (1997: 14) and insists on the inadequacy of the term 'cognatic' for describing most Western societies which in her opinion, should, preferably, be called 'bilateral'. However, it is not uncommon to classify bilateral societies as 'cognatic', in order to underline the fact that they have a far more inclusive mode of descent than unilineal ones. Nevertheless, not all societies that can be broadly termed 'cognatic' show the same degree of inclusivity, with regard to simultaneous membership in particular kin groups. These degrees of inclusivity vary with the importance given to genealogical closeness in the definition of socially significant kin. Societies that place great emphasis on this principle of closeness (abbreviated hereafter as 'GC-societies') have less potential sources of kin-friends. This often appears to be the case in Europe and in the United States, where the set of socially significant relatives is limited to the nuclear family, grandparents, immediate uncles and aunts and first cousins. Since the members of such societies, in general, also have more autonomy with regard to meeting their kin, they have fewer opportunities to get to know one another well and to convert relatives into friends. On the other hand, the fact that people belonging to GC-societies can be more selective in their interactions with relatives has a positive effect on the overlapping of friendship and kinship. The more control people have over their gatherings with kin, the more means they have to construct kinship as a relationship that can be coupled with friendship.

The question of which categories of kin are more likely to become friends depends on a variety of factors, some of which will be discussed further in a later part of this chapter. First, however, I would like to examine data that give a concrete idea of the relevance of kinship in the choice of friends in a non-Western society with a cognatic descent system. The main source is Gulliver's book *Neighbours and Networks* (1971). Here, focusing on the Ndendeuli of Tanzania, the author sketches roughly the friendship networks of 76 male household heads and illustrates the importance of kinship for friendship, with the following empirical results: only 20 of the men of his sample had more than two friends that were non-kin (Gulliver 1971: 302). These numbers, which seem to speak a clear language at first sight, should nonetheless be taken with caution. Their representativeness is limited, due to Gulliver's own difficulty in distinguishing clearly between 'mere' visitors and friends. Had he not faced such problems, he would probably have been able to identify more friendships among Ndendeuli men.

This point is also made by Gulliver himself, who apparently found only one obvious case of deep and enduring friendship developed outside kinship among the household heads of the 73 hamlets for which he collected data on friendship. In his brief discussion of this case, Gulliver does not simply mention that the nonrelated men concerned were close friends of many years' standing, ever since their labour migration together as youths. He also reports that, in practice, they treated each other as if they were kin, and were regarded frequently by others as being quite closely related, given the strength of their friendship (Gulliver 1971: 63). However, Gulliver additionally emphasizes that Ndendeuli men preferred to recruit friends among kin, but, unfortunately, does not provide much detailed information about how related friends are genealogically linked to one another. These kin-friends are usually about the same age and generation and are often described simultaneously as 'brothers'. The quotation marks surrounding this kinship term indicate that Gulliver uses it metaphorically in accordance with one of its broader meanings found in Ndendeuli society. That such terms do not always have an immediate genealogical denotation is also suggested in the first passage of the book stressing the exceptional character of close and long-lasting extra-kin friendships between Ndendeuli men and the passage in which he mentions two outstanding friendships involving brothers-in-law and second cousins respectively (Gulliver 1971: 303).

Apart from Gulliver, there are many authors who have observed that friendship 'loves to masquerade as kinship' (Pitt-Rivers 1973: 90), particularly, in non-Western societies. The fact that friends are often figuratively called 'brothers' or 'sisters' obscures the visibility of friendships for outsiders, including anthropologists (see also Santos 2010), and favours misinterpretations of the true nature of the relationship existing between unrelated persons, who apply the idiom of kinship to friendship. At the same time, it increases the risk of underestimating the real significance of friendships in 'exotic' contexts and may reinforce the view that friendship is a very rare phenomenon in non-Western societies. However, these societies do not form monolithic blocks. They, too, comprise groups exhibiting variations from one to another, with regard to patterns of friendship that are interrelated with levels of wealth, prestige and education. Thus, it has been stressed that educated African elites and members of the lower class justify their choice of friends by referring to the same principle, namely, social equality. Nevertheless, as Jacobson (1973) points out for Uganda, all those who use this principle do not necessarily define equality in the same way. For the senior civil servant elites he studies, this notion means primarily similar career trajectories and socioeconomic status (Jacobson 1973: 80; see also Werbner in this volume for Botswana). By contrast, social equality among unskilled labourers is strongly associated with shared ethnicity (Jacobson 1973: 73). Another characteristic of the members of this group is that their friendships 'are marked by an emphasis on exchange of goods and services' (1973: 70), and seem to be more instrumental and less expressive than those of the elites. However, the existence of such class-based differences has been documented for other contexts and also with reference to Western societies. With respect to the United States, for example, earlier accounts of the influence of class and income on the nature of friendships were provided by Liebow (1967) and Stack (1974), whose works on poor 'Black Americans' suggest that friendships are largely utilitarian in economies of scarcity. Drawing on the aforementioned works, it has been inferred that these Americans have a greater propensity to cultivate the instrumental aspect of friendship than rich people (e.g., Adams and Allan 1998b: 9). Nevertheless, it is arguable that friendships between wealthy people are just as utilitarian, but their utilities involve different things (obtaining business or political opportunities, being admitted to universities, etc.).[6]

As the preceding observations imply, the opposition between instrumental and expressive friendship is rather one of degree than an absolute one (e.g., Paine 1969; Du Bois 1974; Allan 1979). Not only are all friendships both utilitarian and emotional, but their 'instrumental aspect validates the affect' (Pitt-Rivers 1973: 97). However, the extent to which the utility of friendship is overtly recognized varies with degrees of commitment between friends and according to social settings and circumstances. The number of friends people have also seems to play a role in this context. Those who have few associates of this kind may talk more readily about the usefulness of friendships, because they are more dependent on them than people with a larger circle of friends. At the same time, they may be more tolerant towards friends who disappoint them by failing to maintain a balance of exchange for too long. Although they can opt to terminate the relationship they are increasingly dissatisfied with, they may be more hesitant to do so, given that, according to Rusbult's (1980) investment model, the costs linked with the dissolution of inequitable friendships appear to be higher for them than for people with a larger number of friends.

The evaluation of the costs of breaking up a friendship possibly involves the existence of other networks of relationships. For example, it is conceivable that the way in which people deal with disappointing friends is also influenced by the local (non-)availability of relatives. Whether people with many relatives living in the vicinity are quicker to end friendships, which they have come to perceive as problematic, than those lacking kin in geographical proximity, is a question that cannot be definitively answered yet, because it has been largely ignored by research. In part, this may reflect the fact that friendship and kinship are often treated separately in the literature. Furthermore, it may be related to the fact that, so far, greater empirical attention has been paid to the process of forming and maintaining friendships, rather than the process of ending them. In addition, it seems to be linked to the growing disenchantment with exchange (e.g., Homans 1961) and interdependence theories (e.g., Thibaut and Kelley 1959), which are indeed eager to incorporate principles of learning and conditioning uncovered in laboratory experiments involving animals, also used in reinforcement theories (such as 'We like people who reward us and dislike those who punish us'; e.g., Byrne and Clore 1970) in the analysis of interpersonal relationships, rather than subcultural differences.

However, it remains true that mutual understanding between friends is generally promoted and reinforced by a high level of interaction. Conversely, a decrease in frequency of interaction often leads gradually to a decrease in the sense of 'communion' and the capacity to show empathy for one another. This evolution is more likely when the friendship tie has a relatively short history of shared experiences and when homogeneity in the socioeconomic position between the partners has been replaced with heterogeneity. As numerous studies stress, status changes and increasing differentials of wealth and power tend to affect friendships negatively. This is not surprising. After all, friendship is a relationship founded on several contradictions. The first lies in the fact that although it is common to view the favours of friends as freely granted, nevertheless, they must 'be reciprocated if the moral status quo is to be maintained' (Pitt-Rivers 1973: 97). The second one, and more relevant here, is that although friendships are ideally portrayed as elective relationships based on interpersonal 'liking' and trust, they are not solely a matter of individual choice. They are also structured and constrained by external factors, such as ethnicity, gender, class, caste, age and geographical location (e.g., Allan 1989, 1996).

To this current and often-cited list of factors influencing friendship should be added, apart from the above-discussed modes of descent: patterns of inheritance, socially prescribed patterns of relationships between affines, and – as I will suggest in the second part of this chapter – postnuptial patterns of residence. Generally speaking, one can oppose partible to impartible inheritance.[7] In the latter system, parental property is transferred to a single heir. The rule, for example, that family land is passed onto only one son or daughter often forces the noninheriting siblings to look for a livelihood elsewhere. They may then stay in the vicinity, work on other people's land and seek to improve their position by marrying a landowner. They may also engage in nonagricultural activities and move to another area. They may certainly leave for reasons other than the fact that they cannot expect to take over plots of land. However, it seems that theoretically impartible systems favour migration more than partible ones. As a consequence, it may be assumed that they are fertile ground for the development of 'serial' and geographically dispersed friendships. The same is true for such a mode of production as pastoralism, especially those forms based on an extensive use of pastures. Indeed, herders often find it essential from an economic point of view to have spatially distant friends. This is the case in Africa, for example, where herders largely live with the threat of localized drought and diseases decimating their herds. One risk-minimizing strategy consists of lending animals to friends residing in a different area, in order to have reserves in the event of disaster.

These friends, more commonly known as 'stock-partners' or 'stock-friends' in the literature,[8] may be kin or non-kin. In practice, it seems that preference is sometimes given first to unrelated men and then to genealogically distant kin. One reason for favouring distant relatives rather than near ones appears to be linked to the importance attributed to genealogical closeness in the distribution of rights and obligations among kin. The more closely related, the more difficult it is actually to get back what was lent out, if the trustee is not inclined to respect his part of the contract. A further explanation may be that potential competition tends to be structurally minimized by genealogical distance. Since distantly related kin are less likely to become direct rivals for inheritance and dominance than close kin, they may be associated categorically with relatives who can be more easily trusted. A similar point has been made by Schlee in an article on intra- and interethnic networks of northern Kenyan pastoralists (1984: 69). In the context he refers to, brothers, especially those who are full and half-brothers, in a narrow genealogical sense, are strongly involved in competition over the above-mentioned issues. This competition and the resulting mutual distrust that often pervades the relationships of such brothers are factors that encourage the development of stock-partnerships with individuals belonging to other kin categories. As Schlee stresses, in East Africa, such institutionalized partnerships, in addition, may either largely include or exclude affinal relatives. According to him, differences in tendencies observed locally are interconnected with differences in kinds of bride-wealth. These may be divided into two ideal types which, in the pastoral societies compared by Schlee (see also Schlee 1989, 2012), correlate with two contrasting types of postnuptial relationships between affines. The first type of bride-wealth involves the transfer of a *fixed* number of animals which may even be handed over all at once to the wife-givers. It is rather prevalent in societies where affinal relationships are generally characterized by avoidances and a high degree of formality. The second type corresponds to open bride-wealth and is widespread in societies, where relationships between affines are customarily marked by less reserve and more co-operation (1989: 418). And precisely because relationships between affines are both less restricted and have more positive connotations in societies with open bride-wealth than in those with fixed bride-wealth, it can be assumed that the former societies leave more room for affinal bonds to overlap with friendship.

One advantage of having affines as friends is that their support often offers the opportunity to reduce one's own dependence upon agnates, i.e., kin with whom relationships tend to be more competitive in societies with a strong patrilineal bias. Such dependence varies with age, a criterion which has repercussions both on the outcomes of conflicts and rivalries between relatives and on the importance of extra-kin friendships for defeating competitors. This can be illustrated by the example of two siblings separated by approximately twenty years. One of the implications of a large difference in age is a temporal inequality in powerful friends or friends whose assistance can enable effectively to overcome rivals, in particular, senior ones. Another implication is a significant difference in time between marriage periods. Since the younger sister/brother marries far later than her/his older sibling, s/he is – at least in early adulthood – likely to have a smaller number of affines s/he can also mobilize against competitors. And, because s/he has fewer kinship resources s/he can use potentially to her/his benefit in case of conflict with either kin or non-kin, s/he may also have – for a certain period of time – a greater need for friendship with nonrelatives than her/his much older sibling.

Coming back to the question of which kin make 'better' friends, I would like to discuss further some of the data presented by Gulliver in his aforementioned Ndendeuli work (1971). On the basis of his findings alone, it cannot be really concluded that the people he studied either gave priority to genealogically distant relatives over close ones or to immediate affines over closely related cognates, because it is fallacious to draw generalizations from simply two cases of outstanding friendships. However, it remains interesting that one of these cases of particularly deep and enduring personal friendship identified by Gulliver actually involved brothers-in-law, i.e., close relatives by marriage, and the other second cousins, i.e., relatives who tended to be on the margins of acknowledged kinship. These men had indeed in common that, by virtue of their formal status as relatives, they had few obligations towards one another. With regard to the pair of second cousins mentioned by Gulliver, it is also possible that their chances of staying friends increased because they had largely divergent sets of kin, with whom they maintained active relationships of kinship and close co-operation. This suggestion is partly derived from Gulliver's observation that, among the Ndendeuli, such tertiary relatives had usually fewer overlapping sets of kin, with whom they indeed chose to actively cultivate ties of mutual kinship, than either secondary relatives (e.g., first cousins) or primary relatives (e.g., brothers; Gulliver 1971: 15, 296). Given that the respective kin-sets of relatives included in the last two categories entailed a larger number of kin acknowledged as being common, their members were more likely to face problems of conflicting obligations and responsibilities, if some of them competed or quarrelled with one another. Since primary and secondary relatives were also more likely to be linked by kinship to both opposing parties, they appeared to be less able to avoid taking sides. In addition, they seemed to be less free to choose whom they supported among those kin who were current rivals or overtly against one another, because they were less able to ignore the opinions of their other relatives whose kin-sets greatly overlapped with their own. It was particularly important for them to take these opinions into account, given that the risk of being disapproved of often increased with the degree of kin-set overlap. The higher this overlap, the more people have to fear that competition and disputes between particular individuals will negatively affect their personal relationships with other relatives, who acknowledge kinship connections to the primary adversaries. Consequently, the more closely interlinked kin-sets are, the higher the probability that particular friendships within these kin-sets, too, become endangered by friction and conflicts between other kin living in the neighbourhood.

This point is not explicitly made by Gulliver[9] who, in his discussion of friendships, focuses more generally on the preference given to kin in the recruitment of friends. According to him, the Ndendeuli explained their preference and consequently their supposed disinterest in having friends who were neither connected by cognatic nor by affinal ties, as follows: 'whereas a kinsman could be trusted and had to accede to requests of assistance *because* he was a kinsman, an unrelated man was unlikely to be so concerned, ... and had no need to entertain obligations nor rights to make demands' (Gulliver 1971: 302). The sociological interpretation is that an unrelated person would suffer conflicts of loyalty when his/her help is simultaneously required by his/her own kin and his/her unrelated friends (1971: 302).

The avoidance of conflict and its significance in relation to the choosing of friends among kin is also stressed by Campbell for the Greek sheep herding Sarakatsani (1964). His informants stated that friendship was only possible with relatives; and apparently, the (male) kin with whom such ties were preferentially established were first cousins, whose families of origin were not involved in co-operative sheep management (Campbell 1964: 121). Given that working together on a daily basis is generally a source of economic conflicts, they were less likely to maintain close friendships with patrilateral parallel cousins (i.e., father's brother's sons) than with cross-cousins (i.e., father's sister's sons or mother's brother's sons) and matrilateral parallel cousins (i.e., mother's sister's sons). The last two categories of cousins not only differed from that of patrilateral parallel cousins to the extent to which co-operation in pastoralism was generally developed, they were also more likely to live in different neighbourhoods since postnuptial residence was patri-virilocal. By virtue of the fact that physical separation is often a factor diminishing the risk of information disclosed by friends under a seal of secrecy becoming known to a wide circle of persons, it is all the more understandable that cross-cousins and matrilateral parallel cousins are categorically thought of as being endowed with a greater chance of being good friends than patrilateral parallel ones. The matrilineally organized Senufo of the Ivory Coast, too, seem well aware of the above-mentioned potential advantages resulting from geographical distance between friends. These people have an institutionalized form of 'best friendship' which can be found among both women and men, and which is characterized by a limitation of the choice of a friend for each partner (Sindzingre 1985). Here, the 'best friend' is recruited preferably from outside one's own matrilineage and subethnic group. Furthermore, it is preferable for her/him to live far away from the respective counterpart (Sindzingre 1985: 73). Although one rarely meets this friend, s/he is someone in whom one confides easily. This is because the restrictions put upon the actors in the choice of their 'best friend' seem to reduce the dangers of betrayal and gossip.

These dangers can also be minimized through the bestowing of asymmetric relations on formally symmetric relationships, an asymmetry which in itself limits the possibility of exchanging confidences and intimate information from the outset. Such a structure is at the heart of an institutionalized form of 'best friendship' that I encountered in northern Cameroon among women belonging to subgroups of the Fulbe Mbororo commonly referred to as Aku. One singularity of the aforementioned form of institutionalized friendship is that it is modelled on kinship. Once ritually entered into – after having at least reached the age of puberty – it implies a greater formalization of behaviour, i.e., an increased display of reserve and restraint towards one another. This formalization, which is notably marked by a specific way of addressing one's friend (using thoroughly the term *belayDo* instead of her first name), is linked to the fact that the friendship form under consideration entails the partial adoption of the restraints of older sister/younger sister roles.[10] The latter characteristic points to the importance of kinship in Fulbe society. At the same time, it pervades a kind of friendship which, due to its similarity to kinship, is from the start contracted with the expectation that it could last longer than less formalized variants of friendship. This expectation is also often justified with the idea that one has already to feel genuine sympathy and affection for one another to agree to enter into and participate in a kind of friendship within which one's behavioural and interactional room for manoeuvre is particularly limited when other friendship options are available. Since institutionalized friendships are widely recognized to demand more self-discipline than less formalized variants of friendship, they are not contracted lightly and in large numbers. Given all this, it is not surprising that these friendships are highly valued and considered to embody the purest form of friendship existing within the Aku section of Fulbe Mbororo. However, the very fact that such friendships are reserved to women, and lack male equivalents, seems to fit well with ideal images of women as being more readily disposed than men to making sacrifices in the name of love. This uneven distribution of institutionalized friendships across genders is also a phenomenon that tends to reduce gender differentials in the ability to maintain friendships over longer periods of time, differentials which are structurally promoted by patri-virilocality. The composition of the scope of friends involved is yet another interesting feature of these institutionalized relationships. Although the partners can belong to different clans, there seems to be a greater tendency to choose women from within one's own subclan. These privileged partners, in turn, can be divided into two groups: on the one hand, women with supposed but not known genealogical connections and, on the other hand, relatives who are on the margins of genealogically traceable kinship (e.g., third cousins).[11] In the latter instances, friendship clearly reinforces kinship and is thus endowed with a function that, to my knowledge, has never been documented in the literature on institutionalized forms of friendship.

However, with reference to other kinds of friendship and concerning different contexts, it is theoretically possible to argue that unrelated friends are more vulnerable than kin-friends. Du Boulay (1976), speaking generally, notes that confiding in unrelated friends is more dangerous than confiding in relatives, because the structural features of friendship make it more likely that the relationship 'will sooner or later suffer a setback or come to an end and when this happens the secrets' already entrusted are also more likely to be revealed to the community (Du Boulay 1976: 398). Given this, it may be wise to develop friendships within kinship. On the other hand, the kin-friends in whom confidences have been made may suffer conflicts of loyalty, when they know of things supposed to be kept from other relatives. In addition, by virtue of the closer association of kinship with permanence, once their personal relationship has deteriorated, kin-friends seem to be granted a special ability to hurt those who have entrusted them with secrets. Compared to nonrelated friends, these kin-friends, in principle, have more opportunities to exercise to their advantage the power they have gained over a former friend, given their former role as confidants; they also have greater occasion to use earlier confidences as a means to enhance their own position once the friendship has terminated. Moreover, since even friendships with kin, in practice, often end in enmity, their demise remains a development which renders the further fulfilment of reciprocal kin-obligations particularly precarious.

Friendships between Veiling and Unveiling

As already suggested in this contribution, friendships cannot all be expected to be easily identifiable for outsiders. In some settings, they need to be veiled; in others, they need to be made public. In this section, I focus on the first phenomenon and delineate the conditions in which it appears particularly desirable to remain secretive about friendships. Furthermore, I discuss two sources of veiling: the actors themselves and anthropologists. With regard to the latter, I especially consider their failure to capture adequately observable realities when dealing with friendships between ethnic strangers and between women in certain contexts. I provide possible explanations for the above-mentioned failure, while pointing to studies in which statements made about friendship or methodological approaches adopted remain problematic. Here too, I draw attention to kinship as a field that influences friendship.

First, however, the meaning of 'unveiling' needs to be clarified. In the present context, this term refers to my own analysis of the ease with which some anthropologists have 'conspired'[12] with their informants to conceal the actual significance of interethnic and female friendships. To a certain – but not negligible – extent, the latter inclination is grounded in adherence to popular, normative representations or to theoretical assumptions which, in part, have been increasingly criticized over the last decades. As will be stressed at the end of this section, this criticism particularly applies to earlier assumptions made in connection with friendships between women.

However, it is important to recognize that friendship is difficult to observe. This is especially true of the measurement of trust and more generally of levels of friendship. Such an enterprise is notably complicated by the fact that self-disclosure and mutual confiding (i.e., intimacy) and frequency of interaction are not always reliable indicators of closeness.[13] The same is true for qualitative labels such as 'best', 'good' and 'casual' friends (e.g., Allan 1979: 35–37; O'Connor 1992: 50, 60). This can be illustrated by taking the example of the Fulbe of northern Benin and northern Cameroon among whom I conducted fieldwork, and to whom I will refer often in the present section. These people, who notably share the commonality of having strong ties to cattle, adopt a double standard in their labelling of friends, especially good and close ones. When friends are chosen from within their group, it is very likely that the strength of their friendship will also be indicated by employing the local terms denoting higher degrees of trust and intimacy. The same does not apply to good and close friends from different ethnic backgrounds, who, in practice, are simply called 'friends'.[14] Such variations in the use of the local terms available with regard to the quality of friendship are to be found elsewhere as well. Indeed, friendship discourses are identity discourses. They entail personal evaluations of others and selves not only as particular individuals, but also as representatives of broader categories (ethnic fellow/ethnic stranger, Christian/Muslim, woman/man, etc.). Thus, one characteristic of narratives on friendship is that they often entail discourses in which members of larger in-groups (co-ethnics, co-religionists, co-gendered, etc.) tend to be portrayed more positively than those belonging to larger out-groups (see also Barcellos Rezende 1999). Given this, they should principally be treated with circumspection. Otherwise, there is a considerable risk of perpetuating clichés about others who are not at the centre of one's study. There is also a significant danger of underestimating the importance of friendships in the lives of those actors who are the main focus of research.

In the following, I will discuss some accounts illustrating these points and focus on publications that underevaluate the significance of interethnic friendships, a form of sociability still neglected in anthropological studies.[15] One problematic work is that of Campbell on the Sarakatsani entitled *Honour, Family and Patronage* (1964). As mentioned above, in this classic monograph, friendship is asserted to be simply an intra-kin relationship and nonexistent with ethnic strangers, especially villagers and townspeople. Underlying both assertions is the awareness that kinship makes particularly strong claims on individuals in the community studied. According to Campbell, these claims are so overwhelming that sympathetic relationships with unrelated persons could hardly lead to more than an economic contract (Campbell 1964: 205; see also Loizos and Papataxiarchis 1991: 20). It may be true that many of the amicable relationships between nonrelatives and, by extension, between Sarakatsani and villagers, are interest based and better described as patronage. However, certain arguments presented in Campbell's study lead one to question whether 'real' friendships with ethnic others were indeed totally absent. The arguments that are unconvincing seem to coincide with those advanced by the Sarakatsani themselves in the realm of discourses which essentialize differences and primarily associate 'others' as a single whole unable to embody the same virtues as those highly valued in their own community. Given that such ethnocentric discourses are part of public discourses on interethnic friendships, I believe that Campbell should have been more critical of the actors' narratives. Another shortcoming is that he did not take into sufficient consideration that friendships with ethnic strangers may have a hidden nature.

The hypothesis that such friendships among the Sarakatsani have a veiled aspect is supported by the observation that competition between unrelated families is an important basis for their integration into the wider community (Campbell 1964: 9). Since these families – and by implication a great number of co-ethnics – are strongly engaged in mutual rivalries, they all appear to have vested interests in keeping their own kinship resources as high as possible. In principle, the capacity to achieve such a goal is proportional to the ability of mobilizing *both* kin with whom one is already on good terms and those with whom actual relationships are more strained. A good strategy to maximize the effective support given by the latter kind of relatives is to nurture the impression that alternative resources are lacking. This can be done by keeping secret extra-kin friendships. In practice, this strategy is all the more profitable since it also helps to reduce conflicts within kinship and to continue obtaining information, favours and goods, which, in turn, allow people to acquire new resources and recurrently increase their ability to ensure certain outcomes.

I would argue that, more importantly, one particularity of face-to-face communities is that they tend to share characteristics that are conducive to the veiling of extra-kin friendships. In many of these communities, relationships between relatives continue to be particularly demanding and quite tightly organized around differences in power positions assigned along genealogical lines. In such communities, overt opposition to kin occupying higher positions is strongly disapproved of socially. In these circumstances, kin occupying lower power positions need to handle some of their power resources more discreetly than those in higher positions. Accordingly, they have a greater incentive to conceal their friendships from public view, especially those developed outside kinship. Keeping in mind that the interpersonal relationships between kin who are normatively granted different power positions (father/son, paternal uncle/nephew, etc.) are often troubled, it can be stipulated that strategies of secrecy with regard to friendship are far more common in face-to-face communities than is currently acknowledged in the literature.

A further argument supporting this view is that kin are made up of idiosyncratic individuals who, as such, differ from one another in personal traits, character and willingness to provide mutual help. This point is often stressed in practice and it cannot be denied that, in everyday life, kin assistance underlies an 'emotional economy', i.e., a disposition to distribute goods and services on the basis of the *actual* feelings experienced towards other people. Given that actors are well aware of their emotional economy, they often fear that some of their relatives would increase their attempts to escape their kin-obligations, if they knew that those asking for help also had access to supplementary means of support (or to additional means of gaining power),[16] namely, friends. In fact, the same applies for these friends. On various occasions, the probability of providing one another with the help currently required is effectively increased through the veiling of the existence of other friendships.

Another point that needs to be considered in the analysis of friendship is that it can be a relationship that is strongly discouraged by norms governing certain roles, in the exercise of which people may interact regularly and come to like one another personally. Take, for example, professional roles. There is a norm that judges should be impartial. Thus, they should not be friends with lawyers with whom they work even though this occurs occasionally. Furthermore, there is a rule in the military that proscribes friendship between people of different ranks, because it can lead to dysfunctions in the chain of command. Here too, compliance is reinforced by the application of legally determined sanctions against those who circumvent the rule by, nevertheless, establishing friendships with one another. When circumventions occur in such contexts, it becomes obvious that people cannot be so easily brought to ignore their own emotional economy. With regard to this economy, it can be assumed that the more it is in contradiction with certain prevailing norms, the greater the likelihood that friendship will be veiled.

Yet, given that veiling strategies seem to be more widespread, in practice, than acknowledged in previous accounts, there is reason to believe that the tendency to underestimate the actual significance of friendships is far more pronounced among anthropologists than already conceded. In certain contexts, it becomes particularly evident that some of our limitations in analysing friendship cannot even be overcome through fieldwork conducted over a longer period of time. This can be illustrated by reflecting on my own experience as a researcher investigating friendship among the Fulbe, primarily in northern Cameroon and peripherally in northern Benin. Earlier in this chapter, I have indicated that the interpersonal friendships between these people and members of other ethnic groups are qualitatively more diversified than suggested terminologically by the Fulbe, who refer to them by using the vaguest and least emotionally laden word of the vernacular vocabulary of friendship. The latter kind of 'naming politics' seems to be less systematically developed within groups from whom the Fulbe choose interethnic friends. This difference does not appear to reflect differences in degrees of ambivalence towards friendship as dissociated from kinship. In practice, both the Fulbe and their neighbours equally recognize that part of the problem with friendship stems from the fact that many of its functions are similar to those of kinship. Both groups acknowledge that it is notably because friendship and kinship are greatly overlapping functionally that friendship behaviour can be so easily associated with anti-kinship behaviour and surrounded by suspicion. Taking into account that both the Fulbe and their farming neighbours place high value on kinship, it may be presumed that, in theory, both groups have the same interest in veiling how important their interethnic friends really are for them personally. Such a supposition is not entirely inaccurate, but it seems somewhat contradicted by the empirical finding attesting to the existence of an ethnic-based contrast, as described here in connection with interethnic friendships. Striking for this contrast is not only that it is consistent with cross-cultural differences in attitudes towards self-expression. It is also strengthened by the fact that the Fulbe cultivate a more introverted type of personality and thus ideally ought to display a greater predilection than their neighbours for keeping things implicit and for talking in a restrained manner. Surely this ethos ought to be approximated first and foremost during interactions outside one's own home. But one of the audiences before whom it is expected to be more intensively expressed is that composed of people who are culturally close. Now, it is worth noting that I found myself recurrently included in the latter category while conducting fieldwork. Since the Fulbe identified me more strongly with their own group than with that of the farmers, they felt regularly compelled to embody reserve and self-control in my company, i.e., qualities they tend to elevate as central markers of their ethnic identity and which they tend to deny to members of farming communities. And the more they granted me a sort of 'sister' status, the more they strove to demonstrate these qualities while speaking with me about sensitive issues. Quite obviously, interethnic friendship is also considered to be a delicate topic, because it is a relationship of solidarity that involves a double tension between 'sameness' (the friend as another self versus the co-ethnic as a 'brother') and 'otherness' (the friend as both a non-kin and an ethnic stranger). If this kind of friendship were not associated with this double tension, it is probable that the Fulbe would have made less effort to present their interethnic friends to me in a tempered way, i.e., by simply using the generic term for 'friend', as they would do with people who actually share their own culture and ethnicity, but not necessarily in the presence of third persons belonging to farming groups. The corollary was that, paradoxically, an increasing integration in the field counteracted my ability to quickly get a good overview of how close the friendships were among some of the people studied.

This problem, which has certainly been encountered by other anthropologists spending a longer period of time in the field (including Campbell mentioned above), is still downplayed in the literature. One reason for hedging around a discussion of the methodological disadvantages of being more strongly associated with one ethnic community than with another is that many scholars believe that these disadvantages are still insignificant compared to those of using questionnaires as the main tool for studying friendship. An example supporting this point of view is the work of Gareis (1995), who studies intercultural friendships on a U.S. campus, stressing that foreign students are far from lacking friends among Americans. While calling into question some estimates and approaches presented in older publications, she acknowledges the importance of addressing both partners of the friendship dyads mentioned during the research process. However, since she herself omitted to include American students in her survey, the great discrepancy between her findings and those reported in former accounts on friendships between foreign and American students remains slightly troubling. This discrepancy seems to be reinforced by the fact that Gareis did not take enough time in the field to establish whether those described as 'close friends' by her informants were similarly defined by their counterparts. Another criticism is that Gareis reproduces many clichés about American friendships. Once again, this shortcoming is related to the absence of American students in her sample. Furthermore, it is related to the questions asked. One of the first questions was: 'What is ideally friendship in your culture?' (Gareis 1995: 158). It is not surprising, therefore, that the students she worked with mainly stressed differences between American friendships and others, and saw greater value in those they associated with their own culture.

To some degree, Gareis's approach of friendship is similar to that of Reina (1959), who belongs among the anthropologists who have veiled the importance of friendships in the context of their areas of study. In his now classic article entitled 'Two Patterns of Friendship in a Guatemalan Community',[17] Reina claims that Indians and Ladinos have different concepts of friendship, although he only had one-sided sources and did not observe practices in each of the groups under discussion. According to him, the contrast between friendships among Indians and among Ladinos clearly involves emotion versus calculation. His ethnically based dichotomy is all the more questionable since he compares 'apples with oranges', namely, friendships between young people in one group, with friendships between adults in the other group. However, all the friendships he focuses on involve men. Those defined as characteristic for Indians seem to be very passionate and often have a homoerotic aspect. They correspond to friendships developed between young men within this ethnic group. The second type of friendship referred to as being typical for the Ladinos coincides with that identified among adults. This type has more economic functions and, in fact, bears resemblance with patron-client relationships. Such relationships were surely to be found in both contexts discussed by Reina whose study explicitly reminds us that friendships change throughout one's life and are not always harmonious relationships. They have problematic aspects, such as conflict, unpleasant competition and feelings of jealousy, hurt, betrayal and anger. But how much dissatisfaction, however, are we willing to tolerate in friendships? Obviously, the level of tolerance depends partly on the degree of commitment to the relationship and on the scale of investment already made in that friendship. The greater the investment, the more costly it is to end it (e.g., Rusbult 1980).

This principle is stressed in many settings, including African ones. As Piot shows in an article on the Kabre of Togo (1991), the continuity of certain kinds of friendships may also be enhanced by the fact that they are built up slowly and gradually evolve into costly affairs. This article is interesting because it adopts a processual approach – an approach still too rarely taken in anthropology – and emphasizes the correlation between spheres of exchange and stages of a growing relationship. Drawing on Bohannan (1959), Piot distinguishes three spheres of exchange and ranks gifts and countergifts within each sphere, as follows: food in the lower sphere, wealth items in the middle sphere and women in the highest sphere. While all these spheres may be mobilized in the case of what I will call 'best friendships' (third stage), the same is not true for inferior forms of this relationship. Yet, even the economic costs related to the elevation from the first to the second level of friendship seem to be too high for many Kabre to afford. Here, 'good' or 'best' friends do indeed increasingly become a luxury. If it is the case, this is partly because the relationship between such friends is not considered simply as linking two individuals together, but two families as well, as reflected in the special meaning given to commensalities involving all their members. Taking into account that these families are large in size, it becomes better understandable why the making of 'good' or 'best' friends is now a process that appears increasingly difficult to achieve successfully.

The combination of a processual approach with an economic one is also a useful entry point for the analysis of friendships which are less ritualized than those discussed by Piot for the Kabre. In many cases, it helps to understand why people often state that intraethnic and interethnic friends are of different kinds. There is little doubt that the tendency to oppose strongly these two categories of friends can be reinforced by the fact that the actors concerned belong to groups which do not all cultivate an ideal of friendship as an interpersonal bond of affection culminating both in the arrangement of marriages and in the creation of kinship ties. It should not be forgotten, however, that a great propensity to contrast intraethnic friendships with interethnic ones can also be a side effect of a high degree of convergence between (some of) the friendship concepts and values developed by the groups, to which the participants are respectively affiliated. The latter applies, for example, to the Fulbe of northern Benin and to the Fulbe Mbororo of northern Cameroon, who share with many members of adjacent communities the view that matrimonial alliances represent the apex of close friendships (for Burkina Faso, see Breusers in this volume). Here, the problem is that these Fulbe show a strong preference for group endogamy. As they rarely intermarry with ethnic strangers, they are not only prone to experience friendships forged across ethnic boundaries differently from those established among themselves, but are also quick to support the fiction that their friendship concepts and values are principally dissimilar to those of various other peoples, with whom they co-reside and among whom they have friends.

In addition, Piot's account of Kabre friendships is interesting because it discusses a form that is not per se reserved to men, but which becomes clearly gendered at the third stage. Since, among the Kabre, marriages are officially arranged only by men, 'best friendships' are not available to women. Given this, it is comprehensible that Piot does not focus on female actors. Although greater attempts have been made over the last two decades to break the invisibility of women in the literature on institutionalized friendships in Africa (e.g., Scholz and Schultz 1994), there is still very little information on the significance of such ties for women. To a certain extent, the same can be said for other forms of female friendship.[18] This situation undoubtedly reflects the persistence of the idea that the most important social relationships for adult women are within the family and with relatives. Such an assumption is critically discussed by Kennedy (1986) and Uhl (1991), for example, who studied female friendships in Crete and Andalusia respectively, i.e., regions in which friendship has long been perceived primarily as a male phenomenon in the literature. Both authors stress that this perception is locally supported by men as well by women and that the latter actively perpetuate it by more regularly disguising their own friendships linguistically and by keeping them more hidden from public view than men. By doing so, women do not only give 'conventional' performances of femininity, and maintain the impression that they do not call the hegemony of men into question; they also allow themselves to increase some of their power, notably in the domestic sphere.

Apart from pointing to the veiled aspect of female friendships in southern Europe and uncovering how women, too, cultivate this, Uhl and Kennedy challenge earlier observations made by anthropologists about the decline in women's friendships after marriage (e.g., Leyton 1974; Gilmore 1975). They both emphasize that women have more friends than has been suggested in the literature previously. In part, their findings are certainly influenced by the perspective they took. The more closely one focuses one's gaze on women, the more one becomes aware of the number of friends they actually have. However, in the case of the female actors studied by Uhl (1991), a further factor, namely, the pattern of postnuptial residence that seems to predominate in Andalusian towns, may help to explain why they appear to have more extensive friendship networks than had been often supposed by earlier researchers. As noted by Gilmore (1998: 98–99), in many of these towns the preferential pattern combines neolocality *and* matrivicinity. Given the importance attributed to geographical proximity to the wife's mother's home – and by extension to the wife's parents' home – in choosing a new place of residence after marriage, such a pattern can be assumed to allow greater continuity in women's friendships than mere neolocality or both patri- and virilocality.

In fact, not enough attention has been paid so far to postnuptial patterns of residence in friendship studies. If these had been taken more into account, it is probable that women would have been portrayed less readily as having fewer friends than men. Generally speaking, patrilocality versus matrilocality and virilocality versus uxorilocality are all (ideal-typical) patterns with gendered implications. Since viri- and uxorilocality can be regarded as extensions of patri- and matrilocality respectively, their gendered effects on friendships are quite similar to those of the two last kinds of residential patterns. Therefore, it is not necessary to detail how each of these patterns influences friendships. In the following, I will concentrate rather on virilocality and uxorilocality. In communities that favour virilocality, women leave their parental home after marriage to move into that of their husband. As they are usually the ones who relocate in these circumstances, to some extent, they are more compelled to build new friendships in a certain phase of their lives than men. This situation is the reverse in the case of uxorilocality, as it is characterized by postnuptial changes of residence undertaken by husbands. However, the practising of either uxori- or virilocality can also mean for newly wed men or women that they become transplanted into an environment, where their own consanguineal kin are missing. Then, and like many members of communities favouring neolocality (i.e., establishing a new residence after marriage independent of the domicile of both spouses' parents) or any people who lack relatives in the proximity, these wives or husbands will have fewer opportunities to interact with their own kin, including those whose company they particularly enjoy. As they are deprived of 'good' kin (i.e., kin they particularly like and to whom they feel especially close) residing nearby, they will have to invest more strongly in friendships, in order to satisfy their emotional need for acceptance, trust and support.

By stressing that friendship becomes a greater necessity in the absence of kinship, I do not mean to minimize the importance of the first kind of ties in settings with a relatively high proportion of relatives in the vicinity. In these settings, friendship is all the more significant since relationships among kin go beyond standardized roles. As already mentioned, they include competition and hostility, which can either be mitigated or strengthened through friendships. Indeed, friends do not always advise one another to be magnanimous towards rival kin; they often take sides and play a determining role in the outcomes of rivalries in which their own friends are involved. In particular, in clashes over power, the support they provide in the assertion of competitive claims of kin often appears to be more decisive than norms existing in view of the respective situation.

Conclusion

A general premise of this chapter is that, in some respects, friendship does not differ greatly across societies, even if it may take different shapes. This premise is based on the observation that both in Western and in non-Western societies, variations in the way in which friendships tend to be patterned often reflect variations in aspects of the broader social and structural context within which these relationships occur. Specifically, I have stressed that friendships are partly influenced by modes of descent and other organizational aspects of kinship, such as genealogical positioning, socially prescribed patterns of behaviour between affines and patterns of inheritance and of postnuptial residence. While analysing how each of these features may affect the relationship between friendship and kinship and their degree of overlap, I have drawn parallels between societies and emphasized principles with cross-cultural relevance that have been largely neglected in the literature on friendship.

This neglect is notably due to the fact that friendship is still largely studied apart from kinship. Such a state of affairs is regrettable for a number of reasons. First, it is hard to ignore that friendship is usually an ideal model for relationships between kin. Second, it is undeniable that friendship is frequently transformed into kinship. Third, it should not be overlooked that even in contemporary settings where first marriages largely continue to be arranged by relatives of ascending generations of the future spouses and where alliances between certain categories of kin are still clearly preferred, the kin constellation opted for in practice is often the one simultaneously reinforced by already existing bonds of friendship between relatives enjoying greater rights to arrange marriages. All of the above proves that kinship and friendship cannot be easily separated from one another (see also Reed-Danahay 1999; Rodgers 2010). Rather, they are like a couple who may get divorced, but even then still has a lot of trouble in clearly splitting up.

However, there are other reasons for advocating greater consideration of kinship in friendship studies. In the previous literature, it has been argued that there is a positive correlation between ambivalence towards friendships and both strength of kinship structures and degrees of overlap between neighbourliness and kinship. Given that friendship is still largely studied in isolation from kinship, however, some implications of this correlation have been neglected by research. One of them could be that in contexts where kinship structures remain strong and where many relatives still live in close geographical proximity, the tendency to keep friendships hidden also increases. If this is true, our ability as anthropologists to grasp fully how important friendships are for those we study is even more limited than indicated in this contribution.

In practice, the identification of other people's friendships is undoubtedly complicated by the fact that these relationships are often linguistically disguised. Such identification is also problematic both because, as was shown in the second section, friendship is related to questions of identity and power, and because its development sometimes underlies an emotional economy that is at odds with certain norms which, in turn, favour the veiling of friendships. These points, taken together, suggest that the actual significance of friendships has been underestimated in most studies and social settings. However, the latter assertion applies to a greater extent to non-Western countries, given that less research has been done there than in Western ones, especially in the last decades.

The recent tendency to focus increasingly on the West is, on the whole, consistent with the sociological stance that friendship gains significance in societies which have 'abandoned' kinship as an organizing principle. Furthermore, it conforms to a dualistic thinking of kinship versus friendship that is all the more inappropriate since friendship plays a considerable role in the activating, verifying and creating of kinship ties in many places, including in non-Western societies. With regard to the latter, it can be argued that it is precisely because they comprise groups of people whose everyday life is still strongly structured by kinship that they belong to the societies in which friendship is of particularly great significance. Such an assumption is notably supported by the fact that non-Western societies also entail a larger number of face-to-face communities. Since actual relationships between relatives are often, in practice, more strongly felt to be both quite constraining and burdensome within such communities, there are grounds to believe that it is rather in non-Western societies than in Western ones that friendship, conceived here as an extra-kin relationship, is of special importance.

Acknowledgements

I am very grateful to Bettina Mann, Stephen P. Reyna and the late Mahmoudou Djingui for their comments and suggestions on this contribution. I also wish to thank Günther Schlee and the Max Planck Institute for Social Anthropology (Halle/Saale) for their support and the Volkswagen Foundation (Germany) for funding the multidisciplinary project entitled 'Freundschaft und Verwandtschaft: Zur Unterscheidung und Relevanz zweier Beziehungssysteme', in the context of which parts of this chapter have been written.

Notes

1. For the significance of size in alliance building in conflict situations, see Schlee (2008).
2. For a shorter version of this article in German, see Guichard (2007b).
3. Both expressions are borrowed from Paine (1969: 508).

4. For an interesting study dealing with this topic in connection with a European context, see Spencer and Pahl (2006).
 5. For early use of the term 'amity' in the anthropological literature on kinship, see Fortes (1969).
 6. See also Reyna in this volume.
 7. In practice, there is a variety of intermediate patterns between these two extremes (see, for instance, the work of Rogers and Salamon [1983] on French and North-American farmers).
 8. See Gulliver (1955), Schlee (1989, 2012), White (1990) and van Dijk (1994).
 9. This is surprising since Gulliver seems to acknowledge the validity of the principle according to which networks with a high degree of multiplexity contain a greater potential for interpersonal conflicts to draw in large numbers of people than less interconnected networks. But one reason for this omission could be that the Ndendeuli appear to have been remarkably quick in moving away from kin-neighbours which whom they came into conflict, i.e., to move away from neighbourhoods in which they found that they could not enjoy 'good company'.
10. This friendship form is disappearing. During fieldwork in 2003–2004 (Adamaoua region), I mostly found it among women who were over fifty years of age.
11. Third cousins can indeed be considered to be on the margins of genealogically traceable kinship given that the memory of Fulbe Mbororo rarely covers more than three ascending generations and three degrees of collaterality.
12. See also Uhl (1991).
13. Here, I rely on the accepted notion in the existing literature that trust and intimacy can largely be perceived as both defining qualities and gradients of friendship.
14. The generic terms for 'friends' are *pasiiBe* in Benin and *soobiraaBe* in Cameroon. Each of these terms can also be used to refer to 'casual' friends and be opposed to those meaning 'good' and/or 'close' friends (*beldiiBe* and *yiBBe* respectively in Benin; *yiBBe* notably for both in Cameroon).
15. For the importance of interethnic friendships, see, for example, Jacobson (1973); in this volume, see Breusers, Grätz, Tadesse and Guichard.
16. For an analysis of friendship in terms of power, see Reyna in this volume.
17. Reina's study of friendship became better known through the work of Wolf, in which the latter author revitalized the classic opposition between expressive or emotional friendships and instrumental ones (1966).
18. For accounts on women's friendships in Africa, see, for instance, Werthmann (1997), Meier (2004) and Pelican (2004, 2012).

Chapter 2

Comradeship and the Transformation of Alliance Theory among the Maasai

Shifting the Focus from Descent to Peer-Group Loyalty

Paul Spencer

Introduction

In considering the topic of friendship among the Maasai of East Africa, it is useful to recall Simmel's (1950) analysis of dyads and triads as fundamental building blocks of society. A dyad, he noted, entails a very personal relationship that can involve a range of close emotional bonds, and it may be regarded as the basic element of any personal network of friends. But this relationship is often ambivalent and essentially fragile. Even where the pair is united through warm fellow feelings, this union cannot survive the death or desertion of either partner. The only lasting future lies in breaking down the exclusiveness through third parties, in effect becoming part of a more inclusive threesome. The triad, he argued, can survive the critical loss of one member, although it also opens up a wider range of possible relations: a majority of opinion between two against the third, perhaps conspiring and sharing secrets – a dyad within the triad – and the possibility of shifting relations between them with each shift in context. Simmel's point was that while the transition from a twosome to a threesome is radical, this is not true of a transition from a threesome to a foursome or a fivesome. With the presence of a third party, the triad can contain many of the elements of a larger group and presents a microcosm of society at large. Clearly, this argument has limitations as the scale extends to the impersonality of groups that reach beyond the personal network of individuals, but in introducing the constraining effects of third parties on personal relations, it bears on the more permanent and overarching constraints of social institutions, which Malinowski later highlighted as the crux of social anthropology (see Firth 1957: 29, 59, 137).

Among the Maasai, the relevance of third party constraint on individual friendships and rivalries is well illustrated by their age system, which is *the* dominant institution governing their society, looming over their interaction, even to the point of suppressing individuality itself. The notion of close and warm friendship among age-peers is institutionalized, and expectations for hospitality and sharing are sacrosanct, extending towards total strangers from another Maasai section. To evade these expectations can lead, it is held, to the most terrible age-set curse. The stereotype of a total stranger who also happens to be an age mate provides a vivid illustration of the ambiguity that underpins Simmel's third party.

Marriage and Career Fulfilment among Maasai Women and Men

The development of friendships among Maasai women in the course of their lives contrasts quite strikingly with that of men. Their experience seems to be typical of many other societies in this region, where they are treated by elders as chattels for arranged polygynous marriages and then expected to produce sons as heirs and daughters for further arranged marriages. The sharp demarcation of male and female domains corresponds to quite different career profiles.

Marriage is a particularly bleak point in a Maasai girl's life, but it is also the first step towards building up her personal 'ego-centred' network of friendships which accumulates as her family grows and her children marry to produce children of their own. The development of this network is chequered by the pattern of pastoral nomadism, which changes the configuration of neighbours with each move. It is the men as family heads who make decisions to migrate and may choose to live near friends of their own choosing, disrupting the friendships that their wives may have formed locally. However, this also opens up the possibility of making new acquaintances and renewing old friendships. By the time a married woman emerges as a grandmother and often a widow also, she will have moved many times, renewed many friendships, and had a good chance of establishing herself as a pillar within the women's domain, wherever she goes. From a position of subservience, she reaches her full potential in old age. This broad profile contrasts in almost every respect with the life careers of Maasai men, who are in a stronger position at first but find themselves increasingly marginalized as they grow old, although still respected.

The Maasai have a male-centred age system, evoking an obsolete ideology of warriorhood that has survived the virtual abolition of intertribal warfare. Elsewhere (Spencer 1965), I have argued that this anachronism stems from the persistence of a high degree of polygyny, which creates a shortage of marriageable women. This is resolved by delaying the marriage of young men, typically until the age of about thirty. Elsewhere in Africa, a high rate of polygyny often leads to family tensions, because sons have to wait – and wait – while their fathers take on further wives and deplete the family herd. Among the Maasai, these young unmarried men are known as *moran* (sing. *morani*), and the organization of *moran*hood, which is controlled ultimately by the married elders, may be viewed as a means of creating a queue discipline among impatient bachelors, leading eventually to their marriages when they become elders. It is the age system that delays their marriages and not individual fathers, thereby protecting the family by diverting competition for wives. While this may be seen as a functionalist argument, the persistence of this institution over a period of radical change leads one to search for some kind of stabilizing mechanism such as this. Functionalism ignores the possibility of change, but it does provide an insight into resistance to change, and the Maasai are renowned for the tenacity of tradition.

The Maasai are spread over an area that is considerably larger than Austria, and this is divided into sixteen 'tribal' sections. Within any section there are typically three or four *manyat* ('warrior villages', sing. *manyata*). Defence of the *manyata* territory provides the *moran* with a public role, and they are the most flamboyant and ritualized sector of Maasai society. This does not resolve the competition between younger and older men for women, but it does structure it. The behaviour of *moran* extends from close bonds of loyalty to one another when they sport themselves as the epitome of Maasaihood, to various forms of delinquency. Thus, the *moran* are poised somewhere between childhood and adulthood throughout their twenties. In this sense, they may be viewed as passing through a period of adolescence that is socially constructed and quite distinct from biological pubescence. Boys in their early teens are still dominated as herders by their fathers, pinning them down in a regime that trains them to become herd owners in their own right one day. Meanwhile, they anticipate their *moran*hood in their spare time at night, singing, dancing, parading through the bush and cultivating a sense of group identity. This display of a shared trust and growing confidence in their own ability is ultimately self-fulfilling in persuading the elders that the time has come to initiate them to form a new set. It is then time for the ageing *moran* to retire to elderhood.

Following their circumcision in their late teens, boys become *moran*, and they are co-opted by their age-peers to form a new *manyata*, together with their mothers. This is their opportunity to break away from paternal control, and fathers are expected to comply with this and to want their sons to develop within the discipline of the *manyata*. Some fathers may try to make a reasoned plea for dispensation, but they will be forcibly held down by the *moran* if they try to put their weight as elders behind this request. Exceptions to the rule of *manyata* recruitment are made on their merit – if there is good reason to avoid this duty – but it is the local body of *moran* who have the final say. Elders (and fathers in particular) are highly respected, and even feared for their power to curse. But in the context of the recruitment of their sons and senior wives to the *manyata*, they have to respect the wishes of the body of *moran*. The formation of a new *manyata* is a high point in a young man's career.

The Peer Group, Loyalty and Comradeship

The critical period for inculcating the bonds of loyalty that characterize the Maasai age system is during the years that *moran* spend together at the *manyata*. The glamour of *moran*hood centres on the *manyata* and it is there that they cultivate and parade an ethos of sharing. They shun any form of self-indulgence in public. Any disloyalty to the *manyata* is a breach of faith and will be punished. To abscond and stay away without permission is an offence. *Moran* should always keep one another's company. They cannot drink milk by themselves and, coupled with other food prohibitions, this means that they must go hungry on any morning or evening when they happen to be alone until they have found the company of at least one other *morani* to offer them milk. In popular imagery and self-esteem, this sharing of milk with its strict etiquette is the epitome of *moran*hood. Away from the family dominated by the father (and older brothers) *manyata moran* build up a rich store of experiences that they continue to share anecdotally in later life. These extend throughout the territory defended by the *manyata,* even to diplomatic visits to neighbouring *manyat* and beyond. The Maasai are mesmerized by the notion of *moran*hood, which also has a vicarious spell on women. Women of all ages do not simply dote on this ideal, but they also experience the *manyata* as unmarried girls when they may reside there as shared lovers of the *moran,* and later as proud co-opted *manyata* mothers. Young wives should avoid *moran* and the *manyata,* but as suspected lovers, they, too, are involved more covertly with these young men. *Moran* are suspected of having affairs with married women, of being stock thieves, and generally of lacking respect for older men: adolescence has its deviant aspects, especially when it is prolonged as among the Maasai. But no-one suggests that disloyalty to the *manyata* could ever be a further vice among *moran,* so intense is the popular image that they project.

Bonds of friendship between age mates grow out of the *manyata* episode. The latter is characterized by an excessive display of 'group indulgence', opposed to any suggestion of self-interest. This male age bonding is expected to form the basis of friendship for the rest of their lives. A traditional expression of friendship would occur when two *moran* pledged themselves together in battle. They would defend one another to the end, and if one were killed, the other would risk his life to lay out the corpse properly. However, the notion of such 'friendship' also has an ambivalent ring if it implies any sense of pairing or cliquishness, excluding others. Thus, 'comradeship' would better express the ideal of the *manyata,* with the emphasis on unity and sharing. In a similar vein, no *morani* should claim exclusive access to any girl who is his lover, for this would be to display jealousy towards his peers' right to share. Inevitably, some friendships may be closer than others, but such intimacy should not be displayed in public: no other *morani* should be excluded from their company. Exclusive pairing threatens the comradeship of the *manyata* and is anathema. It is disloyal and a denial of sharing.

Eventually, as they are challenged by uninitiated boys displaying their unity and strength, the ageing *moran* begin to tire of their way of life. Some are forced to marry or to take over from their ageing fathers. Morale at the *manyata* begins to slump, and the older *moran* are further dispirited by the switch of attention of the girls to younger *moran* – and even to boys. Increasingly, they accept the inevitability of retiring to elderhood. After an extended period, the *manyata* is disbanded. However, the comradeship that was built up during their *manyata* period persists throughout the remainder of their lives, and their age-set continues to develop.

The most significant ritualized step towards elderhood is taken when each *morani* is made to drink milk by himself, offered by an elder rather than an age-peer. *Moran* who have performed this ceremony say that they have difficulty in swallowing the milk, and for some time afterwards they lose their appetite and age visibly. They may even seek out age mates informally to share milk as they did in the past; but they no longer enjoy the experience and find that the spell of *moran*hood has been broken. Whereas the ideal of equality among *moran* was enacted through sharing company, milk, girlfriends and anything else that could be shared, this ideal is compromised when they become elders.

This is a time when they begin to marry, around the age of thirty, and cultivate their family and herd. They turn to herding, and this highlights considerable differences in wealth between families, and in their devotion to herding which, coupled with luck, can increase these differences. The bonds of age-set sharing remain, and as elders they continue to share food and also the sexuality of their wives with their age mates. As hosts, they may go hungry to satisfy their peers. As fathers whose children may have been (visibly) begotten by other age mates, they should express delight and gratitude that these liaisons have produced offspring and show no jealousy or discrimination towards these children. It is an ideal demonstration of age-set unity. But the sharing – even the sexuality of their wives – is of consumables. They share milk, meat and the marital bed with age mates; but the living herds and the children remain their own. Regardless of paternity, each child is a new asset to the family, and differences in wealth persist.

After they have married, age mates do not necessarily live together in the same village, and of course they, too, move around. But there are always age mates in the vicinity, and it is with these that they tend to look for company in their leisure time, which increases as their sons become old enough to manage the family herd. The very fact of their nomadism brings them constantly into touch with other age mates, and so do feasts on various ritual occasions, when they again share meat together. As dispersed elders, they are scrupulous in maintaining bonds within the age-set as a whole. If two of them fight, then they will both be punished severely, even if the fault is one-sided, for the anger of their age mates can constitute a terrible age-set curse. It is the development of this power to curse with elderhood that gives this bond a sinister edge. For a curse by his age-set leaves a man totally isolated, even from his age-peers; it is sometimes described as the most terrible curse of all. When an elder is summoned by his age mates to lend his support by attending some gathering, he dare not refuse. If an articulate or popular elder is asked by some age mates to speak on their behalf locally or to lead a delegation on some issue, there may be a certain coyness in accepting this role, but again the expected response is that he dare not refuse. It would be a disloyalty to his age-set to do otherwise. Even if just two age mates make a reasonable request of a third, then they act as representatives of the age-set and their request has a coercive power. Men are bound by their age-set. In the eyes of women and younger men, elders are self-indulgent and mean hypocrites, who put their own selfish interests above those of their families and have a terrible curse over younger people. The popular image of the sorcerer may be seen as a grotesque caricature of the worst side of elderhood. But the view from within the age-set is that loyalty to age mates is still the highest virtue, and this reveals a strong sense of group indulgence, which persists almost to the very end. As Richard Waller has noted (personal communication), as members of an age-set die off in old age, the handful of survivors claim to lose further interest in life. Friends die, while the notion of comradeship persists until there is nothing left to live for.

In addition to the sinister power of the curse that characterizes elderhood, there is a further ambiguity that undermines the idyllic image of the peer group in later life. The activities of *moran* are centred on the territory that their *manyata* is bound to defend, which comprises just one part of the total tribal section, whereas elders migrate freely across the whole of this section, and very occasionally even across the borders into a neighbouring section. This brings elders into regular contact with age mates whom they do not know so well because they had been *moran* at different *manyat*. They may come to know one another better as mellowing elders, especially when they find themselves allied politically against other age-sets at formal gatherings. But they do not share the same *manyata* experience and this leads to a more formal relationship among age mates, which tends to stress the element of age-set obligation and duty. The relationship lacks the spontaneity of friendships stemming from a shared youth. Thus, when elders visit their age mates, the host is obliged to vacate his wife's hut for the night, in effect offering his wife – if she consents. This is a punctilious obligation, but visiting friends from *manyata* days may invite the host to remain in his hut, so that they can continue to share one another's company overnight. So long as such lapses are in the spirit of age-set unity, no harm is done, for the visitors in effect give dispensation on behalf of their age-set. However, if a man were to avoid this obligation in any other circumstance, then a wider group of age mates could raid his village, kill a prized ox for a feast, and force themselves on his wife. The host is then expected to show his gratitude, for this would be undertaken with a view to quelling their anger and avoiding their age-set curse. Worst of all would be if a visiting age mate from another tribal section is denied full hospitality in any way, for his resentment would have the automatic effect of an age-set curse. The stranger who is also an age mate is one of the most threatening images of Maasai elderhood, and the observance of age-set obligations and generosity is more than just scrupulous: it becomes almost obsessive. This reveals a spectrum of relations within the age-set. The closest life-long friendships tend to relate back to the *manyata* experience, and then as elders they may formally relax age-set obligations in a spirit of total trust. At the opposite extreme, obligations towards the stranger age mate from across the section border become excessively rigid with the bleak spectre of an age-set curse. As a stranger, he is dehumanized and represents the faceless age-set at large.

The Shallowness of Descent

It is virtually impossible for a Maasai to belong to the same age-set as his father, but beyond that the father's age-set does not influence or restrict the future age-set of any son. To this extent, the Maasai are atypical of other age-based societies in East Africa and theirs is an age system based more purely on age alone. They are also atypical in the degree to which kinship bonds beyond the extended family are largely ignored. Shallow lineages peter out beyond the generation of the father. Few Maasai know the names of their grandfathers (although they will normally know their age-set). A responsible elder is in a strong position to manage his own family even before his father has died; and afterwards he goes from strength to dominance. Surviving fathers' brothers might be involved in some critical event, such as a divorce that leads to the return of marriage payments or dealing with the disruptive behaviour of some member that threatens to bring the extended family into disrepute. These senior men are respected and may even have a hand in arranging the odd marriage. However, it is towards age mates that men look for support rather than their brothers or close patrilineal kin. The Maasai also have clans, but these are largely significant only by default, and even clan exogamy has dwindled in the course of the twentieth century. For whatever reason, clanship seems to have been a casualty of colonial rule, while the age and *manyata* systems have persisted, despite attempts to stifle them by colonial and postcolonial authorities.

The diminution of clanship can be pursued somewhat speculatively in relation to Maasai history. Generally, the Maasai recognize that clan exogamy was more strictly observed in the past, and there are clues in the early literature, notably Merker's *Die Masai* (1904), that clanship had been more pronounced in earlier times. *Moran* bore clan markings on their shields, and debts and feuds were pursued with force between clans, apparently without restraint from the wider society. This would have been anathema more recently, when hostility between *moran* of different clans would have undermined the unity of their shared *manyata*. In fact, Merker's outline of earlier times evokes a society rather similar to the Samburu further north, where Maasai-type *manyat* have been absent and clanship has remained strong. Clan exogamy is characteristic of the Samburu, and the prime loyalty among *moran* is to age mates of their clan rather than to their age-set at large.

According to Maasai oral tradition, the nineteenth century was a period when two charismatic prophets, Supeet and Mbatian, had a dominant influence and were largely responsible for unifying Maasai *moran* against powerful enemies. This suggests that their policy of unification sought to build up altruism and group indulgence as a *manyata* virtue, overriding family feuds and clan hostilities in the interests of Maasai dominance throughout the region. This is to imply that some of the characteristics of friendship which have been discussed in the previous section only emerged since around 1860 with the decline of clanship. Expressed in another way, this suggests that the major sense of identity among Maasai has shifted from the membership of a clan, shared through common descent, to the membership of an age-set, shared through common experience as age-peers.

Alliance Theory and the Elementary Structure of the Maasai Age System

A very general term for friendship among the Maasai is *shoreisho*, expressing a casual sense of rapport and shared company between friends (*il-choreta*, sing. *ol-chore*). In a more formal sense, implying a trusted exchange partner, a friend in need is *o-sotua* (pl. *i-sotuetin*), someone who has given help and asked for help in the past, perhaps to restock his depleted herd, and he may be relied on at any time. The term *o-sotua* also signifies an umbilical cord, and this draws attention to the very specific and formalized 'friendship' between a man and his father-in-law. Rather than coining the term 'bride-wealth' for the Maasai, it is more useful to speak of a 'marriage debt'. Even before the marriage of his daughter, an elder may solicit cattle from his prospective son-in-law, building up a debt with his daughter as security. After he has given her away in marriage, the indebtedness is reversed and the father-in-law may solicit further cattle without end. Father- and son-in-law display a pronounced show of respect, but they are also *i-sotuetin*, firm exchange partners, and these payments of the marriage debt are 'cattle of friendship' (*inkishu o-sotua*), responding to the priceless gift of a daughter. The mutual giving is in a metaphorical sense the umbilical cord, a link to further life.

With this in mind, I wish to invoke Lévi-Strauss's (1969 [1949]) theory of alliance between exogamous groupings. This was an elaboration of Mauss's

(1990 [1923–1924]) notion that formal gift exchange underpinned society as a binding moral force, and of Tylor's (1889) suggestion that extended families were too small to survive without exogamy: they faced the practical alternative between 'marrying out and being killed out'. This may be compared with the widely quoted East African expression, 'We marry our enemies'. Lévi-Strauss's explanation of the horror of incest and the regulation of marriage as the bedrock of social morality is nowadays treated as an odd episode of anthropological history and wholly inferior to his more mature structuralism that followed (e.g., Leach 1970). He himself regarded his theory as largely irrelevant to African societies, which only rarely have prescriptive forms of cross-cousin marriage. Among the Maasai in particular, clan exogamy is lax, and concepts of incest with relatively close 'sisters' or 'mothers' are not a matter of general concern. Yet oddly and quite unexpectedly, Lévi-Strauss's theory does have some relevance for the Maasai. This arises from their very strong concern for even a hint of intimacy between a man and any woman who can be classified as a 'daughter', and notably the daughter of his age-set, which I have elaborated on in more detail elsewhere (1988). While Lévi-Strauss has sometimes been criticized for confusing exogamy with incest prohibitions and marriage with sex, a point I would note here is that the Maasai quite explicitly link these together, and they are particularly unprudish on the issue of marriage and sex, with this one exception. A man must *not* have intimate relations with or marry any woman whom he would avoid as a 'daughter', and this involves a considerable proportion of all women.

Lévi-Strauss argued that the system of alliance between lineages and clans through the exchange of women (as chattels) could be threatened by in-marriage. This led him to suggest that the horror of incest extends beyond the biological family to the culturally defined wife-giving group precisely because it stems from a social rather than a biological incongruity. This has to be modified to adapt it to the Maasai context, where hypersensitivity over incest concerns age-set 'daughters' rather than clan 'sisters'. It is the strict avoidance of each 'daughter' by the age-set of her father that structures the system of marriage. They are the wife-givers, and her husband's age-set are the wife-receivers.

It has to be borne in mind that a Maasai daughter is uniquely linked to her father's age-set. She can have only one father, whereas, as a mother or sister, she can have sons or brothers in two or even three different age-sets. Elders of an age-set can assert exclusive possession over a category of marriageable women – their 'daughters', whereas they have no such claim over their 'sisters' or 'mothers', who are also 'sisters' and 'mothers' of other age-sets. This correlates neatly with the absence of a widespread concern over the possibility of incest with either 'sisters' or 'mothers'. The term 'age-set exogamy' may be coined in relation to marrying 'daughters' out, corresponding to the notion of clan exogamy in relation to 'sisters'.

Unlike clans, age-sets are not self-perpetuating groups. They dwindle into old age, and the general flow of daughters is towards more junior age-sets. This provides a basis from which the more senior age-sets can exercise power over their juniors, demanding respect as real and potential fathers-in-law with the power to withhold their 'daughters'. This downward flow of 'daughters' is the clear norm. An upward marriage to a more senior age-set would not be regarded as 'incestuous', but it would be anomalous and unlikely. It would place the older husband in the incongruous position of having to respect a younger man as his father-in-law. The age mates of both parties could oppose the match, effectively prohibiting it. A highly polygynous and feared prophet might conceivably rise above such an anomaly, but it would be contrary to the emphasis on age-set conformity among ordinary Maasai.

The tension between age-sets should be stressed. It is provoked with each new age-set by the delinquencies of the *moran,* which infuriate their seniors, and then it is fanned by the competition for wives and the jostling for power between elders of different age-sets. The ideal of loyalty within an age-set corresponds to an undercurrent of rivalry with other age-sets, contradicting the outward display of respect for older men and of dignity in the presence of younger men.

Given the competition for wives between age-sets and the strong bonds of friendship within each age-set, one may ask: what if age mates *were* allowed to marry each other's daughters? A system of exchange of daughters within the age-set would then be possible. In the spirit of age-set sharing and loyalty, a father could be under irresistible pressure from age mates to give them priority over suitors from junior age-sets. To prefer some other suitor could be construed as an act of disloyalty to his own age-set, and even provoke an implicit age-set curse. Such a request would be dangerous to refuse. This would then encourage 'in-marriage', and 'daughters' would accrue as wives of the most senior age-sets instead of being handed downwards. Younger men could be starved of wives and of the opportunity to generate daughters of their own. This could even drive them to rebellion against the senior generation for wives, reminiscent of the change-over of generation-sets in northern Uganda, on the one hand, and Freud's scenario in *Totem and Taboo* (1931 [1910]), on the other. Paraphrasing Tylor (1899), each Maasai age-set is faced with the simple practical alternative between marrying 'daughters' out (and down) and families dying out. In forbidding 'daughters' to one another as age mates, elders are ensuring the future succession of their families as fathers.

What at first sight might seem a negative example that throws further doubt on Lévi-Strauss's argument concerning the link between notions of incest and clan exogamy turns out to be an impressive vindication of it in another respect. Intense rivalry between age-sets is held in check by a system of alliance, expressed again in terms of marriage rules: the transition of women from being 'daughters' of one age-set to becoming 'wives' of another. The way in which the horror of incest is expressed is consistent with the social solidarity of the 'connubium' of age-sets. This involves a type of 'hypogamy', with the avoidance of 'daughters' and their downward marriage to younger men, while these younger men, in order to qualify as eligible suitors, are obliged to show respect for their seniors. The strict avoidance of 'daughters' is the bedrock of social morality in a society where institutionalized and casual adultery characterizes the relationship between men and women in general.

Among the Maasai, the fury of junior elders whose wives have been repeatedly seduced by adulterous *moran* cannot be overstated. They may convene as an age-set and refuse all *moran* their 'daughters' in marriage, and also insist on the return of those that have already been given away, exercising the threat of their curse. This could precipitate the total breakdown of any 'marriage alliance' between age-sets. But the threat cannot be sustained, and the *moran* find themselves obliged to offer very substantial gifts of cattle and other commodities to the offended age-set. Elders of more senior age-sets may then try to mediate, and they encourage the junior elders to accept the gift without loss of face and to lift their threat. The system of alliance is restored, and the age-set of *moran* have transcended a serious obstacle on their path towards elderhood. The junior elders then become their 'fathers-in-law', a popular Maasai term for the next age-set up, and the stage is set for a new confrontation with the next age-set of *moran* as they step into the limelight.

Conclusion

The formalized pattern of comradeship among Maasai men contrasts with women's ego-centred networks of friendship, which extend outwards and through their children as they grow older. From the initiation of each new age-set, young men are constrained into comradeship, and this exclusive bond corresponds to a general situation of rivalry between age-sets of all ages. Given the weakness of the concept of 'descent' beyond the Maasai family, these disruptive tensions are linked to a system of 'marriage alliance' between age-sets that is essential for the perpetuation of future generations. Seniority endows older men with power, and their ability to dispose of their daughters in marriage is a key element of this. Thus, surprisingly, Lévi-Strauss's theory of alliance becomes relevant once it has been transformed to match a society whose social organization is based on age rather than descent. 'Age-set exogamy' ensures the marriage market for *moran* as they settle down and the continuity of Maasai society.

Among those East African societies with age systems, the avoidance of age-set daughters is widespread, although the significance of this elsewhere tends to be masked by the greater importance of lineage and clanship, and a range of other sexual avoidances (Spencer 1988: 195). In these other age-based societies, the avoidance of 'daughters' does not always stand out as a category that is a class of its own, as occurs among the Maasai. The Maasai case appears to be pronounced because it is so clear cut. Indeed, the institutionalized handing downwards of daughters seems to be as central to age organization in this area as generational constraints are to the age systems of their distant northern neighbours, with a shift from a concern for 'descent' in the north to uncompromising peer-group loyalty in the south. As an ideal type, the Maasai system is uncomplicated by descent and generational considerations, and the ramifications of age as the dominant feature of social organization become more manifest.

Part II
Friendship and Ethnicity

Chapter 3

Friendship Networks in Southwestern Ethiopia

Wolde Gossa Tadesse and Martine Guichard

Introduction

This chapter deals with friendship in a region where friendship is still a largely institutionalized practice and an important feature of social organization. It focuses more specifically on bond-friendships established across ethnic boundaries, drawing primarily on data collected by Tadesse among the Hor (also known as Arbore) from 1994 to 1996 and secondarily on a series of brief visits and research work he conducted among the Konso between 1984 and 2002. The Hor are agro-pastoralists whose language 'belongs within a "Macro Somali" (now "Omo-Tana") group [which is itself] a major division of Lowland East Cushitic' (Hayward 2003: 317). They live in the South Omo Zone of the Southern Nations, Nationalities, and People's Region (SNNPR) of Ethiopia. The Hor occupy the plains of the Rift Valley located at the northern end of Lake Chew Bahir (formerly called Lake Stephanie) and in proximity to the Kenyan border. They number approximately 5,000 and constitute a much smaller group than the Konso who are largely farmers and reside in highlands situated northeast of Hor country.

Some useful data is currently available that illustrates the existence of a complex network of relationships covering this extensive landscape of southwestern Ethiopia. The works of Almagor (1978), Sobania (1991), Gebre (1997), Girke (2010) and Sagawa (2010), to mention just a few, indicate how forms of bond-friendship abound in southwestern Ethiopia. Examination of some of the contexts in which these networks have sustained within and beyond the territory of particular groups merits some characterization. In much of the area covered by such friendship networks the state is distant, if not totally absent from the daily lives of people in the region. In Hor country, for example, only a police station mainly with a road-block function and a small school exist outside the limits of Hor villages (*dir*) that testify to the presence of the state. Hor indigenous structures of governance remain intact to this day, benefiting local and regional needs and filling the gap one naturally assumes to be covered by the state and other commercial and financial institutions as is the case in the West. This chapter is not about the absence of these institutions but rather about the existence of other kinds of local institutions that are layered at different levels and widths, connecting different cultures and people. These institutions coexist with state institutions and in some cases institutions of the state need them for their own benefit of reaching the wider public through them. In Konso, state presence is more pronounced. In that area, thriving institutions of traditional governance exist side by side with institutions of the state (with visible presence) in the district town rather than in rural villages, where only a few schools mark state presence. This intactness of traditional governance structures and remoteness of the state in the region are factors contributing to the persistence of the kind of friendship networks that are at the centre of this contribution. These networks of bond-friendship established across ethnic boundaries are also a preferred form of institution since they are sensitive to specific needs of each member group and people. They operate within a framework of seniority that is common to various ethnic groups and serves both as an organizing principle and a dynamic for moving forward socially and culturally. In this framework, certain group members are entitled to prerogatives that support the continuation of ties of interethnic bond-friendship and work towards strengthening their relevance and usefulness for the people in the region. Unlike relations with state representatives, such networks are accessible, satisfy the needs of partners to the friendship and are trusted. Where there is betrayal of trust each partner knows where to go and which bell to ring to reclaim lost trust or to redress harm caused by loss of trust. Most of all, friendships follow lines of relatedness and acquaintance which make things easier, less bureaucratic, stress-free and full of adventure.

In the following sections, we will show that interethnic bond-friendships are still important channels for the circulation of wealth between various groups occupying different and contrasting ecological zones in southwestern Ethiopia. As practised today in the research area, these bond-friendships and the networks associated with them show many similarities with those described for other regions or other times.[1] In his now classic article entitled 'Feasts, Famines and Friends: Nineteenth Century Exchange and Ethnicity in the Eastern Lake Turkana Region', Sobania (1991) illustrates how trade routes and intrasocietal bond-partnerships of gift giving and exchange – i.e., interethnic bond-friendships – weaved together in the nineteenth century and how this weaving related to the needs of communities that were constantly adapting to changing circumstances, maintaining flexibility of identity and residence. Sobania sees two pathways of bond-friendship that begin in Konso and Bachada Hamar reaching eastern Lake Turkana north to south. Our contribution builds on Sobania's work and focuses on networks of friendship that cover Sobania's pathways as well as the wider region between western Omo extending to the Boran-Somali border area and to Boditi in the north (Wolaita territory). This chapter adds that it is not only the routes and traders that matter but a number of institutions that facilitate movement through landscapes and traditional routes bringing ideas, knowledge, gifts and valuables of secular and religious value to people in other lands.

While dealing with interethnic bond-friendships, we will give insight into the kind of gifts exchanged between bond-friends and into some of the activities shared by friends during visits. Then we will illustrate how seriously such friendships are taken by both individuals and the communities to which bond-friends belong. Furthermore, we will point to the importance of interethnic bond-friendships as a source of mutual assistance in times of hardship. After giving examples from data collected among the Hor, we will focus on the friendship networks of Konso craft-workers and traders locally known as *hauda*.

General Information about the Hor

The Hor depend primarily on sorghum cultivation and animal husbandry for their livelihood, and secondarily on trading, fishing and hunting. They are patrilineal and practise clan exogamy. They are organized by age in a system that notably works by placing a generation in power for a definite period of time, and have four major villages, each with their own age organization and ritual leaders. These leaders who are referred to as *qawot*s hold hereditary positions and come from bracelet-wearing clans, i.e., from clans that are all mystically powerful but not all to the same degree. The most powerful among these leaders are those who act as senior and junior *qawot*s and claim to have influence over the natural order of the region. This claim is widely accepted by members of neighbouring groups who, like ordinary Hor, bring them prescribed ritual gifts acknowledging their power. Elders of the ruling generation complement the power of the *qawot*s and manage animals, distribute fields and organize calendarical activities, including life-marking events such as initiations.

Although the villages of the Hor are politically autonomous, there is a strong sense of unity between them all that notably becomes manifest in case of conflict with surrounding groups. The latter are categorized as having sweet blood or bad blood. The Hor say they go to war or raid animals from the first category of neighbours and avoid any conflict or shedding blood of members of the second category of surrounding groups. Paradoxically, however, the Hor have friendship networks with both categories of neighbours. Yet, it appears that their sweet-blooded enemies have been changing over the years from the Samburu to Maale and to Boran in the early 1990s.

The Hor have been a self-administering autonomous community managing their affairs without external interference. Whenever external threats appeared, they had managed to evade threat by moving villages, settling in remoter parts of their country and even abandoning their territories only to reappear when threats diminished, hence making it difficult for outsiders to track them. With the nation-state and development coming ever closer to their lives, their earlier strategy of evasion may not be well suited. Although they are not officially acknowledged as contributing to the national economy, their contribution to the regional economy has been immense. Like many other people living in pastoral and rural areas in Ethiopia, they are not well integrated into the cash economy, but – and as will become clear later in this chapter – they supply many of their neighbours with sorghum and livestock and, in exchange, receive various essential items from neighbouring groups. In practice, they have also been sending their animals to the north along the footpaths for many years now and have long received products from the north that they need for their subsistence.

A Partial Overview of Institutionalized Friendships in Hor Country

Forms of institutionalized friendship are still widespread in southwestern Ethiopia, especially in South Omo. In this area, these forms of friendship include variants differing from one another in the extent to which they entail obligations and commitment between partners. With regard to male friendships, for example, the Hor distinguish between *miso*,[2] *abujal*, *baami* and *jal*. The term *miso* is usually used to describe friendships started in childhood, when boys have reached the age of herding young stock. While sharing such activities, children often hunt small animals such as birds and lizards. If they like one another, they may agree to bite the ears of one of the animals they have killed and thereby enter into a formalized friendship with partners referred to as *miso*. Such friendships have a dyadic structure and link young boys who are considered to be witnesses of each other's valour as killers. Their relationships are hoped to later resemble to a relationship between initiated men who have gone to battle together and in which a warrior helps a friend who has killed an enemy to achieve a 'man killer' status by severing the genitals of the killed enemy. However, as friendships formed at a young age, *miso* friendships are primarily associated with ties that are not particularly binding. Given this, they can be contrasted to those between *abujal*. The latter kind of friendship is established in adolescence and usually links a group of four to twelve older boys who are affiliated to the same age-set. Its formalization begins when one of them slaughters a big he-goat, habitually stolen from the herd of a mother's brother. They then make strips of the stomach fat (*mor*) of the goat and wear them around their neck and also rub the stomach content (*ur*) on their bodies. They roast the meat on an open fire and divide it according to their order of seniority. These procedures are repeated from time to time until the other members of the friendship group have each taken turn in killing an animal. Once the killing of the goat is reciprocated, their friendships are fully instituted and the partners start to address each other as *abujal*. Those who are in such relationships may refuse to flog friends when seniors impose a punishment of flogging on one of them. These friendships, however, are generally asserted to involve a lesser degree of mutual commitment than the friendships between partners referred to as *baami*.[3] The friends designated by that term often have maintained a very privileged relationship with one another since childhood and are hence reputed for having regularly drunk milk from the same calabash during that period.[4] They frequently dine together after marriage and avenge each other's death if one is killed by an outside enemy. They are best friends and considered to be closer than brothers or other people related by blood. They exchange gifts, but not with the clear expectation of return gifts, as is the case between friends who call each other *jal* and whose friendship is referred to as *jala*.

In Hor country, the term *jala* denotes a bond-friendship initiated by men, the establishment and the maintenance of which formally require 'seeing the hand of the other', i.e., the receiving of gifts, and 'showing the other person one's own hands', i.e., the giving of gifts.[5] This variant of institutionalized friendship is contracted with members of out-groups. It encompasses relationships infused with trust and generosity that are particularly enduring and link families together over time. Such relationships are in some cases 'inherited' from father to son or transferred from husband to widow after the death of one of the original partners.

Jala friendships established across ethnic boundaries are considered to have a strong binding character and it is often stressed that they should persist even when the groups of the men involved in such relationships are at war with each other. As will become clear later in this chapter, they indeed show a remarkable capacity to survive episodes of violent conflict between groups. In practice, they are so binding that they do not culminate in marriage in the next generation (see also Thubauville 2010). In the latter respect they do not just differ from best friendships between *baami*, but also from friendships that have not been entered into ritually, especially those having evolved into good and close friendships. However, institutionalized best friendships can also be the prelude for matrimonial unions between the friends themselves, provided that these friends are of different sex and belong to marriageable clans.[6] As noted earlier, among the Hor, marriage is notably regulated by clan exogamy, a rule that is now devaluated as 'backwards' by members of some evangelical or born-again churches. These churches, which have proliferated in Ethiopia since the 1990s, provide new avenues for friendships in the research area.

Interethnic Friendships of the *Jala* Type and Their Routes

As noted above, *jala* friendships are institutionalized friendships established across ethnic boundaries. Such bond-friendships are kept alive and strengthened by mutual visits and by using old caravan routes away from the 'modern' roads controlled by police officials. To a great extent the latter roads are avoided because of the tendency of officials to confiscate part of the goods one travels with and to elevate bribes as a precondition for being able to pass without much difficulty the numerous checkpoints they control. But the preference for old caravan routes is also reinforced by the recognition of the growing strength of an organization of craft-workers and traders, the centre of which is located in Konso (Purqud'a). This organization, which is known as *fuld'o* in Konso and has grown more powerful since the fall of the military regime of the Derg (1991), has a branch in Tabya, the administrative centre in Hor country. There it is called *fund'o* and has a Konso ritual leader at its head to whom a rather large number of groups show allegiance in his capacity as major local representative of an organization reputed for keeping the region going. In practice, the *fuld'o/fund'o* certainly plays an important role in ensuring safe movements of goods and persons throughout the region. It ensures that a certain code of conduct is observed while using old caravan routes. According to this code, traders who travel together – and the bond-friends who are part of their travelling team – should support and help each other on journeys along these routes. They are obliged to participate together in the search of lost animals and not to continue with their journey until the searching team finds the lost animals. Those who fail to fulfil such obligations are fined by the *fuld'o/fund'o* which also acts as a guarantor of compensation payment to traders in the case that the latter have been robbed by bandits operating on old caravan routes. This compensation is expected to be paid by the group on the territory of which the goods have been stolen and failure to comply with this expectation would cause the *fuld'o/fund'o* to withdraw all assistance to the group in question. Furthermore, all trade with members of this group would be banned.[7]

The establishment of a *fund'o* branch in Hor attests to the geographical significance of that country for regional trading activities.[8] This significance is also partly reflected in the fact that people of various origins show allegiance to the Hor ritual leaders who belong to mystically powerful clans and assume the function of senior and junior *qawot*. These two *qawot*s are not just ritual leaders of special importance for the Hor who believe that they have strong power to bring rain and fertility over their land, people and animals as well as victory over enemies. They are also held in high regard by members of other groups who recognize their spiritual power and therefore largely solicit their services at the regional level. Among these services are the prayers and blessings they perform for traders and bond-friends planning a joint trip outside Hor country. Such prayers and blessings are believed to be especially potent in guaranteeing a safe journey. In practice, there is no doubt that the *qawot*s work complementarily to the *fund'o* in ensuring safe travel on old caravan routes and thus in facilitating the operation of *jala* friendships established across ethnic boundaries.

The portions of old caravan routes used in connection with *jala* friendships are all the more various since the Hor have bond-friends in a large number of groups, including the Konso, the Tsamako, the Wata, the Dassanetch, the Hamar, the Boran, the Karo and the Nyangatom. These groups cover much of the large area that lies between Somalia and South Sudan. As is well known, relations between these groups are not always peaceful and some groups tend to have more relations of simultaneous enmity with their neighbours than other groups. Over the last decades, the Hor have ceased to have more than two enemies at the same time. This development has allowed them to make more effective use of their networks of bond-friends than in the past.

Exchange of Goods between *Jal* Bond-Friends

Interethnic bond-friendships are pathways through which the Hor obtain goods and tools that are essential for their food production and the performance of their rituals. Among the ritual items that the Hor receive from bond-friends are coffee and honey. Coffee is the medium through which blessings and prayers are made possible. Honey, in its brewed form, is used for initiation ceremonies, supplications of pardon and cleansing ceremonies. Both items are also used for marriage agreements and for bride-wealth payments. Coffee can be bought in local markets but at prices that most Hor cannot afford easily. The same is true for honey which the Hor notably get from bond-friends of Hamar ethnicity, together with tobacco, tobacco seasoning, baking pans, knives, headrests and cotton blankets. These friends obtain goats, heifers and sorghum from the Hor.[9] From their Konso bond-friends the Hor require and receive unhusked coffee beans, tobacco, cotton blankets and sorghum – especially if the Konso harvest was good and the Hor have suffered from drought. The Konso, in return, are given donkeys, small stock, heifers, cows and oxen. They also receive ostrich feathers, game skins, giraffe tails and ivory, which the Hor may get from across the Kenyan border – or perhaps from hunting expeditions with their Hamar bond-friends in Karo land in the Mago National Park. The Dassanetch need and obtain cowhides for roofing their houses, donkeys, tobacco seasoning, ostrich feathers, ammunition and cloths from their Hor friends.

What bond-friends of one group require from bond-friends in other groups depends largely on what is available among them to meet their needs. As the Hor consider it a taboo to grow coffee, to keep bees, to make clay pots and to engage in metal work, they seek to obtain coffee, honey, pots and metal goods from bond-friends belonging to groups that produce such items or have themselves friends in those groups. Characteristic for the prohibitions of production mentioned above is that they actually provide an important basis for interethnic interactions and for the contracting of bond-friendships across ethnic boundaries.

However, the very fact that Hor are very keen to receive certain items from bond-friends in other groups may also be linked to the fact that these items cannot be found in their local markets in the amount needed or may not be available at all. As already reported elsewhere, Tadesse cannot recall having ever seen any knife, axe, hoe blade or clay pot on the markets held in Hor country (Tadesse 2000). Knives are tools of production that are essential for irrigation work, for clearing the bush, for harvesting sorghum and for building houses and animal enclosures. Pots are used for cooking and making coffee. Among the Hor, all these items are first accessed through channels of interethnic bond-friendships, before being secondarily dispersed through society via other lines of connection. Accordingly, the Hor depend very much on bond-friends to perpetuate themselves as a group.

In the Hor community, it is therefore often stressed that it is good to have bond-friends in as many places as possible. This ideal is more successfully achieved, in practice, by wealthy and locally influential men than by other Hor men. Those who are particularly able to have a large number of friends in different out-groups are actually the members of the generation in power who have been appointed as leaders of the age organization, their predecessors, and men who have become spokespersons of their respective settlements by mere competence. Many such people boast about the size of their friendship networks and about the amount of gifts between themselves and each of their twenty-something friends.[10]

More ordinary Hor may have up to three bond-friends across ethnic boundaries. The very poor, however, rarely have *jala* friendships, although they also strive to establish such ties with out-group members and share the view that formalized interethnic friendships are *important investments in the future*. Indeed, one characteristic of *jala* friendships is that their maintenance requires great displays of generosity. Part of that generosity, manifested in hospitality and in the offering of gifts, can seem costly and difficult to afford, when one is particularly weak economically.

Poor Hor mostly report of bond-friendships within their own group, i.e., about friendships through which they are more prone to receive agricultural and pastoral products than exotic items such as coffee and honey. Among them, these items are largely obtained through links of kinship with men having bond-friendships across ethnic boundaries. Such friendships are also important for those who do not have any such relationship on their own because they can enable them to travel safely to neighbouring territories. This state of affairs is at least facilitated by two facts. First, men who have bond-friends in other groups often visit these friends accompanied by friends, kin, spouses or other women. Second, visiting bond-friends and their accompanying team are all entitled to full protection of the host community while in the territory of that community.

Visits to bond-friends are often announced in advance, but it is usually upon arrival that the visiting friend specifies what kinds of items he needs and tells his host when he plans to go back with these items. Before he leaves, the things he requires may be ready for him to take. If times are bad, he will be told to come back at some other time. If the visiting bond-friend is trying to use his stay for selling firearms and ammunition, but is unsuccessful to do as planned, he may leave them with the host partner for him to look after or to convert into livestock.

As suggested above, visits may serve as occasions for guests to trade with members of the host community. In practice, bond-friendships allow to bypass barriers to trade resulting from intergroup conflict. In such circumstances, friendships with members of groups that are not involved in the conflict can be mobilized in order to buy or sell items in the territory of current enemies. For example, if a Boran wants to sell his rifle or ammunition in Hamar country, but is unable to go there because the Hamar are fighting, he may ask a Hor man to help him to achieve his goal. The Hor man will then visit a Hamar bond-friend and make use of his rights to free lodging and to food and security when he travels within the bounds of the territory of his bond-friend's group to sell the above-mentioned items as requested by his Boran friend. He will also use the contacts of his Hamar bond-friend to bargain the sale of these items for a reasonable price.

In practice, however, visits to and from bond-friends involve much more than just exchanging and trading goods with members of out-groups. This point will be dealt with in more detail in the next section. For the moment, we would like to stress that visits are social events marked by great displays of hospitality and conviviality. In Hor country, guests are welcome at the liminal time of dusk – the time when cattle are brought home and the time when it is neither hot nor cold. It is the time assigned for coffee and evening prayers. It is time for rest and peaceful conversation. During this time, noise and disorderly behaviour are avoided.

The atmosphere that reigns in the host's compound after the arrival of a visiting friend is comparable to an atmosphere of festivities where there is plenty to eat and drink and a lot of time to rest. If the situation in the land of the host is good, a goat will be slaughtered. Honey wine will be brewed and served generously together with food. To be sure, hosts take great pains in ensuring that friends are well catered for during visits. But visits to bond-friends are not simply occasions for guests to spend leisurely days of eating, drinking and chatting with their hosts. They are occasions for forming closer ties with one's counterpart. The closer the ties, the higher the probability that friends will treat one another as almost kin and offer one another a part of the bride-wealth they receive from the marriage of their daughters. The closer the ties, the greater the probability that the friendship will be passed on from one generation to the next generation.[11]

However, visits are often arranged so as to be able to witness important events in the life of one's partner and his family. In practice, bond-friends often attend weddings organized in one another's homestead. They may also go to weddings and ceremonies held in other places as they are entitled to move freely in the territory of their host's group and to take part in the social life of that group during visits. If a communal meeting is held during that period, they can attend it and be helped to find an appropriate sitting place in the public assembly. The same applies to the persons who have come together with the visiting friend as guests. But then if members of the host community go on a raid, they are not invited to join the raid. This privilege is reserved for bond-friends who as 'co-raiders' are entitled to a fair share of any loot distributed according to the tradition of the host community.

As the above passage indicates, the activities in which bond-friends take part during visits can be numerous. On such occasions, friends may also work together on the fields of the host and thus get further opportunities to deepen their knowledge of one another as particular individuals and as out-group members. In practice, bond-friends are very familiar with the way how neighbourly groups do certain things. They are well acquainted with the customs of the groups from among which they take friends.

Jala Friendships and Some of their Further Meanings

In the previous section we have already mentioned that *jal* friends rarely visit their counterparts on their own. They usually come together with other persons who, like them, are all entitled to full protection as guests of the host community during visits. In these instances, any offence against the friend – and those who accompany him – is considered as an offence against the host, punishable by flogging. The visited community must recognize and acknowledge him as a friend of one of its members. This principle is highly valued even though incidents occur, as can be illustrated by taking the case of a Hor man called Ello whose visit to a Boran bond-friend took an unexpected turn. After his arrival in Boran, his host asked him to go hunting with the host's younger brother and to bring back game meat. Ello did as requested to please his bond-friend. On the way back from hunting, the bond-friend's brother shot Ello from behind in the arm and Ello fell bleeding. Boran from a nearby settlement carried him to his bond-friend's camp and from there he was carried to a clinic in the nearest town. The camp members paid for his treatment and fed him goat meat until he recovered. Later on, they held the younger brother of the host and, after handing him to the police, intervened to pay a compensation of a couple of bulls to Ello. They then accompanied him back to Hor country. This treatment of the wounded man, and the compensation the Boran gave him, pleased Hor elders and no revenge was taken.

However, special protection should be given to bond-friends in times of conflicts. This ideal was, for example, realized in October 1991, when Hor and Boran became involved in a conflict that would cost hundreds of lives. At the beginning of the conflict, there were a few Boran bond-friends in Hor villages who did not know what was going on. Hor hid them, protected them and sent them off with an escort only after the fighting had ended. They took charge of their property and looked after it so that it could be collected at a later date.

Since 1991, and despite the peace treaty of 2003 negotiated with the arbitration of the nongovernmental organization (NGO) Farm-Africa, group relations between Hor and Boran have remained strained. This treaty was the culmination of a process in the course of which so many peace-making meetings were organized that it is difficult to recall them all. One of these meetings, however, is well documented in the literature on southwestern Ethiopia as it was notably supported by anthropologists and the Addis Ababa University. The meeting in question is that held in the Hor village of Gandaraba in March 1993 and described by Pankhurst in an article entitled 'A Peace Ceremony at Arbore' (2006).[12] Prior to this intergroup meeting, visits between Hor and Boran bond-friends had been suspended, as it is usually the case during serious conflicts between groups and in the wake of conflicts having cost many lives. Shortly after the peace-making ceremony of Gandaraba some Hor and Boran bond-friends began to visit one another again, but only some friendships could be reactivated in that way in 1993. The main reason for this is that most of the Boran sections that had participated in the fighting of 1991 had refused to attend the peace-making ceremony mentioned above. Consequently, the agreements made during that ceremony were not really binding. The very fact that these agreements had still not entered into force in 1994 did not prevent Baqalu, a Boran man from El Kunne in the northern part of Boran land, from following with his desire to meet again with his bond-friends in Hor country. The Hor friends of this Boran man, who belongs to a Boran section that had refused to take part to the peace-making ceremony in Gandaraba, included the late Arbla, a well-reputed Hor warrior who had become a wealthy man in Egude; Jarsa Ghino, a wealthy Hor man residing in Kulama; the late Iyya Bokao, ritual leader of the Tsamako then living in Kuile; and Hunna Arshal, the late junior *qawot* of Gandaraba.

Arbla was away on a visit to his Hamar bond-friend when Baqalu came to Hor country, accompanied by his Boran wife, a Wata woman, and a Boran man and his Hor wife who was originally from Murale, one of the Hor villages which together with Egude is located in the eastern territorial section of Hor country commonly referred to as Marle. Before reaching Hor territory, Baqalu sent a message from Wata Wando to announce his impending arrival and that of this travelling team, and asked for an escort as the group relations between the Hor and the Boran were still particularly tense at that time. Baqalu's team was brought in with the help of an escort just in case. He also brought a cow with him that had been kept at El Kunne (Boran country) and descended from a heifer that Arbla had left behind with Baqalu before the 1991 Boran-Hor fighting. When Baqalu arrived, Arbla's wives laid out a cowhide and served him coffee, milk and sorghum dumplings. They could not kill a goat for him, as this is a man's responsibility. His arrival was big news. Children and adults alike gathered around to see him and the Boran who accompanied him. Baqalu brought news to the Hor about developments in Boran country. Previously, the Hor had only received news about the northern Boran indirectly from Konso traders who travelled between Hor and Boran countries. But, as the Konso and the Boran were long-standing enemies, the news tended to be prejudiced.

Baqalu's news included information about Boran bond-friends of the Hor, about their health, their property, their families, etc. Baqalu also provided information about the conditions of water wells, pastures, cattle and crops in the northern part of Boran country he was coming from. Furthermore, he brought news about whether the members of the northern sections of the Boran and their representatives were meanwhile ready to enter the cattle gates of the Hor *qawot*s, bringing animals for peace.

However, Baqalu's visit and that of his travelling team was greeted with suspicion. In the evening preceding their arrival, an urgent meeting was called in Marle. Young people at the meeting threatened to kill all the Boran visitors. Some communal curses were articulated against Boran. Arjan of Egude, a land distributor (*mura*) and official of the age organization of the Hor, stressed: 'People do not take their eyes off as they do their rubber sandals when they enter your house.' With this statement he was not encouraging hostility against the visitors, but was urging caution and vigilance. He was referring to the fact that the guests would use their eyes to ascertain the situation in Hor country and that Baqalu would report what he had seen and heard there to the Boran of El Kunne when he went back.

Although most Hor were wary of his visit, Baqalu was granted an escort to arrive safely in Hor country. In practice, many people felt that Baqalu had indeed the right to enjoy the privilege of being protected and entertained as a guest by his Hor counterparts in spite of the difficult group relations between Hor and Boran. But Arjan's suggestion that Baqalu should be given a clear impression of Hor vigilance was well accepted. This vigilance was ostentatiously displayed and witnessed by Baqalu who was welcome to report to his people that Hor youth were only to be seen heavily armed in Hor villages and in the surrounding bush.

As the case of Baqalu illustrates, reconciliation between groups is not a necessary requirement for being able to revisit bond-friends after violent intergroup conflicts. However, Baqalu was not the only Boran man who met again with his Hor bond-friends in Hor territory at a time when his section had still not officially shown any readiness to make peace with the Hor. Characteristic for most of the men from such sections who, like Baqalu, revisited their Hor friends as early as 1994 was that they had actually developed strong loyalty to their counterparts.[13] Such loyalties can transcend group affiliation and then be demonstrated through the passing of advance information about the ill intentions of one's own group against the group of one's partner. There were, for example, cases in 1991 in which Boran bond-friends alerted their Hor counterparts about Boran preparations to attack the Hor.

Another point that can be deduced from the recounting of Baqalu's visit is that stock-friendships are parts of *jala* friendships and do not constitute a friendship variant on their own in southwestern Ethiopia. But there, too, the practice of lending cattle to friends partly serves the function of reducing vulnerability in adverse climatic conditions. Pastoralists who disperse their herds internally and externally can also better cope economically with the impact of losses due to livestock epidemics. Furthermore, loans of cattle reinforce friendship between the parties involved and make available resources evenly distributed in a wider landscape, enabling recipients to gain access to milk and butter as well as additional animals whenever the loaned animal calves. Most of all, they are long-term investments as they will trigger further reciprocity.

However, the significance of *jala* friendships also comes to the fore, for example, when the dry period is unusually long in the territory of the friend's group. In that case, bond-friends from the group living in a territory that is climatically better off will host their counterparts who come to their country with their families and pack animals to get grains. If these people are, for instance, Hamar who hardly possess livestock and have a good nurtured friendship with Hor bond-friends, they will normally stay for around a week, pack their animals and move back with loads of sorghum given by a Hor friend who generously hosts them. The Hamar who are wealthy will need fewer gifts of grains from their Hor bond-friends as they will themselves come with animals to sell and exchange for sorghum.

The very fact that gift exchange remains an important feature of *jala* friendships certainly helps to make the latter particularly suitable to risk-spreading in contexts where people live under ecologically volatile conditions as is the case for the Hor and many of their neighbours. Such friendships are undoubtedly still valuable and relevant for the Ethiopian situation, which is currently characterized by recurring famine. Today an important threat to their persistence and to the attributes which give them prominence is the attempt by some NGOs to appropriate peace-making from its traditional practitioners (*qawot*s, etc.) and also to appropriate the very central feature of friendship, *rendering emergency assistance in times of need*. This threat, in turn, is accentuated by the fact that *jala* friendships are still largely based on relations of voluntary economic interdependence between members of different groups.

Hauda Craft-Workers and Traders of Konso and Friendship Networks

Let us now move on to Konso, a society within which people have been historically divided into two occupational groups: *edanda* (farmers) and *hauda* (craft-workers and traders). It is true that the Konso used to be either *edanda* (majority) or *hauda* (minority) and that the members of each of these two categories had a different status in Konso, did not intermarry and had differential access rights to land in the past.[14] In recent times, however, differences between these two categories of people have become less pronounced. Since the land reform of 1975 the *hauda* have owned land and married farmer women. Today they assert their equality with the *edanda* who, for their part, have become increasingly involved in trade and weaving over the last three decades.

Within this society, however, the itinerant *hauda* craft-workers and traders still constitute the group that takes a lead in establishing bond-friendships across ethnic boundaries. For them, friendship is an interpersonal relationship that can have an enduring character or just die out because it has been made with a person who has not proven to be trustworthy. Once contracted with the right kind of person, it becomes a basis for expanding a friendship network in a new place and with people who are friends of the original person. Members of the *hauda* group take full advantage of the friendship networks of their partners in other communities and so do the partners. During visits in Konso, these partners, including those of Hor ethnicity, are provided with food and lodging and have the freedom to travel and to benefit from their stay in the foreign environment. They are also able to use the friendship network(s) of their *hauda* partners and the security it gives to them if they, for example, travel to Hamar, Dassanetch or to Boran country with their Hor friends. The very fact that the *hauda* are members of the *fuld'o* certainly improves the ability of their friends to travel safely through the region. Other social networks can be used for the same purpose, but those involving *jala* friendships with *hauda* are largely viewed as the most reliable because of the great ability of the *fuld'o* to enforce the observance of an ethos of amity between travelling companions.

The friendship networks of the *hauda* cover a very large area. To the west these networks stretch from Lake Turkana to Nyangatom territory (border to South Sudan). To the north they extend to the Shashamane (Oromia Region) and Wolaita districts (SNNP Region). To the east the region includes the towns and settlements along the Shashamane-Moyale road (border to northern Kenya). This network area that we just described is more widely visited by itinerant *hauda* Konso than by non-*hauda* Konso traders as the latter still have smaller networks of interethnic bond-friendship across the region. However, both categories of Konso traders share the tendency to visit the southern part of the network area more frequently than the northern part. *Hauda* and non-*hauda* Konso alike have taken residence in the network region delineated above for some time now. A majority of itinerant traders, however, move around traditional routes trading, staying with bond-friends and dealing with local branches of the *fuld'o*, bringing them messages from the main Konso *fuld'o* and taking back messages when they return to Konso. Outside their home territory there are Konso men and women of *hauda* and non-*hauda* origins who reside in towns such as Soyema (Burji territory), Agere Maryam (Guji territory), Yabelo, Tartalle, Mega (Boran territory) and in the Huri Hills of northern Kenya (Gabra territory) and serve as additional contacts among whom *hauda* coming from other places can rest during travel. Similarly in the southern area comprising Hor, Hamar and Dassanetch country there are *hauda* and non-*hauda* Konso residing in the capacity of school teachers, mission employees, civil servants and as workers for development projects. Trading activities are conducted by both residents and itinerants. Resident Konso (usually three of them) join the local *fuld'o* as messengers (*khelita*), but the executive committee is composed of a team of local leaders (Hor, Hamar, etc.) and persons whose livelihood is based on trading.

Links with resident Konso are connections used by the *hauda* to expand their networks of trade. Konso who are not *hauda* may trade and certainly invest in establishing bond-friendships with local out-group members. They, too, often take goods to Konso which they earn through such connections. The *hauda*, however, move around a lot with items of trade and gifts. Characteristic for the *hauda* is also that they more heavily rely on their bond-friendships in other groups to widen their networks of trade. If they plan to travel from Hor to Dassanetch country, for example, they will always ask a Hor bond-friend to accompany their caravan as a master of the terrain, interpreter and as someone who already has *jala* friendships with Dassanetch. This Hor friend will lead the *hauda* to the homesteads of his bond-friends where they will be hosted nicely and offer gifts to the friends of their Hor friend. The *hauda* will also use their stay in the homesteads of the bond-friends of the Hor man to trade on a barter basis with individuals residing in the same settlement as their hosts. In some cases, payment for the items acquired from *hauda* can be delayed. This practice is facilitated by the fact that the Konso and various other people of southwestern Ethiopia have adopted the *fuld'o* system of administering trade relations between trading partners and have connected it to the political system of each group, to the network of friendship and to trading partnerships.[15] An illustration might help to understand this better. If the local political systems of the groups inhabiting the region were to be viewed as a huge tree, the *fuld'o* or trading network would be like a creeper plant that successfully weaves itself onto this tree winding up through the trunk and branches reaching all parts of the tree. The friendship network, too, can be viewed as an additional weave onto this giant tree. All parts of the tree thus have three layers which are interwoven in such a way that each layer reinforces the other. While the political system, trade and friendship networks operate in the specific context of each locality, shared values and purposes guarantee the successful operation of the weave, illustrating the high permeability of boundaries between the groups that sometimes makes one wonder if they actually are different groups. The political system onto which the *fuld'o* network latches itself is valuable for assuring the smooth running of trade and exchange in the region and for clearing the paths from anything that threatens free movement of people, animals and goods. The weaving of these different lines indicates that this is a negotiated rather than imposed institution, one reason why it continues to sustain.

Conclusion

In this contribution, we have shown that interethnic bond-friendships are channels through which much property, knowledge and information is exchanged. As we have indicated, such friendships are connections that are crucial for the Hor as much as they are to others in many ways as they give access to a great variety of essentials. Among the Hor and their neighbours, interethnic bond-friendships not only reinforce existing relations but also help build layers of other connections with people in other groups, paving the way to further expand one's friendship as well as one's trading network.

While discussing bond-friendships established across ethnic boundaries, we have pointed out that the operation of these friendships is facilitated by certain institutions and have given insight into the weaving of one structure of governance of the Hor – ritual leadership – with externally-oriented networks of friendship. Furthermore, we have underlined the significance of the weaving of the Konso system of administering trade relations between trading partners with networks of friendship with members of other groups. At the same time, we have demonstrated that interethnic friendships as practised by the Hor and Konso need to be comprehended within a broader regional context where institutions of various groups work in concert to guarantee continued co-operation and secure movement of essential goods through the reproduction of interdependence to maintain culture and society.

The networks we have focused on in this chapter are still intact, culturally appropriate and dependable sources of mutual assistance both in times of hardship and abundance. However, the institution that is central in this endeavour is currently facing challenges of unprecedented proportion as the region opens up for developments driven by global and Ethiopian institutions. This institution may appear to be collapsing, but like any other human institution it may evolve taking different shapes and will eventually help the groups meet newer challenges. This may also give rise to a new opportunity for forging on new dimensions of friendships to continue benefiting various people of the region. On the other hand, in the very unlikely event of its collapse this will probably have detrimental impacts on both the various groups that are involved in the networks and the landscapes that keep them.

Acknowledgements

We are both very grateful to Christina Gabbert for her comments and suggestions on this chapter.

Notes

1. See, for example, Santos-Granero (2007) and Killick (2010) for Amazonia.
2. *Miso* is initially a Hamar term.
3. The female equivalent of *baami* is *baamira*.
4. In practice, *baami* friendships often evolve from *miso*ship.

5. *Jala* is a term that is widely used by Omotic and Cushitic-speaking groups in southwestern Ethiopia. Whether all the groups mentioned above actually employ it in the same way is a question that cannot be definitively answered given the current state of research on friendship in this region. But the empirical data collected by Tadesse seem to indicate that this term has at least similar meaning among the Hor, the Gamo, the Konso and the Boran.
6. The friendship constellations we refer to in this context are thus those in which one partner is called *baami* and the other *baamira*.
7. For more information about the *fund'o* (*fuld'o* in Konso), see Tadesse (1999, 2000) and Amborn (2009).
8. This significance is not new. It has been documented historically for the end of the nineteenth century by Waller (1985) and Sobania (1991) who note that the Hor acted as intermediaries in the trade between highlands communities and various groups living in the Lower Omo valley at the end of the nineteenth century. At the beginning of the twentieth century, and as shown by Rein (1919: following 358), Hor country was the terminal point of a caravan route that connected ports of the Gulf of Aden to Addis Ababa and continued south until it reached Konso country and eventually Hor country. This route joined an east-west caravan route linking what was then Italian Somaliland with Boran country and eventually with Hor country and Lake Rudolf (now Lake Turkana). What is particularly striking is that the junction of the north-south and east-west routes is situated in the part of Hor country where major villages are located.
9. The Hamar regularly require sorghum from the Hor due to the fact that, contrary to the latter, they do not practise flood-retreat cultivation but rain-fed cultivation.
10. See Tadesse (1999: 261–305 and 302–5; 2000: 156–57) for a list of exchanges between a wealthy Hor man and his numerous friends in neighbouring groups and within his own group.
11. See Almagor (1978) for difficulties related to the 'inheritance' of bond-friendships among the agro-pastoral Dassanetch of southwestern Ethiopia.
12. For a documentation of this peace-making ceremony, see also Bassi (1993) and Strecker and Pankhurst (2004).
13. Meanwhile one can say that the Boran-Hor fighting has had little consequence for the persisting of *jala* friendships that had already existed between Hor and Boran before 1991. Mutual visits began to become more usual than described above by the end of 1996, but it is since 2000 that they have become completely re-routinized.
14. See Hallpike (1972) and Watson and Regassa (2001) for the Konso division of farmers/nonfarmers and the role this plays in regional trade.
15. There is also a *fuld'o* branch in Dassanetch country that can be approached by the Konso if they have issues that may arise as they trade with local people.

Chapter 4

Friendship and Spiritual Parenthood among the Moose and the Fulbe in Burkina Faso

Mark Breusers

Introduction

Ever since the Mossi or Moose kingdoms were created from the fifteenth century onwards, they have been marked by their capacity to accommodate difference. They originated from a pact concluded between a 'conquering' population that still traces its origin to the Mamprussi and Dagomba chieftaincies in the north of present-day Ghana, and various 'autochthonous' groups which came under their control. The initial pact assigned political power to the foreign conquerors, the *nakombse*, and religious authority to the autochthones, the *tengbiise*, who thereby preserved a distinct identity and provided the religious legitimacy for the *nakombse*'s rule and exercise of power. In the course of time, several other specialized groups entered the kingdoms and were incorporated into Moose society without being fully assimilated. Artisan-traders from the Yarse, Maranse and Hausa populations, blacksmiths and different categories of captives were integrated through institutions regulating intergroup marriage, association to the chieftaincies' courts and access to natural resources. At the same time, they were inscribed into a matrix of functional groups, so that group membership corresponded to specific occupations and status positions (Skinner 1970: 193–95; Izard 2003: 150–52).

What resulted was a relatively heterogeneous and open society, where socioethnic statuses were far from absolute and could not be captured in a rigid scheme based on geographical or historical origin, and where identity changes from one population group to another were relatively easy to achieve (Izard 1992: 75–90). One population, however, tends to be absent from most analyses of the history and sociopolitical organization of the Moose kingdoms. The Fulbe, who first arrived in the region not later than the mid-seventeenth century (Diallo

2008: 163), are, indeed, regarded as a kind of parallel society, exterior to Moose society and characterized by separate social and political institutions. There were limits with regard to the extent of otherness a single society was thought capable of accommodating.

The question of how the Moose and the Fulbe relate to one another has hence long been neglected by scholarship, despite the fact that in most Moose kingdoms the Fulbe constituted up to 10 per cent of the population and that their settlements were interspersed among Moose villages. When considered at all, Fulbe relations and interactions with the other population groups present in the Moose kingdoms were portrayed as being intrinsically different from those between 'integrated' population groups. In contrast to intrasocietal relations, intersocietal relations were understood to be depoliticized and nonaffective, generally referred to in terms of 'contract' and 'common interest' (Izard 1970: 384, 1982: 368). Highly important economic relations were contrasted with the poverty of relations in all other domains (Lallemand 1977: 363–66; see also Breusers 2013).

Undoubtedly, such representations were fuelled by the perception that the livelihoods of the Moose and the Fulbe complemented each other both ecologically and economically, the former being mainly crop cultivators, while the latter were primarily herdsmen. More recently, despite the persistence of professional specialization – the Moose continue to be mainly interested in millet and sorghum farming, while the Fulbe still concentrate on cattle herding – both groups have engaged in both crop cultivation and cattle herding. This change, on the whole, has been attributed to growing pressure on natural resources and, as a result, it is often unjustifiably thought of as having substituted economic and ecological complementarity with fierce competition along ethnic lines over scarce natural resources. If, in principle, many kinds of social rearrangements can be imagined, a quasi-'natural' transition from symbiosis to polarization is often taken for granted (Breusers, Nederlof and van Rheenen 1998).

In another publication (Breusers 2002), I have shown that, contrary to what is generally assumed with regard to the Fulbe in Moose kingdoms, the Fulbe of the Boussouma kingdom, like other groups making up Moose society, are accorded a role in the chieftaincies' histories, associated to the chieftaincy courts and included in the realm of political power. I have argued that from their association to higher-level chieftaincies, the Fulbe derive a settlement right as well as a general feeling of belonging to the Moose context. In this contribution, I will explore the relations that enable the Fulbe in the province of Sanmatenga, a province which more or less corresponds to the kingdom of Boussouma, to develop successfully a feeling of belonging in the localities wherein their daily lives unfold. The institutions through which other population groups create and reinforce such a feeling include those regulating marriage and access to land. The Fulbe, however, occupy marginal positions vis-à-vis these institutions. They rarely intermarry with the Moose and, since long-term use of specific plots of land by them is precluded due to the inherent mobility of their production system, they are excluded from the autochthonization processes that enable most Moose subgroups to root themselves in a locality. Moreover, the Fulbe tend not to participate in the Moose's locality-related rituals. Strangers, par excellence, they must find other ways to integrate themselves socially and to belong to Moose-dominated localities, notably through friendship.

The focus of this contribution, then, is how friendship acts both to accommodate and to reproduce differences between the Moose and the Fulbe. To begin with, the meaning and significance of friendship, specific to each group, will be outlined. Subsequently, intergroup friendship will be analysed, and then the following questions will be addressed: what circumstances are conducive to its establishment; how and why does it differ in meaning and significance from intragroup friendship; what is the relative importance of affection and utilitarian motivations; and in what circumstances do these interethnic friendships go beyond two individuals to encompass families or other social networks? In a separate section, it will be argued that despite the quasi-absence of marriage between the Moose and the Fulbe, intergroup friendship, can, nevertheless, become enmeshed in kinship through symbolic exchanges and the establishment of spiritual parenthood. Finally, the integrative dimension and boundary-maintaining aspects of both friendship and spiritual parenthood will be briefly discussed, as well as the issue of how friendship between the Moose and the Fulbe is affected by such changes as the shift, among the Moose, from crop cultivation to livestock rearing, and the growing scarcity of natural resources.

Friendship among the Moose and the Fulbe

Kinship is of primary importance in nearly all domains of social life for both the Moose and the Fulbe. Moose villages consist of several wards, each composed of a number of compounds, closely connected to one another by paternal or maternal ties. The most intensive social interactions take place within the ward. Likewise, Fulbe settlements consist of a limited number of huts, most often inhabited by families which are more or less closely related through kinship. Moreover, access to ritual and political office, as well as land tenure, are governed, to a large extent, by kinship-based rules and procedures. However, despite the seemingly overriding importance of kinship, many aspects of daily life, as well as the perpetuation of certain institutions, cannot be fully grasped without taking into account non-kinship relations, notably friendship.

Among the Moose, several terms denote distinct friendship-like relations. For instance, *reementaaga* refers to comradeship that develops between neighbours who grow up together, whereas *tudentaaga* is a friendship-like relation reinforcing bonds within the context of associations and migration, or trade networks (Martinelli 1999: 362). Here, I will concentrate on *zoodo,* which is the most exclusive notion of friendship characterized far more than the other types of relations by individual choice and affection. Hence, if one Moaga (pl. Moose) can have many comrades in the categories of *reementaaga* and *tudentaaga,* s/he rarely has more than three *zoadamba* (sing. *zoa*) friends. Besides being exclusive, *zoodo* is also, among women in particular, loaded with passionate emotion traced back to the friends' first encounter. When recalling their first meeting, friends emphasize the immediate connection they felt, a mutual 'liking' of one another which sprung up from literally nothing. This coup de foudre aspect (Lallemand 1977: 351), however, must be put into perspective, since, in practice, as I will argue below, friendship grows and matures over time. As observed by Martinelli (1999: 376), the emotion surrounding the initial attraction is exalted in such a way that, as in love, it is validated by a chain of ulterior experiences.

Zoodo is institutionalized in the sense that it stipulates that the partners involved behave according to prescribed expectations, make certain exchanges and, particularly where men are concerned, that their friendship develops in a certain way over time. It implies symmetry between the partners and reciprocity of exchanges, regardless of whether the friends are of approximately the same age or not. As such, it is distinct from kinship, which is generally characterized by hierarchy and a less balanced reciprocity of services rendered. In addition to exchanging gifts over time, friends are also supposed to do their utmost to help one another whenever one of them is in distress (such as in times of illness, or food or money shortages). Equally important is 'just being there' for one's friend on important occasions, such as name-giving ceremonies, marriages and funerals. Friends should share the bitter and the sweet. They are also supposed to be completely honest with one another. To keep a reproach or a criticism to oneself or to withhold gossip overheard about a friend could compromise the friendship.

Indeed, there is no danger in telling a friend everything. Only rivalry over a woman – the pursuit of a woman who is married, or promised to either one's friend or to one of his kinsmen – justifies the revoking of a friendship; all other offences, if avowed, can and should be forgiven. At the same time, such assertions about friendship's strength and durability – 'until death do us part' – point to a prominent threat, namely, the envy of others who, by means of gossip and backbiting, attempt to drive friends apart. Friendship is a treasure to be carefully cherished:

> It happens that a kinsman or someone near to you attempts to harm your friend to see how your friendship will end … Bereavement is not only to lose money or the death of a child, your wife, or a kinsman. It is also what happens if someone succeeds in placing himself between two friends who used to be respected and feared by many because they could not be separated. And then each will be on his side, talking in a way that

could not be heard while their friendship lasted. That is what one calls a loss. It turns into hatred each time the former friends see each other or when they remember the time they went together through all problems, good and bad.[1]

Even if it is maintained time and again that friends should share all that they are able to, and although friendship, from the first moment onwards, carries the notion of complete dedication, both the depth and strength of the relation usually grow as trust is progressively established. Accordingly, the value of mutual exchanges increases as friendship endures, with the 'gift' of a woman being the ultimate and definitive sanctioning gesture. Although less clear-cut than among the Kabre of northern Togo (Piot 1991: 415–18), friendship among the Moose also passes through various phases that correspond to different spheres of exchange.

Similar to Moose friendship, friendship between two Fulbe (*yiggiraagu*) also implies symmetry and reciprocity, and the partners' complete dedication to one another: 'All you wish for yourself, you also wish for your friend, and whatever your friend's problem you come to his help.'[2] Likewise, friendship between the Fulbe strengthens in the course of time with the growth of trust. One way of achieving this is to entrust cattle to each other's herds: 'You mustn't [entrust your animals] for only a short period; they have to last with your friend, so that you are assured that he can be trusted.'[3] But, here as well, the relation is continuously threatened by other peoples' gossip and backbiting. Finally, among the Fulbe, the exchange of women is also considered to be the ultimate mark of friendship (for northern Cameroon, see Guichard, this volume).

If two Fulbe friends have grown up together or are more or less close kinsmen, cementing their friendship by the exchange of women does not have to be a problem. A first marriage with the father's sister's or mother's brother's child is even recommended (Riesman 1974: 45). The Moose, however, observe bilateral lineage exogamy for up to four or five generations. Therefore, friends must be relative strangers to one another, to make the sanctioning of their relationship possible through the exchange of women. A friend is someone one did not grow up with, someone who is a member of another kin or population group. The high value attached to friendship among the Moose, then, cannot be fully understood without situating it in relation to marriage practices. These friendships are established between relative strangers with the establishment of in-law relations as an expected primary outcome. Besides being an expression of individual freedom, therefore, male Moose friendships, in particular, must also be understood as playing a significant role in the never-ending process of creating alliances between kin groups. Hence, especially among the Moose, friendship can be seen as an intermediary phase that transforms strangerhood into kinship, a relation that needs to be coupled with marriage in order to be considered complete.

Martinelli (1999: 357) depicts Moose friendship as a relation that helps to resolve the spaces of uncertainty that arise in encounters characterized by 'radical otherness'. Below, I will explore how intergroup friendship helps to resolve the spaces of uncertainty present in the encounter between the Moose and the Fulbe, which is clearly characterized by 'radical otherness' as well. I will do this, at first, by taking a closer look at three stereotypical contexts in which such encounters take place: host-stranger relations, joking relations and cattle entrustment.

Circumstances Conducive to Friendship between the Moose and the Fulbe

The establishment of friendship between two Moose or two Fulbe does not depend on any particular circumstances, nor are certain people, in principle, more eligible than others to become another person's friend – except that Moose friendship implies a certain measure of strangerhood. Friendship between a Moaga and a Pullo (pl. Fulbe) can arise from casual acquaintances as well, for instance at the market, where two people happen to like one another 'at first sight'. However, it often comes about in specific circumstances and is best understood as a second phase in a process of social integration initiated by a prior relation.

Host-Stranger Relations and Friendship: 'Being Elsewhere' versus 'Feeling at Home'

The Fulbe of Sanmatenga practise transhumance in response to the varying availability of pastures and water, both time and space wise. Their transhumance occurs mainly during the dry season, when a few herdsmen take the herd to a nearby village where pastures and water are more readily available, leaving most family members with some animals in the permanent settlement. At their destination these herdsmen establish a relation with a 'host' (*beero* in Fulfulde, *gãsoba* in Moore), on whose field they camp. Like elsewhere in West Africa, the host-stranger relation is an institutionalized relation whereby a herdsman gains access to crop residues, pastures and water. In exchange, the host's field is fertilized. Other smaller exchanges, like milk for cereals, may occur as well.

Wherever they go and regardless of whether they have been there before or not, the Fulbe consider the presence of a *beero* as a given. To provide a host for a stranger, who is just passing by, or else who needs to stay for a few days, weeks or months, is a practice that both the Moose and the Fulbe understand as having always existed and consider to be a moral obligation for the host population, whether the latter are Moose, Fulbe or any other population group, living near or far from the Moose region. In other words, a stranger is always entitled to *at least* a host. In this regard, it is useful to note that the Moose distinguish the 'stranger' (*saana*) from the '*unknown* stranger' (*zende*). The *saana* is a familiar guest to be received in one's house and village, an identified individual who enters a welcoming social space (Martinelli 1999: 360).

While the host-stranger relation allows a link to be initiated between the Fulbe and another locality, it is a relatively superficial relation as such and does not entail sustained commitment or emotional ties between the individuals involved. It does not result in a feeling of belonging on the part of the Pullo, nor does it imply a durable relation. On the contrary, the relation only makes sense during the transhumance and it signifies 'not being at home'.[4] Transhumance destinations are selected primarily on the basis of the availability and accessibility of pastures and water, and not because of the people one may find there: 'By going on transhumance, we do not join another person, but rather water and pastures for our cattle.'[5]

However, the relation between a Pullo and his Moaga host does not necessarily have to remain ephemeral. If a herdsman returns year after year to the same *beero* or, after several transhumances, decides to transfer his permanent settlement to the village of his host, the relation may evolve into friendship and, hence, will no longer be a given but demand personal commitment.[6] The Fulbe explicitly distinguish friendship with a Moaga from having a Moaga host. Notably, with one's friend, one is 'at home' regardless of whether this friend is a co-resident, or a person living elsewhere, with whom one also happens to stay during transhumance.

Hence, the host-stranger relation has a double significance for the present analysis. First, it constitutes one of the specific circumstances out of which intergroup friendship may grow. Second, the opposition between 'host' and 'friend' – between 'being elsewhere' and 'being at home' – strongly suggests the importance of friendship among Fulbe, in bringing about a feeling of belonging in Moose localities.

Joking Relations

The Fulbe entertain joking relations with the blacksmiths and Yarse subgroups of Moose society. Throughout the West African savannah region, joking relations between the Fulbe and blacksmiths are among the most solid to be found (Bâ 1991: 317). In the Moose kingdoms, their origin can be traced back through accounts which explain how in a mythical time professional specialization – cattle herding and forging – came into being in a previously undifferentiated population. The joking – i.e., the boldness, the teasing, the exchange of mutual insults, the right to 'steal' from one another – is justified by referring to the ruse involved in this original separation of people who were initially 'the same'. The second intergroup joking relation is explained by the existence of a kin relation between the mythical ancestors of Yarse and Fulbe (the former being the latter's mother's brother). Among the Moose and the Fulbe, joking plays a part in the relations between actual mother's brothers (or their children) and sister's sons.

This practice is transposed, as it were, to interactions between groups assumed to be structurally similar in the way that they are situated vis-à-vis one another. The mythical accounts, then, also serve to turn 'the other' into a kinsman, into someone who ultimately becomes 'the same'. As Badini (1996: 109) argued, joking can be understood as a game of receiving the other; joking relations serve as 'bridges' between the Fulbe and certain Moose subgroups and represent a cultural basis for social interaction (see introduction, this volume).[7]

In the past, joking relations entailed a moral obligation of mutual assistance (Bâ 1991: 316–17), and this is still recognizable today in so far as joking helps to ease tensions between members of different groups, when, for instance, Fulbe livestock accidentally enter fields and damage crops. Because joking facilitates amicable settlements, it is said that a dispute between a Pullo and a blacksmith or a Yarga (pl. Yarse) cannot go far. However, the general patterns of reciprocal joking between groups are relatively fixed. They only allow for a specific, limited repertoire of social interactions between individuals, and these correspond to their respective positions as defined by the joking relation. Joking also supposes self-control and refraining from emotional reaction; it is too standardized for personal feelings to be communicated.

Regarding joking among the Moose in the context of kinship and marriage, Luning (n.d.) argues that it should not be the exclusive form of communication, for otherwise it amounts to denying sociability. Only if 'the joke is contained' and embedded in various types of interaction between two individuals, does it add to the sociability of relations. Luning's argument – joking is an integrative force, provided one can also opt out of it and shift to another, more empathic mode of interaction – can be extended to intergroup joking. To go beyond stereotypical interaction and allow for social integration, joking partners must be able to opt out of joking. The joking relations between the Fulbe, the Yarse, and blacksmiths create a context in which social interaction can be initiated and thus represent another realm in which friendships may develop. Such friendships, in turn, are capable of generating sustained social interaction and integration for which joking alone is not sufficient.

Friendship and Cattle Entrustment

Joking relations and host-stranger relations inform us about friendship in the way that they differ from it, and what they lack. The third circumstance conducive to friendship between the Moose and the Fulbe discussed here – the entrustment of cattle – helps us to grapple with intergroup friendship in a more positive way.

The Moose's land use is not exclusively based on crop cultivation. Livestock is crucial to their livelihood. On nearly all Moose compounds goats and sheep constitute a reserve to be drawn on, to meet expenses for children's schooling, health care, ceremonies or, quite often, food purchase. The number of cattle a Moaga rears himself rarely exceeds a few heads, and they are often used for animal traction or fattened for sale. However, cattle also constitute by far the most important form of rural wealth, and are the preferred object of investment. Wealthy Moose, then, can own larger numbers of cattle, most of which they tend to entrust to Fulbe herdsmen.[8] There are various reasons why the Moose entrust their cattle: labour constraints, lack of expertise, the need to hide wealth from fellow villagers and contempt for the pastoral way of life are most often cited. The Fulbe, on the other hand, seek to herd the Moose's cattle of their own accord, be it to secure their livelihood, to supplement or reconstitute a herd of their own or to simply establish good neighbourliness with the Moose among whom they live.

Since the end of the nineteenth century, property relations regarding cattle have changed significantly, as has the economic and social role of cattle, both within production entities and between different production entities and population groups. In precolonial times, cattle ownership among the Moose was not widespread and mostly limited to chiefs. Commoners could own cattle as well, but ran the continuous risk of having their wealth confiscated by chiefs. Both chiefs and commoners usually entrusted whatever cattle they possessed to Fulbe herdsmen (Tauxier 1917: 161–62). During colonial rule, Moose cattle ownership was discouraged by epizootics, droughts, taxation policy and confiscation of pack animals. Nevertheless, animals continued to be secretly entrusted to the Fulbe at this time as well, given that their herds were more 'beyond the reach' of the colonial administration (Marchal 1983: 586). From the 1960s onward, Moose who were successful in migration enterprises in the Ivory Coast or in commercial activities at home were able to accumulate cattle which they continued to entrust, in large part, to the Fulbe. The Moose's involvement in cattle rearing was further facilitated when, during the droughts of the 1970s and 1980s, the terms of cattle trading compared to those of cereals deteriorated. Farmers with cash at their disposal enlarged their herds substantially, whereas impoverished Fulbe were obliged much more than before to look for Moose cattle to herd as a means of securing their livelihood. Secrecy continues to surround Moose cattle and their entrustment, although no longer out of fear of confiscation, but rather because of fellow villagers' envy (Breusers, Nederlof and van Rheenen 1998).

Cattle entrustment involves a number of contract-like arrangements. The herdsman, for instance, is entitled to the entrusted animals' milk production, a heifer every three years and a part of the sales price when the owner decides to bring one or more of his animals to the market. However, owners do not conclude 'contracts' with any arbitrary herdsman. To take care of an asset as valuable as cattle, they seek a partner whom they can trust and with whom they can share a feeling of complicity (especially in view of their wish to hide their wealth). As a consequence, cattle entrustment tends to be embedded in friendship: 'Before a Moaga entrusts a Pullo with an animal, there must be friendship; he does not bring his cattle to a Pullo without knowing him first.'[9]

Although it is generally ascertained that friendship with a Pullo is a prerequisite for a Moaga to entrust cattle – or even to own cattle at all – it is often far from clear which comes first in practice, cattle or friendship.[10] Hence, already before buying an animal, a Moaga has a general idea which Pullo he will entrust it to – most often one reputed to be trustworthy, or with whom a certain measure of confidentiality already exists, but who is not necessarily considered a friend as yet. However, it can happen that a Pullo first 'courts' a Moaga cattle owner whom he hardly knows because of the cattle he would like to add to his herd. Only later is he entrusted with the animals. In any case, it is usually the successful entrustment of cattle which gives rise to growing trust and complicity, and thereby favours both the establishment and the strengthening of friendship. The contractual arrangement is thus enriched by a range of informal exchanges and gestures of mutual support characteristic of friendship. Furthermore, when the herdsman is relatively wealthy, some of the usual obligations are sometimes relinquished (for instance, the herdsman may decide not to receive the promised heifer every three years, 'so that friendship is strengthened even further'). Although such a friendship tends to be enduring, and capable of surmounting setbacks, cattle entrustment engenders numerous complications which constantly threaten the friendship and can undermine the friends' confidence in one another: unaccountable disappearances of animals, frequent disputes over crop damage, disrespect regarding the compensations initially agreed upon, etc. Also, gossip and slander by co-villagers envious of the cattle owners constitute a menace to friendship.

Friendship between Moose cattle owners and the Fulbe is not only established or strengthened if animals are entrusted. The few wealthy Moose cattle owners who decide to take care of their herds themselves, despite the many social constraints discouraging it (in particular, fellow villagers' envy and overtly expressed contempt for the pastoral way of life), likewise tend to have good friends among the Fulbe. Friendship is then fostered by engaging in certain activities together (for instance, pasturing their herds or going on transhumance together) and by sharing similar problems and anxieties in their capacity as herdsmen vis-à-vis crop cultivators (crop damage disputes, fields encroaching on pastures, and water points).

Intra- and Intergroup Friendship Compared[11]

Among the interethnic arrangements conducive to the formation of intergroup friendship, there are at least two which are clearly subject to calculated considerations. The first one is that of cattle entrustment. In this case, the advantages expected are the following: access to pastures, and water in exchange for manure in host-stranger relations; labour, expertise and discretion, in exchange for contractually agreed-upon compensations. For good reason, it is all too often claimed that Moaga-Pullo friendship is initiated by those whose interest is largest or by those who are most in need. Such observations, by contrast, are usually not made regarding intragroup friendship, and if they are made, then the sole purpose is to point out certain undesirable developments. Especially in cattle entrustment, the stakes are usually high. On the one hand, a Moaga cattle owner who lacks expertise or labour, or who is under considerable social pressure to hide his wealth, has little choice but to turn to a Pullo herdsman. On the other hand, although a Pullo sometimes takes a Moaga friend's cattle into his herd only to help the latter, entrusted animals are generally a welcome and often necessary support to his livelihood. For a Pullo, not to have (enough) cattle in his herd for a wife to milk is shameful and may prevent him from being married. Even if a Moaga-Pullo friendship came into being in a disinterested way, cattle will often be introduced into the relation from the moment the occasion arises (e.g., if the Pullo borrows money from the Moaga, he acquits his debt by taking a Moaga animal into his herd; or more generally, the Pullo attempts to be entrusted with whatever cattle the Moaga succeeds in acquiring). Contractually stipulated mutual obligations become then a substantial part of the exchanges between the friends.

Due to its intertwining with cattle entrustment and other arrangements having a calculative aspect – such as those aiming to the resolution of fecundity problems (see next subsection for more details) – intergroup friendship may first appear to be of more instrumental nature than intragroup friendship. However, there are many similarities between both kinds of friendship. In practice, a Moaga-Pullo friendship often implies unselfishness, mutual dedication and assistance. Friends give one another what they are capable of giving (goods, money, advice), provide moral support at difficult moments in life and are present at each other's important ceremonies (name giving, marriages, funerals). Also, like any other friendship, the relation is put to the test especially when one of the friends or both encounter difficulties. In general, the friendship is considered stable, capable of surmounting setbacks and not easily broken. Provided the partners respect the honesty understood to be inherent to the relation, nothing but death or rivalry over women – which only very rarely occurs, because of the prevailing undesirability of intergroup marriage – is supposed to end it. In practice, however, friendship is, as mentioned above, continuously threatened by gossip and slander engendered by other people's envy. This threat is particularly important with regard to Pullo-Moaga friendship because of the wealth (cattle) that others at least suspect to be involved. Physical separation when one of the partners migrates can also, though not always, put an end to friendship. But friendship between a Pullo and a Moaga may also motivate joint migration, which then entails further strengthening of the relation.[12]

Another similarity with intragroup friendship is that through friendship a Pullo is supposed to become integrated into the network of his Moaga friend's close kinsmen (and vice versa). In line with the assertion that 'with one's friend one is at home', the Moaga friend's father, mother, brothers and sisters become like a father, mother, brothers and sisters to the Pullo, who also addresses them as such. In practice, however, things can be a little different, especially if cattle are involved, because of the competition and envy that may exist among kinsmen. Otherwise, such networks are rather antithetical to the exclusivity, intimacy and confidentiality of friendship. Friendship may branch out in several directions through articulation with kinship networks, for instance, but only the one friend with whom it all began is considered *mzoa,* 'my intimate friend'. This does not prevent a person whose friend is in need to call upon a second friend if he has not himself the means to help out. Also, if a Pullo decides to migrate, he may refer his Moaga friend, whose cattle is in his herd, to one of his Pullo friends for the entrustment of the animals after his departure. From this, a new friendship may grow. Similarly, a Moaga who entrusts cattle to his Pullo friend will not only allow the latter's herd to graze crop residues on his field but may also negotiate his access to the crop residues of his kinsmen and Moose friends. However, it would go too far to label such arrangements as occurring in networks of friends.

When one of two former friends dies, certain precautions are to be taken in order for the broken friendship not to cause harm to surviving kinsmen. Each Moaga, as soon as he starts participating in social life, is assumed to release 'impurities' (*reegdo*) into his environment and to simultaneously absorb impurities from whoever and whatever he interacts with (Bonnet 1988: 32–33). An individual's *reegdo,* then, is likely to be most affected by those people who are closest to him: kinsmen, allies and friends. A deceased person must leave behind the *reegdo* he absorbed during his lifetime (symbolically represented by shaving the head); otherwise he cannot join the ancestors. Those who maintained relations with him must be purified as well, and dispose of the *reegdo* they were permeated with by the deceased. In the course of my field research, I found that *reegdo*-related ceremonies involved former friends in case that discords had existed between the latter and the deceased.[13] Former friends, rather than actual friends, are to rid themselves of the *reegdo* in their hearts. Indeed, a broken friendship often turns into a vehemently hostile relation to the extent that former friends come to curse one another. If one of them dies, effacing the *reegdo* becomes all the more important as it prevents further victims. The Fulbe, as well, believe in the power of curses, whether the Koran or Moose-related forces are invoked, and, if necessary, they participate in purification rituals to undo them.

Due to the confidentiality and intimacy involved, in principle, there is no reason for friendship to be transferred from one generation to another, although, of course, if their parents are on familiar terms, children have at least the occasion to meet and so may well take a liking to one another. Cattle entrustment, however, may encourage the transfer of intergroup friendship. If a Moaga cattle owner dies, his children may decide to leave their father's wealth in the herd of his Pullo friend, or, if a Pullo herdsman dies, his children may ask their father's Moaga friend to leave his cattle in their herd. There is a good chance then that a friendship will be transferred. Nevertheless, since friendship with a father does not *automatically* mean friendship with his son, the new partners may be far more interested in discussing the contractual and agreed-upon obligations of entrustment and, as a result, become caught up in endless haggling. Also, it can happen that broken trust, rather than friendship, is transferred. For instance, if the sons of a Moaga already came to the conclusion that their father's cattle has been 'eaten' by his Pullo friend, they may also have resolved never to entrust a Pullo herdsman with their animals again.

Finally, one crucial difference between intra- and intergroup friendship stands out. Especially among the Moose, a successful friendship must be sealed by a marriage arrangement. So instead of transferring friendship from one generation to the next, the goodness initiated in friendship must be prolonged and extended in subsequent generations by establishing relations with the in-laws. Marriage between the Moose and the Fulbe, however, although not prohibited, is strongly discouraged and only rarely occurs. Nevertheless, as will be shown in the next section, the Fulbe can be drawn into Moose kin relations through spiritual parenthood and symbolic in-law relations.

Fecundity, Spiritual Parenthood and Friendship

Like in any society, fecundity is of fundamental importance among both the Moose and the Fulbe. To remain childless or to see children die at a young age goes against the cosmic order and compromises the harmony of a couple's social and economic life (Houis 1963: 20). In their attempts to cope with this eventuality, people are frequently obliged to turn to the 'other', i.e., to people from another population group who are to some extent strangers. Below, I will deal with some of the Moose's practices in this regard, since, especially in their case, solutions to fecundity problems entail the establishment of particular social relations embedded in or intertwined with friendship.

Each Moaga child has two principal constituents. Conception occurs through sexual intercourse when a *kinkirga* (pl. *kinkirse*; 'one of two twin spirits normally residing in an invisible counterworld') enters the womb of the woman, while the twin *kinkirga* remains in the counterworld. The *kinkirga*'s intrusion allows for fecundation, but a successful pregnancy needs the transmission of *siiga* ('vital force') in the third or fourth month of pregnancy. The *siiga* communicates the qualities of one of its ancestors to the child, who is then said to be its *segre* (Bonnet 1988: 35–36). Sterility, miscarriage, children's illness and child mortality are all understood to be *siiga*- or *kinkirga*-related, and explained according to the same interpretative scheme. Hence, a miscarriage is provoked if a capricious *kinkirga* decides to leave a pregnant woman's womb, or because no *siiga* has fixed itself in time. Likewise, an infant risks dying when its *siiga* is captured by a witch or weakened – for one reason or another – by its offended *segre* (the 'ancestor' that returned to the child), or when its *kinkirga* – dissatisfied by its reception in the world of the living – returns to its playmates in the other world (Bonnet 1988: 94–95). If pregnancy is long in coming, or accompanied by unusual pain, or if an infant's illness is not easily cured, or if a mother repeatedly loses her children, diviners are consulted to identify the responsible forces as well as the steps that ought to be taken to conciliate or to deceive them. Below, I will concentrate on those of the diviners' recommendations that refer to or involve other population groups.

One way of deceiving spiritual forces (for instance, 'bad' *kinkirse*) that attempt to lure a Moaga child back to the counterworld is to put the child into fictive captivity by symbolically selling it to a blacksmith or a Pullo. The child is devalued in order to demonstrate the parents' disinterest or even contempt, in the hope that no spirit finds it worthwhile to attack it (Houis 1963: 73–80; Bonnet 1988: 96). According to Houis (1963: 80), to give a Moaga child a Pullo name also constitutes a symbolic substitution used to deceive spiritual forces. Giving the name of a stranger devalues the child and places it outside the kin group and society. However, as we will see, giving a Moaga child a Pullo name can also be otherwise explained, and imply a more positive appraisal of the Fulbe and the establishment of significant intergroup relations.

Diviners often refer a Moaga couple experiencing a fecundity problem to yet other intermediaries who frequently belong to population groups perceived as strangers, in particular the Fulbe. In all population groups, certain individuals, without necessarily being diviners, are renowned for their capacities to mediate with the spiritual world and to conciliate forces that hamper a couple's fecundity. Moreover, the Moose ascribe a special mediating capacity to the Fulbe in general because of their knowledge of the bush with which they are in permanent contact, or so the Moose maintain, and which they are capable of observing closely (Houis 1963: 29). Therefore, although people possessing specific capacities – a *tii lobere* or a 'throw of power' – tend to be approached, a couple can also be advised to 'ask for fecundity' at the cattle enclosure (a place reputed to be inhabited by spirits) of any Pullo. In practice, a Moaga will then consult a Pullo s/he is acquainted with, preferably a friend. In both cases, Moaga couples place their fecundity 'under the custody' of the Fulbe. Their relation with the Fulbe on the whole does not end with the propitiatory ceremonies. This is because the Moaga woman, for whom fecundity is implored, is often advised to use Fulbe utensils, to acquire a sheep with specific characteristics, or else to symbolically represent Fulbe in her daily life. Also, from the moment the woman becomes pregnant, it is recommended that she informs the Fulbe whom she previously consulted, so that if childbirth proves to be difficult, she can go and await delivery in a Pullo's hut.

Moreover, if a child is born and survives, its fate is linked to the Fulbe. This is because, for a child to live, it is of crucial importance to acknowledge where it comes from and what circumstances and forces made its coming into the world of the living possible to begin with. Especially during its first years, a child is tempted to return to the other world. Obtaining the blessings from and involving those who made the child's life possible can only help to make it stay. Hence, the Fulbe benefactors are involved in the name-giving ceremony, which corresponds to the public acknowledgement of the child's 'origin'. The Fulbe give the child a Pullo or a Muslim name, or a name referring to the place where the spiritual forces were implored. Acknowledgement of the circumstances and forces that made one's coming into the world of the living possible is to be continued later on as well, in order to ensure success and to avert misfortune. In this sense, 'each name has its path', as the Moose say, and an individual's destiny is linked to his/her 'origin' and to the workings of the above-mentioned forces (notably the person's *segre* and personalized *kinkirse*).[14] Before turning to the relations established between the Fulbe and the Moose, I will discuss a situation in which a Moaga's fate becomes even more bound to the Fulbe than when a Moaga is helped into this world by the Fulbe from the very beginning of his/her mother's pregnancy.[15]

In some cases, a Moaga newborn is identified to be of Pullo ascendancy; then it is said that *kanga yiitgen Silmiiga*, i.e., 'the bush where (the child) comes from is Pullo'. Most explanations concentrate on the *kinkirse*'s role in the child's conception. As long as a child is not weaned and has no power of speech, its *kinkirga* dominates its *siiga*, even to the extent that it is equated with its *kinkirga*. A *kinkirga* can always opt out of the human world and return to where it came from. Therefore, the child's caretakers must do their utmost to seduce it to stay. Normally, one does so by regularly giving the child sweet foodstuffs that the *kinkirse* are reputed to adore, and to keep it from crying by giving it sufficient attention and affection. However, just as there are Moose and Fulbe in the world of the living, the counterworld is also inhabited by Moose and Fulbe (and other *kinkirse*), and so it is possible that a Pullo *kinkirga* can enter the womb of a Moaga woman.[16] A newborn with certain traits (long, sleek hair, or unusually light skin) may immediately be recognized as 'Pullo'. But in most cases a diviner only comes to such a conclusion after a child/*kinkirga* has 'returned' to the counterworld repeatedly (after a woman has lost several infants in a row), explaining that this 'return' is due to the, until then, unrecognized Pullo ascendancy of the child. If the same child/*kinkirga* is born once again, a Pullo is invited at its name-giving ceremony to give it a Pullo name.

A Moaga of Pullo ascendancy must bear this 'origin' in mind throughout his/her life. At first, this implies that in her/his early years s/he must be recognized and treated as a 'Pullo'. A symbolic environment must be created for otherwise s/he will not feel at home and will return to the counterworld:

> The way of the Fulbe is important especially in the beginning. The Pullo child is like a lost child who follows a path you do not follow. If you go one way, you will encounter Fulbe, if you go the other way you encoun-

ter Moose. Now, this child that came from a Pullo's bush, but appears with the Moose, becomes Moaga; one must seek the child's source and follow [the path of] the Fulbe for that child to live well … We act that way in order to block the roads, so that it can go nowhere else [than with us].[17]

Subsequent to this, however, her/his destiny also remains linked to the Fulbe and their way of life, in line with the idea that health, good fortune and success are dependent on how well one is able to live in harmony with the path traced by one's destiny. Hence, when a child of Pullo ascendancy is ill, his/her Moose parents are likely to consult the Fulbe who were involved in naming him/her as well. Later on in life, it is recommended that a man of Pullo ascendancy establish good relations with the Fulbe to avoid misfortune or failure. Also, diviners may advise him to wear clothes offered by a Pullo, to buy white sheep, to build a mosque in his compound and sometimes even to convert to Islam.[18] Pullo ascendancy becomes part of such a person's identity:

> To tell you the truth, I am a Pullo. I cannot detest the men dressed in white [Muslims, Fulbe, Yarse], I constructed a mosque, and I have my children named by Fulbe … During my whole life, my children will not do what might compromise my ascendancy … Although their lives are not linked to my ascendancy, I want them to respect who I am as long as I live.[19]

Hence, in both cases discussed here, where Fulbe are involved in Moose fecundity problems – i.e., Moose children 'asked for' by their parents together with the Fulbe, and Moose children of Pullo ascendancy – identity boundaries between the two groups are transcended in ritual (notably name-giving ceremonies), and the Fulbe are symbolically represented in the Moose's life world. However, the resolution of fecundity problems also favours the establishment and reinforcement of social relations across group boundaries. First, the friendship between the Moose parents and the Fulbe they called upon is strengthened, or if it did not exist before, it is likely to be established. Indeed, when the Fulbe are asked how their friendship with certain Moose was initiated, they often cite assistance in solving fecundity problems in the same breath as cattle entrustment. Likewise, most Moose, whose child survived thanks to the Fulbe's involvement, claim they can never forget the good done by the Fulbe, whom they regularly present with small gifts.[20] Second, the Fulbe who were involved in a Moaga child's name giving become this child's spiritual parents. They consider the child to be theirs as well, and regularly visit its parents, bringing along gifts. When the child grows up, s/he addresses them as 'father' and 'mother' and pays them respect with regular visits and gifts.

Furthermore, with regard to a Moaga girl, who was 'asked for' by her parents together with the Fulbe, it is considered appropriate to involve her Fulbe spiritual parents in her engagement and marriage. Usually this is limited to the symbolic gesture of giving the girl to her husband (accompanying the girl into her husband's compound). Yet, out of gratitude for the life received, which can be compensated for only by another life, i.e., a wife, the girl's biological parents may also promise her to her Fulbe 'parents', who are then entitled to decide whom she marries. Far from an obligation, this is done especially if a strong friendship exists between the girl's Moaga father and the Pullo benefactor. Since marriage between Moose and Fulbe is rare, the Pullo generally 'passes' the girl to another Moaga friend of his.

However, the Fulbe are not involved to the same degree in the marriage of a girl who was 'asked for' by her parents together with them as in the marriage of a Moaga girl believed to be of Pullo ascendancy. In the latter case, all the various stages of the marriage must follow Fulbe traditions, in order to be prosperous (fecund). In view of future marriage ceremonies, the girl's mother often seeks to keep up her friendship with a Pullo woman, who introduces her daughter into the husband's compound. A marriage, according to Fulbe traditions, not only means that the girl is 'given' by a Pullo (often the girl's spiritual father or a friend of the husband's family) and is accompanied by a Pullo woman into her husband's compound, but also that Fulbe utensils (e.g., calabashes, spoons) are used during the ceremony and that a Pullo hut is built in the husband's compound (so that 'the compound becomes like a Pullo compound'). The newly arrived wife must spend the first few weeks in that hut before joining her husband for sexual intercourse, again to increase the chances of a fecund marriage. The Fulbe are involved in the name giving of all the children born from such a marriage, and sometimes the mother learns how to administer enemas from the Pullo spiritual mother. These children's relation to Fulbeness is similar to that of children 'asked for' by their parents together with the Fulbe.[21]

Although marriage between Fulbe and Moose is discouraged and rarely occurs, Moaga-Pullo friendship can become enmeshed in kinship. First, the Fulbe who are involved in the name giving of a Moaga child 'asked for' by them too, or considered to be of Pullo ascendancy, become this child's spiritual parents. Second, if the child is a girl, her spiritual father can be asked to symbolically 'give' the girl to her husband, or if friendship between the biological Moaga father and the spiritual Pullo father is strong, she may be 'promised' to the Pullo (who 'passes' her to another Moaga friend of his).[22] The result is a kind of tripartite alliance, with the husband considering both the girl's Moose parents and the Fulbe spiritual parents as in-laws. In this sense, friendship between a Moaga and a Pullo can find its fulfilment through spiritual parenthood and symbolic in-law relations.

Friendship, Spiritual Parenthood and Social Integration and Dissociation

Intragroup friendship is a phase in an unequivocally integrative process that effaces boundaries and culminates in marriage arrangements. Ideally, therefore, friendship among two Moose or two Fulbe is concluded by the exchange of women, which completes the double metamorphosis of self and other into people who are alike and known to one another (Martinelli 1999: 359). Despite the possibility of symbolic kinship and in-law relations, the Fulbe cannot accomplish such complete integration and cannot become 'one and the same' with their Moose friends, because of the quasi-absence of marriage between the Moose and the Fulbe. On the contrary, both spiritual parenthood and friendship reaffirm the boundary between the two groups, since the circumstances in which they are established and the meaning and 'function' with which they are infused reproduce differences.

Both the children who were 'asked for' by their parents together with the Fulbe and the Moose children believed to be of Pullo ascendancy are in a double state of liminality, not only between the world of the living and the other world, but between Moose and Fulbe worlds as well. The state of liminality demands that boundaries be confirmed. For a Moaga of Pullo ascendancy, in particular, liminality persists throughout his/her life. The 'origin' of children 'asked for' by their parents together with the Fulbe is not fundamentally altered – it still is Moaga – whereas, in the case of Pullo ascendancy, the person's 'origin' is 'Pullo'. Hence, for people of Pullo ascendancy, it is necessary to reaffirm their strangerhood throughout their lives. They must do this in order to render their stay in a Moaga community viable to begin with, and subsequently to avert misfortune in spite of the fact that they live with the Moose. This is achieved in rituals (name giving, marriage) and other dealings, through which not only spiritual parenthood and symbolic in-law relations are established between the Moose and the Fulbe, but also in which the acts and objects involved refer to stereotypical aspects of Pullo identity, thus accentuating the latter's difference. Calabashes (milk containers) and milk spoons confirm the Fulbe as cattle herdsmen; Fulbe huts constructed in Moose compounds during marriage ceremonies of women of Pullo ascendancy express the Fulbe's mobility or temporary presence; and the construction of a mosque evokes the Fulbe's religion.

In Pullo-Moaga friendship, differences are also reproduced. Indeed, although most Moose and Fulbe engage in both animal husbandry and crop cultivation, the difference between them is chiefly expressed in terms of occupation. The Moose's identity continues to be firstly linked to their occupation as millet farmers, just as the Fulbe's identity remains closely related to their occupation as cattle herdsmen. These stereotypes are reaffirmed in the items exchanged between friends (notably, milk for cereals or sauce ingredients, and manure for crop residues) and are further accentuated if their friendship is complemented by cattle entrustment and all the related contractual arrangements. Therefore, in addition to validating the Fulbe's expertise in cattle herding and reinforcing the stereotypical exchanges, the Fulbe are also appreciated for their ability to move around, given that, when pressure on land becomes too great in one place, they are still able to find vacant bush land elsewhere and to take their herds on transhumance.

Despite this accentuation of differences, and despite the fact that intergroup friendships do not develop into networks and are not usually transferred from one generation to another, the relations discussed here are conducive to the Fulbe's social integration into Moose-dominated communities. This can be clarified by looking into the 'co-habitation discourse', which is one of the ways for actors to express their belonging to a place, and which emphasizes, above all, both groups' long-term joint presence. The Moose and the Fulbe have shared the same space for centuries, and people from both populations find it extremely difficult to imagine the other group not being there: 'What made that there are Moose also is the reason for the Fulbe's existence. Where we are, whether the Fulbe like it or not, [the Moose's] presence is obligatory, and, likewise, whether the Moose like it or not, the Fulbe's presence is obligatory as well. God wanted it like that. If there were no Fulbe, there wouldn't be Moose either.'[23] A similar inevitability with regard to co-habitation is implied in the joking relations between the Fulbe and certain Moose subgroups (blacksmiths and Yarse). Co-habitation is thought to be further facilitated by professional specialization. The related complementary nature of life styles and production systems, realized through various exchanges of goods and services, is understood as serving both groups' interests. However, although the exchange of goods and services implies face-to-face encounters, these encounters as such remain largely impersonal and modulated by utilitarian considerations. Likewise, as explained above, joking allows interactions, according to the joking partners' identity positions as laid down in mythical accounts, but can hardly be considered sufficient for the realization of the Fulbe's belonging or social integration. A third element in the co-habitation discourse fills the void: 'The Moose take Fulbe as their friends and the Fulbe as well seek to establish friendship with Moose. Thus, it has become co-habitation.'[24] Friendship is, indeed, strongly correlated with 'feeling at home'. Likewise, spiritual kinship and symbolic in-law relations contribute to a feeling of belonging to a place: 'Yes, my brothers and I are attached to [that Moose village] ... My wife has [spiritual] children there, which makes our relations there solid.'[25]

The Fulbe and the Moose consider tensions and disputes inherent to all co-habitation. However, when co-habitation is good, they do not usually degenerate into irremediable conflict. It is no surprise that if a problem arises between a Moaga and his Pullo friend, when, for instance, a Pullo's herd damages a Moaga's crops, a solution tends to be easy to find. The herdsman is forgiven or else they agree quickly on the compensation to be paid. The same holds true when spiritual parenthood exists between the parties involved; for instance, a Moaga who was born after his parents had consulted the Fulbe to ask for fecundity maintained: 'If there is a misunderstanding between me and Fulbe and when I then realize how [my life] began, I cannot but forgive.'[26] In other cases as well, there is a strong tendency to settle intergroup disputes amicably. Like in any dispute, the point is not so much to establish one or the other party's guilt, but rather to appease the situation and to have the parties involved accept each other's apologies. Intergroup friendship is instrumental in solving such disputes, since those who have friends in the other group are preferably called upon to mediate.[27]

However, there are also forces of dissociation at work which go against the establishment of friendly intergroup relations. They become manifest especially in intergroup disputes regarding crop damage caused by livestock or livestock's access to water points. Instead of employing a 'co-habitation discourse' that emphasizes complementarity and backs up intergroup friendships, the Moose often shift to an antagonistic discourse which stresses the incompatibility of the two groups' interests. Although a certain antagonism has probably always been an aspect of Moose-Fulbe relations, it has been accentuated due to growing socioeconomic differentiation internal to Moose communities. The Moose hold up an egalitarian image of their community by behaving *as if* they were all equal (whoever has wealth hides it with the Fulbe), and by employing a public egalitarian discourse which opposes Moose millet farmers to Fulbe cattle herdsmen. Impoverished Moose's envy of their co-villagers' cattle is transformed into animosity towards the custodians of this wealth as a group. Both the Fulbe's presence and the friendly relations through which wealth is secured risk losing their legitimacy. In this regard, given that poorer Moose own no cattle, they also lack one possible and important means of establishing or strengthening friendship with the Fulbe. Certain impoverished Moose farmers fuel antagonism by resorting to acts of sabotage. In order to discredit Fulbe herdsmen, but also, allegedly, to profit from compensation fines that herdsmen must pay, especially when those fines may exceed the value of the lost crops due to a mediocre rainy season, they instigate the damage of their crops by sowing fields on or near cattle tracks, or in such a way that Fulbe cattle enclosures become encircled.

Finally, there are indications that the nature of friendship relations has changed. Both the Moose and the Fulbe argue that utilitarian considerations have become more prominent, stripping friendship of its unconditional and unselfish aspects. More than before, one is approached and flattered by people who seek profit, whose only intention is to take advantage of one's means. It has become difficult to distinguish between 'real' friends and impostors. In such a climate of distrust, suspicion is easily stirred up and slander intended to undermine friendship falls on fertile ground. Although these observations are valid for friendship in general,[28] they are particularly relevant to friendship relations in which cattle entrustment is embedded. Whereas in the past cattle entrustment was exclusively the affair of the owner and the herdsman, today it often takes place in the presence of witnesses. Also, more often than before, the cattle owner informs a close and reputedly discreet kinsman. Such practices point to a tendency to disentangle entrustment from dyadic friendship, and to the growing importance of contractual arrangements to the detriment of informal, friendship-related exchanges. Moreover, utilitarian interests in intergroup friendships have been reinforced, due to the fact that certain resources which used to be freely accessible to everybody have been subjected to restricted access. For instance, Moose farmers tend to reserve crop residues either for the livestock they keep themselves, or only allow Fulbe friends' cattle to graze on it. Conversely, Fulbe herdsmen allow only their Moose friends to come and collect manure to fertilize their fields.

Conclusion

In this chapter, I have shown that the relations between the Moose and the Fulbe are socially and culturally rich and not reducible to bare relations of economic exchange and fierce competition. Nor are they doomed to deteriorate inexorably because of the ever-growing pressure on land and other resources. Despite their limitations and vulnerability, intergroup friendship and spiritual parenthood facilitate intergroup interaction and integration. Moreover, since cattle ownership among the Moose has increased significantly over the last few decades and since the bulk of these assets are entrusted to the Fulbe, the establishment of intergroup friendships can only have been facilitated. On the other hand, the growing prominence of utilitarian considerations and deepening socioeconomic differentiation risks compromising and even delegitimizing Moose-Fulbe friendships.

Notes

1. Interview with Raoogo Sawadogo, Moaga elder man, June 2002.
2. Interview with Adama Diallo, Pullo man, December 2001.
3. Ibid.
4. Note that, besides 'host', a second meaning of the word *beero* is 'stranger'.
5. Interview with Issa Barry, Pullo elder man, November 2001.
6. After having transferred his permanent settlement, the herdsman no longer gains access to resources through a *beero,* but rather on the basis of being a 'resident' and by means of arrangements with his co-residents; the place is his new home and where one is at home, one has no *beero.*
7. Other myths explaining the origin of professional specializations and status positions within Moose society in a more comprehensive way, independent from joking relations, likewise reinforce the common cultural basis of different groups. An example can be found in Dim Delobsom (1932: 118–23), where the origin of Moose society is explained in terms of the different tasks (respectively forging, cattle herding, trading and ruling) God attributed to four brothers, ancestors of the blacksmiths, the Fulbe, the Yarse and the *nakombse* respectively.

8. This is not to say that only Moose who own many – i.e., more than ten – heads of cattle entrust them to a herdsman. If a Moaga owns only one or a few cows or bulls s/he may do so also.
9. Interview with Ado Barry, Pullo elder man, July 2002.
10. Similar to the coup de foudre in Moose friendship, we find here again that certain qualities of the relationship tend to be imputed retrospectively in discourse to the very initiation of the entrustment relation, although in practice these qualities often only grow over time with the entrustment of cattle.
11. Although reference is made to relations among the Fulbe as well, comparison of intergroup relations will be mostly with Moose friendships.
12. Both Moose and Fulbe are involved in migrations from the north-central Sanmatenga province to the south and southwest of Burkina Faso. These migrations generally involve the movement of whole households (husband, his wife or wives and their children) in search of better livelihood opportunities (access to better quality crop and/or grazing land).
13. Hence, contrary to what has been reported for the Dagara, these ceremonies do not concern a symbolic transfer of friendship to a member of the deceased's family. According to Some (1971: 21–23), such a transfer occurs, among the Dagara, in a ritual allowing the surviving friend to free himself of the load occasioned by all the goodness received from the deceased during his lifetime – goodness which is considered part of the 'impurities' each individual is likely to absorb during his lifetime.
14. If a *kinkirga* enters the womb of a woman, its twin remains in the counterworld. Hence, from its conception each person has its *kinkirga* in the other world – its double – and, at the same time, remains the seat of a *kinkirga* throughout his/her life. The *kinkirga* has an influence on the person without directing him/her in a determined way. By taking the desires of his/her *kinkirga* into account, for instance, a person can activate good fortune and success.
15. In the first case, these Moose are said to be 'asked for by their parents together with the Fulbe'.
16. In the first case discussed above, i.e., if a child is 'asked for' by its parents together with the Fulbe, its *kinkirga,* in otherwise normal circumstances, will still be Moaga.
17. Interview with Boukary Sawadogo, Moaga man, August 2002.
18. If a Moaga is not of Pullo ascendancy or experiences fecundity problems in his marriage, he can still be advised to become more closely associated to the Fulbe (or Muslims in general), in order to have better chances in life or more security. For instance, he may construct a mosque to be consecrated by a Koran teacher. Muslims passing by or paying a visit can pray there and this helps the Moaga – who has not converted to Islam – to better secure health, good fortune, wealth, etc., for himself and his family.
19. Interview with Sambo Sawadogo, Moaga elder man, July 2002.
20. In some cases, however, the relation between the consulting Moose and the Fulbe mediators is restricted solely to the ceremonies and symbolic representations prescribed by a diviner (see Breusers 2012).
21. If a marriage remains barren, a wife's previously unrecognized Pullo ascendancy may be identified as being the cause. She is then obliged to find herself Fulbe 'parents' and told to go and stay with a Pullo family, where she must wear Fulbe clothes, do Fulbe women's work (milk the cows, cook) and be given a Pullo name – 'so that she becomes these Fulbe's daughter'. Afterwards, this *bagren paga* ('wife [returned] from the cattle enclosure') is accompanied to her husband by her Pullo 'mother' who brings along a calabash, a mat and other Fulbe utensils.

22. Symbolic giving of the hand of a friend's daughter does not only occur as a consequence of or as a part of services rendered to solve a fecundity problem, but also in 'normal' circumstances in the context of a Moaga-Pullo friendship (to strengthen a friendship, a Moaga receives the hand of the daughter of his Pullo friend, to 'pass' it to another Pullo friend of his, or vice versa).
23. Interview with Tasre Sawadogo, Moaga man, June 2002.
24. Interview with Ousmane Ouédraogo, Moaga elder man, January 2002.
25. Interview with Ado Barry, Pullo man, December 2001.
26. Interview with Pate Sawadogo, Moaga man, August 2002.
27. Joking partners may be called upon as well; joking implies the extension of a moral community beyond the actors' 'own' population group and facilitates expressions of displeasure and criticism without provoking degeneration of the situation.
28. In practice, it is now more difficult than in the past to strengthen friendship by marriages in the next generation. Over the years, it has indeed become less easy to marry women without their consent. This evolution also contributes to the growing fragility of friendship.

Chapter 5

Labour Migration and Moral Dimensions of Interethnic Friendships

The Case of Young Gold Miners in Benin (West Africa)

Tilo Grätz

Introduction

Friendship relations have often been analysed either from a structural and functionalist perspective – focusing on their role in uniting smaller or larger groups or even societies, and their assumed intrinsic mechanisms – or with respect to their emotional qualities. The latter perspective points to the significance of friendship in the different phases of an individual's life and how the various local and cultural meanings and practices of friendship differ according to context or situation.

The underlying theoretical approach for the present case study sides with those attempts, in the realm of social anthropology, that try to integrate the two above-mentioned perspectives. At the same time as referring to certain processual aspects of friendship, this study will also consider situated friendship practices and experiences that inform the ambiguous nature of friendship relations. Consistent with recent theoretical and methodological perspectives on the subject (in particular Guichard in this volume; Beer 1998, 2001; Eve 2002; Guichard, Heady and Tadesse 2003; Schuster et al. 2003; Guichard 2007b),[1] such an approach takes into account the transitions that friendship can make between different categories of sometimes overlapping social relationships, such as kinship and patronage, which hitherto have been discussed separately, although it may seem more appropriate to study them in reference to each other (see introduction to this volume; see also Schmidt et al. 2007; Aguilar 2011; Descharmes et al. 2011).

My case study deals with groups of young labour migrants in West Africa, in particular male artisanal gold miners in northern Benin.[2] I argue that friendship relations in this social setting provide an important means of integration despite the heterogeneous nature of social and ethnic origins and the many conflicts and uncertainties that dominate daily life. The character of these friendships is largely influenced by common elements in West African youth culture, but also by specific logics, practices and moral attitudes particular to their socioprofessional life world.

Without overlooking the dramatic social impacts of local mining booms,[3] my perception certainly differs from that found in accounts describing gold diggers as chaotic and voracious, anomic individuals. It helps to cast a differentiated light on mining communities in general, which are characterized by the combination of an extremely risky and unstable economic environment and by patterns of conspicuous consumption that suffer, right or wrong, from a bad reputation.

Gold miners as labour migrants need to adapt to a new social environment. Developing new ties enables them to cope with their workload and their precarious social position. Friendship here is one option that, by virtue of the particular context in which it develops, is given a new or additional meaning. It helps not only in reducing potential problems, but also in creating a minimum degree of trust (e.g., Eisenstadt and Roniger 1999), thus providing the basis for economic transactions. Maintaining friendship relations also makes it easier to deal with the daily uncertainties and emotional stresses specific to the mining camp. Taking such a manifold approach, I mainly understand friendship to be based on a wide range of social practices, without ignoring the emotional aspects or the underlying codes of friendship that exist in mining communities.

In the pages that follow I will explore the logic of friendship bonds among gold miners, their integrative strength as well as their limits. I will argue that economic relations and strategies of risk-minimization largely promote the development of friendship ties among migrants as well as that of parity in income sharing, which, in turn, is more likely to be established among friends than among kinsmen or 'brothers'. Friendship becomes an important counterforce to the social precariousness of the mining fields and is specifically relevant to integrating people of very different regional, ethnic and social backgrounds, who also often have divergent interests.

In order to provide a broad contextual background, my contribution starts with a brief ethnographic account of small-scale gold mining as it is practised today in West Africa in general, and in northern Benin in particular. Taking an analytic perspective, I will then discern various types of friendship relations that differ in their mode of constitution and their content.[4] Furthermore, I will explore the wider cultural context of artisanal gold mining that these friendship relations are embedded in, and pertinent emic representations and statements hinting to both the advantageous as well as the precarious nature of friendship relations among young gold miners. The final section seeks to extrapolate from the case of friendship among migrant miners, to a general discussion on friendship relations in the context of changing African societies.

The General Context: The Current Situation of Small-Scale Gold Mining in Northern Benin

Gold mining in West Africa has seen a boom since the mid-1990s. Old, abandoned mines have been reopened and many new shafts have been explored by small-scale (artisanal) gold miners who apply and refine traditional mining techniques. This growth of nonindustrial gold mining is related to massive labour migration into rural areas (especially in Mali, Burkina Faso, Ghana and Guinea).[5] Miners are fortune seekers, young peasants as well as impoverished artisans, small entrepreneurs and businessmen, all trying to cope with economic crises linked to the decline in agricultural cash-crop production, droughts or reduced soil fertility, political strains like restrictions on out-migration, political tensions like in the Ivory Coast, or community conflicts. Many migrants are also looking to supplement their existing income, especially in the dry season. Gold miners are mostly mobile young men and women in search of assets that enable them to improve their social position, to marry, to invest in housing or livestock, or to start a business in their home region. Taking serious physical and social risks, successful or not, many of them stay for longer periods of time in gold-mining areas, becoming semiprofessionals trying to discover new deposits.

The rapid establishment of new mining sites leads, in most cases, to the development of mining camps in a very short period of time. Immigrant communities rapidly expand with new markets and the spontaneous development of infrastructures and services. Very often conflicts emerge between gold miners and state authorities, between the local inhabitants and immigrants, as well as between local interest groups themselves, concerning the rights of exploitation, land rights and modes of settlement. Often the state is only partially able to control these processes.

These are typical mining-frontier societies (e.g., Turner 1935 [1893]; Dumett 1999; Grätz 2013). The general features of these mining communities are their heterogeneity in terms of ethnic origins, their flexibility as regards their spatial and economic strategies, and the emergence of intricate hierarchies and norms as regards exploitation rights and patterns of conflict resolution (Grätz 2002a, 2011b).

The gold-mining region in northern Benin is located in the Atakora Mountains close to the villages of Kwatena and Tchantangou. This area, some 30 km southeast of the provincial capital Natitingou, is predominantly inhabited by Waaba and Betammaribe peasant groups as well as by Fulbe herders. Inhabitants mainly grow millet, sorghum, corn, yams and peanuts and practise animal husbandry.

In this mountain region, the gold boom started in 1993. Foreign gold miners from Ghana and Togo first migrated to the region. After their initial success, they triggered a gold boom and further massive immigration of labour migrants from all over the region. Although the site close to the village of Kwatena was known to the locals because of its partial exploitation in the colonial period, there was no local tradition of gold mining to that date, mainly because of rigid state control of those zones considered to be state property up to the end of the 1980s. The miners profited from a period of political transition and appropriated the deposits with simple techniques. In the following years, the governmental authorities tried several times to expel the miners by force and confiscated equipment, money and gold. But in the long run they had little success. One reason for this is that a cohort of gendarmes deployed at the site was corrupted, allowing further mining against bribes. However, once the military that had been sent into the region to establish order was withdrawn, many miners simply returned to the gold fields.

Governmental politics shifted towards partial legalization in 1999. Since then a series of negotiations have been started, aiming at organizing gold miners into co-operatives that would sell their gold to the state. This process is far from being concluded. At the end of 2001, new expulsions took place, mainly to drive foreigners out of the mining region.

The gold miners work along the rivers and mountain slopes, exploiting alluvial and eluvial deposits as well as engaging in small-scale mountain mining. They use simple equipment such as pans, sluices, chisels and sledgehammers. The miners developed an intricate system of labour organization including hierarchies and shift work. The gold exploitation is dominated by small teams headed by micro-entrepreneurial shaft owners, *chefs d'équipe,* hiring assistant workers for a given period of exploitation. Reef-mining teams comprise five to twelve workers, with different tasks, working in shifts. The gold miners usually share the gold ore and every individual miner then needs to extract the gold himself. The chief usually gets half of the yield as compensation for his investment in equipment, the feeding of all workers for the period of excavation and his general organizing capacities. All other yields are shared equally among the team members.[6]

The gold ore is processed further by crushing, pounding, milling, sieving and panning to finally obtain gold dust. Women are often employed in much of this work. Gold is sold as soon as possible in small amounts to petty traders,[7] most of them operating locally as trading agents for master traders. They are part of informal heterogeneous trading networks[8] extending to the international gold trading centres (Grätz 2004b). Most gold traders act as moneylenders, thus obliging the miners to sell their gold to them.

Gold mining in northern Benin consists of economic activities that largely flout the mining laws. This generally includes the miners' disregard for licence requirements for exploring and exploiting deposits, disrespect of any commercial registration rules, tax evasion and working in forbidden zones, as well as the smuggling of gold. Furthermore, the mining communities develop their own modes of conflict settlement without appealing to official institutions. The arrangements between the various – in most cases ethnically diverse – working teams as well as those between immigrant gold miners and local inhabitants are negotiated and established on an 'informal' basis.

We are dealing here with the emergence of a distinct economic and social sphere, shaped by the specific method of gold extraction and labour organization, but also by the distribution of incomes, the establishment of markets and patterns of settlement.

General Types of Friendship in the Mining Region

Given the empirical tendency of my contribution, I do not pretend to give an exhaustive definition of friendship. Rather, I present a working concept, which still needs to be refined (further points of debate will be discussed in the final section). In my perspective, friendship is a relationship of *relative* durability, mutual appreciation, comprising shared moral standards, expectations of reciprocity and trust, sustained by mutual affection, equity, support and common ideas of equality. It comprises a set of practices and shares similarities with kinship and patron-client relations. Friendship is characterized by a range of features, and has multiple meanings, comprising both emotional and functional aspects that vary in degree and weight, according to the situation. It needs permanent reaffirmation, often through rituals and favours. Friendship is first of all a dyadic relationship that *may* grow into polyadic/group relations (Eve 2002). The establishment of friendship is contingent on cultural as well as social experiences and practices. Both the ideas and practices of friendship are socially, culturally and politically embedded and thus require a contextual analysis (Adams and Allan 1998b; Carrier 1999; Pahl 2000). One such context is constituted by gold-mining camps – where I initially did not expect so many friendship relations at all. Here, I will distinguish: friendship among gold miners in working teams, friendship among clusters of joint immigrants and friendship between landlords (local French: *tuteurs*) and their guests (Fr. *étrangers*).

These analytical categories are not mutually exclusive. They comprise ties that may overlap in given dyadic and, even more, triadic relationships. The differences between these types are determined by

- The initial social ties that may then turn into friendship;
- Their 'logic', which sustains them and makes them a preferred relationship;
- The specific content of the relationship in terms of forms of exchange, reciprocity, rites and affection;
- Their social effects in the mining region in general.

The Moralities and Meanings of Friendship among Miners in Working Teams: Reciprocity and Sharing as Ways to Promote a Preferential Relationship

Friendship among miners may grow out of comradeship and is largely a result of everyday working relations, especially among members of the same working team. As regards the social composition of the mining teams, it typically involves a high proportion of interethnic bonds. Mining teams are set up, right on the spot, on a contractual basis for a minimum of one exploitation cycle, which can last from several weeks to several months. The majority of team heads try to compose their team out of experienced and hardworking gold miners, often regardless of their ethnic origin. In most cases, half the team is made up of peer groups, being people who may have immigrated together, and the other half is made up of migrants who met each other in the mining region. Among them, a high proportion of strangers become work mates and potential friends.

However, friendship does not only develop when sharing the hardships of work, the risks[9] and the yields, but also during leisure time in the mining camp, when workers exchange information, favours, help of all kinds and comradeship. Friendship between gold miners is both a result of the interactions among the members of a mining team and a condition for their functioning. The latter aspect points to the specific sharing ethic and the preference that miners have for friendship as opposed to agnatic kin and age-grade relations.

Many of my interlocutors stressed the fact that sharing among friends ideally means getting an equal portion of gold ore for all members of a team who engage in the same way in gold extraction. According to my informants, this would be quite different when working with relatives: in the latter case, seniority, status and even gerontocratic aspects may dominate the sharing rules.

> In case I work together with my brother [in a large classificatory sense, also including father's brother, father's brother's sons, mother's brother's sons, etc.] or with my father, it may be that after all, he demands a higher portion of the yields, and I cannot refuse this. (Kiki, Kwatena, January 2001)

> The advantage of working with friends instead of kinsmen is that the elder kinsmen they want to be called senior. Because you are younger, even when they only give you little [of the yields], you don't have the right to insist [on an equal portion]. With friends, however, you will find an understanding. You will do the sharing in equal parts, and that's it. But with the kin, you won't have that chance. (Djoto Raoul, Perma, August 2002)[10]

These statements hint at an important difference when comparing the logic of sharing in the mines with that characterizing the agro-pastoral households in that area. In the Atakora region, social relations in all ethnic groups are generally shaped by strong norms of social age and status, especially in the same patriclan, both politically and economically. As a result, the elder heads of a household are privileged in managing the bulk of its products and income; there are only limited guarantees of equitable redistribution. This may be seen, however, as a kind of delayed reciprocity, as the young men themselves will, one day, be promoted to a higher age status and may enjoy similar privileges.

But in the context of the mining camps, where the wish to accumulate money in a short period of migration and the possibility of being able to spend a large part of it on the spot predominate, these kin-based systems of reciprocity are seen by most young miners as largely inappropriate. They prefer to share among friends, as peers and equals who 'neither cheat each other nor claim too large a portion because of their age' (Kiki, Kwatena, January 2001).

When I mentioned the possibility that an elder brother who is granted an unequal share may invest his earnings, in one way or another, for the benefit of a family unit in general, from which all members would profit, the counterarguments – as indicated in the following statement of a young gold miner – pointed especially to the reality of migration and life in the mining camp.

> The elder brother or father may spend all the money in the market; on the other hand, I need cash for my part to nourish myself to remain strong, but also to enjoy life with my friends. (Donné, Tchantangou, December 2001)

'Needing cash' means to be able to reinvest immediately into the network of friends in the mining community. It is a way of reinforcing the bonds of friendship and thus the logic of their preference. Migrants say that this does not mean they exclude kin totally from their expenditures or that they are only interested in individual consumption. They return home bearing gifts, for example. Nevertheless, they need cash in the mining camps immediately and in large amounts because they have to pay for rent and food.[11]

It could be argued that the household-based mode of providing economic security does not necessarily need to be respected by gold miners in the mining teams, first, because of the spatial separation between these economic activities and their homes, and second, because of the patronal system of labour relations.[12] The head of the team, who is charged with guaranteeing the basic living standards of all members of the team, is able to do so because of his larger share in the yields. This system of patronage and contract has more in common with craft guilds than with family-based economies in the agrarian sector. Team leaders try to employ the members of a certain team according to their physical capacities, social virtues and experience. Ethnic background or even kinship is less important, as compared to these skills. Team leaders know that the performance of a team depends on mutual understanding and respect among all of its members. Another reason given is that team leaders cannot wait until relatives, eager to engage in mining, may or may not show up. This results in many ethnically mixed teams, largely outnumbering those that primarily work on the basis of kinship (to various degrees). An important 'glue' for their internal cohesion is, aside from the (unwritten) contractual relations, common economic interests and prestige, given by the importance of friendships.

Gold miners try to earn a good income during their often limited period of migration. They are, of course, often inclined to earn their part at the expense of others. According to my observations, however, these strategies are limited by representations of shame and honour: severe personal misbehaviour, like repeated theft and betrayal, is highly disapproved of, whereas there are reciprocal norms, like helping and sharing ethics, which act as ideals guiding the actions of the individual miner. Those who follow these norms are called 'good fellows' and/or, (less often) 'friends', especially when in addition to this, they show respect, conviviality and amity. A friend is someone 'who does not cheat you. Of course, everybody tries to get his part, but a good friend will never try to take more than he ought to' (Donné, Tchantangou, December 2001).

Livelihood and Life Style of Young Artisanal Miners

This sharing ethic is not limited to the gold-mining work itself; in a wider context of everyday life in the mining camps, it also applies to leisure time, as can be illustrated with the case of Kiki.

Kiki is a young gold miner. He is from Natitingou, but usually lives in Kwatena where he rents a room with a local landlord. He was in school until the sixth grade, and later became a truckers' apprentice. Lacking money, he was not able to write the exams to get a driver's licence. He has been working in the mining fields for four years, primarily in a team lead by Ikro, where I first met him some years ago. They were exploring a promising new shaft without having found any veins yet. Ikro is of the same ethnic origin as Kiki, but from another village. They first met in the mining fields. Kiki says that only some members of his mining team are at the same time close friends:

> My friends are Ikro [the team chief], Raoul, Mohamed and Ismail. Ikro is a Waaba, Mohamed is a Semere. Raoul is Kabye from a village close to Chabi-Kouma. Ismail is a Waaba. There are no problems between us. With two of them I used to work together, Ikro and Raoul, but with all of them I hang around and stick together. We eat together and drink and go out to look for girls together, usually in Natitingou. There we go out to dance each Saturday, maybe in 'Le Village', 'Sixteen' or 'Basilic'. There the ambiance is cool. We take the moto-taxi and there we are. In

the 'Basilic', we meet all the 'Joes', the big ones who party all the time. (Kiki, Kwatena, January 2001)

One factor that facilitates the development of friendship ties among miners of diverse ethnic backgrounds is the existence of strong peer relations among men who are about the same age, and who share similar life worlds.[13] Miners also share the same semantic field, their own intimate codes which they constantly re-create. With the category of semantic field, I refer primarily to internal, discursive and communication practices among gold miners. These practices include common codes, symbols, particular neologisms, gestures, speech acts and narratives that miners develop, and they contribute to the emergence of distinct modes of interaction and consequently to cultural integration. I will only mention one element in detail here: nicknaming.

Miners usually call themselves by nicknames. These nicknames generally refer to distinct personal features, virtues or attitudes, or else to certain events or circumstances in their biography or, by way of analogy, to military grades, prominent politicians or cult musicians and actors. There are not only big guys like 'Gaddafi', 'Ben Laden' or 'The American', but also 'The President', 'The Ambassador' or 'The Captain'. *David toujours propre* ('David always clean') is obviously a reference to his vanity on arriving and leaving the mining site with extremely clean clothes. 'Washington' is known to listen regularly to the 'Voice of America' and 'Rasta Man' dreams of buying a good guitar and performing as a reggae star. *Dix Tonnes* ('Ten Tons'), *Paul Acier* ('Paul Steel'), *Paul Marteau* ('Paul Hammer') as well as 'Tarzan' are undoubtedly tough guys in the mountain works.

Nicknames also indicate that ethnic identity becomes less prominent, to a certain extent, and that the youths are judged according to their behaviour at the mining site, irrespective of their origins. *Moussa Cetaci* ('Moussa four-legs') moves fast in the shafts like a dog.

Young, unmarried miners especially demonstrate a particular mode of conspicuous consumption.[14] This includes extensive drinking, smoking and eating practices, certain hair styles and other dress codes, but also partying to various degrees (*faire de l'ambiance*). The partying ranges from joint visits to *discothèques*, bars and video-cinemas, well established in all these mining areas, to creating dance styles and endorsing particular musicians and athletes that miners identify with and imitate. In their spare time, they dress in good clothing. It is the combination of all these elements, how they dress and wear their hair, as well as their gestures and the way they talk and walk together which make up the external, public performance of these youths (*être un jô, faire le grand*, etc.).

Some of the young miners spend their money in ostensive ways as quickly as they earn it.[15] This public behaviour contributes to images of miners as being mad, unsocial and reckless, and of mining camps as sites of decay. On the other hand, investing in drinking is an investment in the peer group.[16] I cannot describe in much detail all the representations of masculinity (particular symbols, practices and idioms of strength) that young miners create, in relation to their self-image and attitudes; however, what is important to mention here are the core notions of trust and understanding. Surprisingly, trust and the positive aspects of mistrust are part of the special social and cultural embeddedness of gold mining. 'You cannot trust all, but a good comrade is somebody to trust because he will be fair to you' is a widespread statement in this respect. The second notion is mutual understanding: 'somebody you work with and the works go fine without much talk, who simply knows what you are suffering from without saying' (Jonas, Tchantangou, December 2001).

This is a semantic field relating to a shared life world, characterized by familiarity and the common experiences of labour migrants who find themselves in a new environment. It relates as well to the bonds that are consciously created within that mining culture,[17] which go beyond (yet partly include) local and ethnic cultural references. Moreover, it is one of the elements that create the basis for friendship, especially among migrant miners.

The Dual Thrust of Friendship

From this perspective, friendship presupposes that the partners do not only share the same norms, but that they also take each other into consideration, so that that they act and behave appropriately when one or the other is in a situation of stress or need. Moreover, the other should come to the *same evaluation* of the situation and share the same attitudes, so that it is easier to come to terms with the situation and to understand one another.

Friendship in this situation could also be considered as a survival strategy (e.g., Mizen and Osofu-Kusi 2010) and moral claim, supported by many 'cultural aspects', such as public rituals and masculine rites, which helps to sustain camaraderie and to indirectly reassert cohesion,[18] despite the heterogeneous origins of the team members, the many sources of quarrels and their diverging interests. In this double logic, friendship among miners (excluding all nonminers) is both advantageous and compelling for the individual – reminiscent of the double face of the gift (Mauss 1990 [1923–1924]).

Seen in this light, however, friendship among young gold miners does not allow itself to be reduced to instrumental aspects and the rationale of material exchange alone: in their view, their relations as friends are first and foremost about mutual understanding and esteem, and only secondarily about demanding mutual assistance, affirming rather than establishing their bond.

The norms of reciprocity and equity between miners of the same team state that a miner will also get the same share if he has been absent for some time because of illness or family affairs. By contrast, his portion may be reduced if he has been lazy or unreliable. Moral obligations include a fair and equal division of hard work and the acceptance of sanctions, but they also require the miners to accept that different tasks will be distributed according to a person's level of experience, expertise and physical capacity.

Elements of a 'moral economy' (e.g., Scott 1976; Thompson 1991) are important aspects of the rules and modes of organization in the mining teams. Apart from these informal rules, there are also more concrete institutions that help to guarantee benefits for all and to organize redistribution. The fact that mining entrepreneurs, team leaders or successful traders are supposed to contribute more than others is important because this may hinder them in direct accumulation. Some team leaders contribute to fundraisers (Fr. *caisses*) intended as a sort of insurance.

This is especially pertinent to mining communities where immigrants live close to the locals or even settle in their villages, as it is the case in the Atakora region of Benin. But taking the more isolated mining camp as a whole, there are multiple modes through which solidarity is organized in the quarters.

Friendship among Clusters of Immigrants

Let us consider the second important pattern of friendship relations in the mining area, those among immigrants from the same region. Many miners arrive in the mining villages of Kwatena and Tchantangou together with mates from the same area, the same village or/and ethnic group. Although many of them are relatives, a high percentage of them are simply mates or acquaintances. Some of them are already organized in peer groups, age-sets or village quarters that are as relevant as formal kin relations among them.

Friendship may be a component of these initial bonds. They are, however, given a new (additional) meaning in the mining camps, as they are linked to the joint labour in the mining fields, the common or complementary economic strategies and the modes of settlement and reproduction. In this context, loose ties become significantly more important and may turn into strong friendship relations.

These clusters of immigrants are built only, in part, upon conviviality in the same compounds or village quarters. The individual members often live separately from one another. This is due to the fact that there is a general scarcity of available accommodation and landlords are rarely able to offer many rooms at the same time. Immigrants, therefore, have to accept living in a compound with the locals and other immigrants of diverse origins. They may move in together if possible. In Kwatena, for example, there are only two small areas of the village where immigrants of the same regional background are living more or less closely together. The majority reside among the local population, either in their own houses or, in most cases, with local landlords. Some of the ties to the local landlords may grow from pure contractual relations into patron-client relations and further, into enduring friendship bonds.

Dyadic Friendships after the Boom Period

In 2002, gold-mining activities declined in the Atakora Mountains of northern Benin, due to lower yields and intensified state interventions. Some gold miners stayed, concentrating on alluvial mining on the few river banks tolerated by the authorities. Others left the region, continuing their migration into other regions, or shifted to agriculture, trading or day-to-day labour in their home regions or the district capital Natitingou. I followed many of these returnees as best as possible, and came up with a surprising picture.

In numerous cases, friendships which had first been forged while temporarily working in a specific mining camp had become transformed into friendships supposed to endure for life.[19] In practice, friendship bonds of former work mates largely proved to be stable over time and many young migrants who had left the gold fields indeed managed to maintain strong ties with those who continued to work in these fields. The young migrants who began working and living in Natitingou or Chabi-Kouma, for example, regularly visited their comrades in Kwatena or Tchantangou, especially on festive occasions, market days, or on Sundays. Not all former work mates maintained this kind of intimate relations, but a remarkable number of them, at least a third, were still close. Friends helped each other to get new jobs in town, visited each other regularly, and pooled their money together for investment in businesses such as trading.

To complete my survey, I also collected cases of terminated friendships. In most of these cases, they ended because of a betrayal or a fraud in the 'moral matrix' of friendship in the gold-mining area, i.e., unequal shares in yields, or the abandonment of common ventures. In a few cases, the rift was caused by 'problems about women', but insults and simple quarrels also led to disagreements that had still not been resolved by the time of my survey.

Friendship Ties Developing on the Basis of Host-Guest Relations: Integration and Distancing

A third type of friendship ties I encountered in the mining region was quite different in nature from the previous cases and developed in connection with the institution of *tutorat* (e.g., Chauveau 2006). This institution is a variant of the host-guest institution which is long established and linked to the history of trade and labour migration into prospering regions of West Africa (e.g., Cohen 1965; Breusers, Nederlof and van Rheenen 1998; Bellagamba 2000; de Bruijn 2000; Diallo 2000).[20] The latter institution indeed includes a special form of arrangement that is often entered into by landlords and labour migrants in rural areas.

In certain mining areas of West Africa, *tutorat* arrangements are frequently part of the relations between immigrant gold miners, renting rooms or houses, and their local landlord. In most mining areas, however, there are separate camps for strangers, some distance away from local villages. They are called *zongo* (in Hausa), *jaare* (in Moore, i.e., Mossi language) and so on, designating both a camp and a market, where the frequency of economic and social transactions is considerably higher in relation to 'normal' villages.

The *tutorat* relations based on patronage may play an important role for establishing friendship relations, especially in cases where there are no special quarters for immigrants, or where immigrants may not find landlords of their own kin. In northern Burkina Faso, such relations between gold miners and landlords are widely found in Karentenga. In northern Benin, they are largely developed in the mining area surrounding the villages of Tchantangou and Kwatena. In these villages, the immigrants rent rooms or houses that are either part of the compound of their landlords or a nearby extension, usually straw huts built for that purpose, on a daily or monthly basis.

In case a tenant stays for a longer period, the landlord (*tuteur*) becomes much more than a provider of a room: s/he becomes responsible for 'her'/'his' guest (*étranger*). In case the lodger gets into trouble, e.g., with some other villagers, the *tuteur* is supposed to act as his primary mediator, in the worst case accompanying him to hearings with the village authorities. The latter may charge the *tuteur* with a certain minimum amount of public responsibility as regards the general behaviour of his guest. Both *tuteur* and *étranger* engage in a variety of mutual favours and obligations, ranging from sharing some of the income to helping in agricultural work or lending money.

Younger migrants, especially, often develop close contacts with sons of the compound head, who in many cases are also work mates in the mining shafts. According to my observations, many of these relations, when they last over many years, turn into stable friendship bonds.[21] Many of the tenants even marry into their host families. In some cases, the host visits the home village of the guest. Subsequently, the landlord often stops asking the guest to pay any rent, while the latter begins to voluntarily contribute to the household in one way or another.

I mention this kind of relationship because of two important underlying logics. Although many immigrants try to build relationships with clusters of mates from the same region, many of them have limited choices: they have to accept the accommodation which is available upon their arrival. With time, a stable relationship with the landlord may develop to include multiple levels of sociability, assistance and amity, which are the essential grounds for friendship bonds.

This dyadic kind of friendship complies with approved institutions (Eisenstadt and Roniger 1999) and enables the immediate creation of a common frame of reference. At the same time, however, it continues to imply a considerable degree of social distance, which inhibits immigrants from having a direct and full access to land, even if they may be entitled to use rights or tenancy rights. Even when immigrants are married to local women/men, a fundamental disparity tends to remain. It requires indeed more than a generation for strangers to become full members of the local community.

We can consider the institution of *tutorat* as an element promoting a differentiated integration of immigrants into the host communities. I use the term of 'differentiated integration' because the immigrants are integrated as strangers and will be regarded as different 'good friends' to the local inhabitants. But it is nevertheless a kind of integration into a network of social obligations, norms and practices, allowing exchanges in many spheres of everyday life. It is a common frame of reference for both sides to claim responsibility and liability. As a way of establishing authority, many locals participate in a very pointed discourse of autochthony. At the same time, they accept the presence of strangers, as long as the latter do not claim more than use rights.

Friendship, Cohesion and Networking among Migrant Gold Miners

I have tried to develop the many reasons, social processes and logic that are the basis for different kinds of friendship ties in the gold-mining camps of Benin. The common social context of migrant miners, especially in that shared liminal space of migration,[22] helps to bring about friendship relations. These may turn into networks, but not necessarily. The social process that leads to the establishment of a set of connections or network associations is contingent upon many other factors. I will limit my account, touching only on some of them: the role of persons with integrating abilities and the effect of social events.

Extraordinary events did not only affect the relations miners had with the central state; they also helped, at least for a certain period, to form a clear identity and cohesion among many miners themselves. This was due to the continued control missions by the gendarmerie that miners had to face. In this period, they were relatively united and used a similar discourse of 'we the miners', regardless of ethnic origin. Even foreigners, very much persecuted by the police, were integrated as 'our brothers and friends'.

Tracing the diverse personal relationships of miners in their interconnectedness, it becomes obvious that often the same persons are quoted by different informants as being their (and thus common) friends. Looking more closely at these persons and asking more details about them, it also becomes clear that they were leading figures of some sort who all enjoyed a certain reputation and who were exceptional either in their organizational skills, speaking abilities or in their capacity to represent others, acknowledged as 'those who know'. They were often pioneer migrants in the business or the location, and usually very mobile and dynamic people, acting as mediators and small investors. Among them were many team leaders and traders.

Comparison between the Types of Friendship

As I have already stressed, the various ideal types of friendship are not mutually exclusive. An immigrant who has been living in the region for a longer period of time and who has built a house may operate himself as a *tuteur* for new immigrants from his home region. His initial landlord will still continue to be his *tuteur*. A local landlord may, at the same time, be a co-worker with his guest in a small gold-mining team and so on. In this respect, friendship ties also overlap with other social bonds. But the types differ in their basic mode of constitution and their content. It is the initial bond between the persons involved as well as the different quality and intimacy of the relationship that creates the basis for my analytic distinction.

As it has been argued before, a friendship between host and guest develops out of a patron-client relation, grows into good neighbourliness and eventually friendship over a longer time span. But it implies a social distance because it still refers to roles of 'strangers' and 'locals', whereas the friendships among young migrant gold miners develop on the basis of common interests, permanent co-operation, shared livelihood and, above all, shared life style.[23] This potentially forms the basis for the creation of a corporate identity as a group apart in its own right. From the point of view of intensity, relationships between individual gold miners are the strongest.

Friendship among clusters of immigrants can be regarded as an intermediary relationship, with the possibility of leading to more intense bonds or of simply remaining a basis for networks of trust and assistance. The relationship does not need to transcend common identities as regards regional or ethnic origins. This very often comprises a transition into patron-client relations (in the context of the mining community primarily between gold miners and gold traders).

Furthermore, the potential for growing into larger networks differs from one type of relationship to another. The largest networking processes certainly link friends originating from the same region, because very loose ends may be tied together by reference to regional and ethnic origin, which is a predominant discourse in that region. Dyadic relationships between (local and immigrant) friends as neighbours, however, follow a complex route through the networks of the local community (the friends of friends, the relatives of relatives, the guest of the *tuteur*, etc.) before becoming more and more extended to link many 'guests' with many 'hosts'. To marry into the local community certainly helps to advance such a process by way of also linking into women's networks.

The Ambivalence of Friendship as a Social Process

Friendship ties among gold miners are not chosen straightforwardly and not only conceived positively. These friendship bonds, however, like those established in other contexts, are fraught with ambivalence: between necessary closeness and distance, between implicit moral obligations and embarrassment in demanding them and between confidence and deception.

As friendship in this context is characterized by shared spheres of communication in a liminal space with growing proximity, a friend may know much – too much – about oneself. What happens when a friendship is terminated one day? Will the former friend use that knowledge against the other or make some personal information public, revealing weaknesses and secrets?

> I prefer not to have too many goods friends ... One or two are just right to deal with. Too many friends mean too many opinions to adjust to, too many people knowing too much about you. (Jonas, Kwatena, August 2002)

This informant, too, clearly marks the difference in degrees of relatedness, corresponding to shrinking circles of trust and intimacy. Another miner was even more sceptical:

> Me, I am staying alone. It's better for me, I don't want too many friends, because if you have too many friends, this brings about 'politics'.[24] You risk to quarrel. Because they will tell something to your friend that you never said. He, when he has no courage to withstand, will start to quarrel. That's what happened to me one day, and I don't want that happen to me again. (Tchorowé, Tchantangou, September 2002)

As already quoted above, a good friend is generally 'someone who won't betray you, someone you may have confidence in'. But are there many such partners that would fulfil these criteria? Asked about this, many informants readily restricted their choice to fewer names, or to one person as their 'best friend':

> My best friend is the one who knows my secrets. What kind of secrets? Well, it may be about some business tricks that help me making some money and should not be known to all. Or that I have done something wrong in the past, back home. (Jonas, Kwatena, August 2002)

That intimacy, of course, could become problematic when it comes to the breakdown of the relationship.

Many sociological and philosophical definitions of friendship stress its noninstrumental nature. This position is questionable. Friendship as a nonutilitarian relationship is a romantic Western ideal (Silver 1989; Carrier 1999).[25] Assistance, support and help are probably part of all friendship ties. I would phrase the question in another way, pointing to the perspective or sequence of causalities: it is a small, but quite decisive difference whether somebody supports another person *because he recognizes him as friend,* or the other way round, whether somebody recognizes another person as friend *because of the support* he may expect from him ('I help you because you are my friend' or 'you are my friend because you help me'). In the former case, the relationship may resemble more the ideal of a 'pure' friendship than in the latter. But both also involve many more aspects of generalized, direct or delayed reciprocity – a term which seems to be most appropriate here. The ways in which this reciprocity is maintained may be of quite a different nature depending on the situation.

I am not arguing in favour of mechanistic causalities, but I suggest that it is useful to point out these differences in order to explain why some particular dyadic relationships among gold miners develop more easily into larger networks and groups on the basis of firm mutual ties and cohesion. On the basis of a comprehensive framework of shared habitus as migrant miners, many commonalities and thus a greater sociability in many parts of everyday life emerge. The ties of cohesion become stronger, reinforce themselves, involve more and more persons, become more complex and develop into networks.

Recording individual accounts on dyadic relationships in interviews, I also realized that in many cases I was dealing with friends of different ages. This often does not represent a major issue for those involved. They primarily regard the essential conditions – mutual understanding and mutual support – as given and thus see themselves as friends. Age is still relevant, but comes into play here only on a secondary level. Differences in age give rise to a different degree of personal experience and the younger partner often expects some guidance from the elder one. It is often the elder one who is more generous, far from exploiting the younger one.

Conclusion

In this contribution, I examined three types of friendship bonds in the gold-mining region of northern Benin, the most pertinent type being dyadic relationships between young miners who are part of the same working team. In that region, friendship bonds certainly do not represent a more predominant form of social ties than patronage, clientelism, kinship or business networks. Nevertheless, there can be no doubt that friendship bonds are there especially of great significance for young migrant miners. These friendship bonds can be seen as being part of a broader social strategy to accommodate a particular migratory situation in a typical mining camp, and as a sort of 'total social institution' (Mauss 1990 [1923–1924]). It is the highly flexible economic and social setting in which the migrants live that makes it more likely for these types of relationships to be created. Furthermore, I identified the underlying logics of friendship within the mining community, demonstrated by various practices, such as the way that miners share. I argued that in many cases friendship is more preferable to kinship, especially when ensuring a 'fair' distribution of the yields.

In addition, friendship – combined with typical elements of a young gold miner's life style – enables the rapid creation of support networks, which help to build confidence and to empower migrants with heterogeneous origins. This process is relevant in the miners' everyday life beyond the work sphere. Seen from an analytical perspective, many relationships, not officially coined as friendship, may fit into our frame of analysis. Among these are relationships between various kinsmen, who having migrated together and having become fellow co-workers in a mining team, may find themselves sharing more labour and leisure time than they ever did before and, as a result, becoming close friends. Remote relatives may become partners, peers and friends only in the mining region.

The same applies to patronage and age-grade relationships versus friendship. Although miners may have a different position in the hierarchies, they often experience such relationships as intimate and interpret them as close friendships. A strong opposition between these categories is hence not helpful. A friend, especially a member of the migrating group from the same region, may be called a 'brother'. In this way kinship provides the dominant idiom through which friendship is expressed, ritually reaffirming 'we-feelings' that have provided a basis for becoming close.

Friendship among gold miners can certainly be perceived as being partly structured and constrained by external factors (see introduction to this volume; see also Adams and Allan 1998b). At the same time, it cannot be denied that it has informal and flexible qualities. By alluding to common realms of sociability, ethos and understanding, I want to go beyond the simple aspects of exchange theory that dominate many other studies on friendship. Moreover, to the extent that migrants share a common group situation, in an unstable social setting, I point to the polyadic dimension of friendship (see also Eve 2002). To conclude, processual approaches may adequately explore the various and shifting social logics inherent to friendship bonds among gold miners.

Acknowledgements

This chapter is based on field research in northwestern Benin between January 1999 and March 2004, as part of a research project on the social and political context of artisanal gold mining in West Africa, financed by the DAAD, Bonn, and especially the Max Planck Institute for Social Anthropology, Halle/Saale (Germany). I thank both these institutions for their support. I am also particularly grateful to Erdmute Alber, Tsypylma Darieva, Youssouf Diallo, Martine Guichard, Barbara Meier, Boris Nieswand, Michaela Pelican and Katja Werthmann for their useful comments on this chapter in its various stages of improvement.

Notes

1. Besides earlier studies by Eisenstadt (1956, 1974), Cohen (1961), Wolf (1966), Paine (1974) or Du Bois (1974), Robert Brain's *Friends and Lovers* (1976) was an thoughtful attempt to discuss friendship in a cross-cultural perspective, a perspective that has been recently revitalized in sociology and social anthropology (e.g., Bell and Coleman 1999a; Devere 2007; Schmidt et al. 2007; Desai and Killick 2010; Descharmes et al. 2011).
2. This chapter represents a basically revised and enlarged version of an earlier paper (Grätz 2004a). In northern Benin artisanal and small-scale gold mining are forms of mining that are often interrelated and combined with one another. A differentiation is therefore not applicable for that region. For a definition of each of these forms of mining, see, for example, Hentschel, Hruschka and Priester (2003: 5).
3. Social impacts include: rapidly changing consumer practices, alcohol and drug abuse, the monetarization of everyday life, mining accidents, the creation of winners and losers and the use of violence in many gold-mining areas.
4. This account refers exclusively to male gold miners. Friendship networks among female migrants are as important as those among men, but overlap only partially with them. 'Young' in this context refers to their social age: most gold miners are unmarried men between sixteen and thirty.
5. See also Carbonnel (1991), Yaro (1996), Werthmann (2000, 2003a, 2003b, 2008, 2009, 2010) and Luning (2006, 2008, 2010) for case studies in Burkina Faso and Vwakyanakazi (1992) for the Democratic Republic of Congo/Zaire. For detailed historical accounts on artisanal gold mining in West Africa, see Arhin (1978), Chauveau (1978), Garrard (1980), Kiethega (1983), Schneider (1990), Pillet-Schwartz (1993) and Dumett (1999). For publications explicitly dealing with contemporary gold mining in various African countries, see, for example, Hilson (2006), Panella (2010), Werthmann and Grätz (2013).
6. Gold miners may receive less when being reprimanded for a bad work ethic, i.e., not working like the others, being late, quarrelling too much, betraying others and the like.
7. For a hard day's work, miners may earn between 1,000 and 30,000 Francs CFA (€ 1.50 to 40).
8. Gold trade does not fit into the 'ethnic argument': it is neither embedded in kinship relations nor does it constitute a distinct corporate group with an exclusive group identity, at least not yet.
9. See also Grätz (2003a).
10. The elder brother may offer, however, some protection: 'There are also advantages to work with your "brother", because he may help you obliging others to work correctly. When you are with your "brother", he will look after you and advise you how to not tire yourself too much. He will protect you.' (Djoto Raoul, Perma, August 2002)
11. It is thus not surprising that I primarily found more kin-based working units of gold miners in Kwatena, Tchantangou or Koussigou among the local inhabitants, members of local households with full subsistence production and reproduction. These younger men considered the comparatively less-rewarding assistant work for their fathers, elder brothers or agnates as an investment into their own kin group and the household they were integrated into, where they enjoyed economic security, including access to clan-based arable land in the long run, but only in relation to the achievement of seniority and status.

12. For a similar account on Congolese gold miners, see Vwakyanakazi (1992).
13. Friendship relations among gold miners, independent of their degree of intimacy and interethnic nature, are expressed openly. This contrasts to the case of Fulbe friendships with farmers in Borgou (northern Benin), examined by Guichard (2000, 2002), where these ties tend to be hidden because of strong distinguishing public discourses and the wish on both sides to disguise the actual extent of cattle entrustment.
14. As traders and service providers immediately follow a new gold boom, the supply of goods (and temptations) in these places is usually extensive: from video-cinemas, bars, coffee shops, gambling of all kinds, discothèques and other entertainment facilities. Established in a simple manner, shops offer fashionable clothing, hairdressing, sunglasses, athletic shoes, radios and even motorbikes and cars.
15. This applies above all to young, unmarried migrants.
16. Extensive practices to entertain each other include reciprocity as well, but certainly not in a balanced way. In this sphere, representations of fairness differ from those in the working context.
17. For a similar account on life styles of diamond divers, see De Boeck (1998).
18. In this respect, relationships among miners are similar to those in other settings and groups such as construction workers, soldiers, athletes, etc.
19. For friendships with especially long-lasting character, see Pritchett (2007) and Werbner in this volume.
20. For accounts on the role of host-guest institution in establishing friendship bonds, see also Pelican (2004) and Breusers in this volume.
21. In this respect, it is easy to observe different degrees of social proximity, from more distanced contacts to a growing familiarity in everyday interactions.
22. Especially young, new incoming gold miners are exposed to a kind of double initiation: an initiation into the socioprofessional world of miners, a male group featuring a distinct life style, work ethic and behaviour. The migratory cycle as a whole could also be conceived as an initiation (in a larger sense of the term).
23. On identity processes and life style among migrant gold miners in West Africa, see Grätz (2003b, 2009, 2010).
24. Intrigues, conflicts and disputes.
25. See also Reyna in this volume.

Part III
Friendship, Politics and Urbanity

Chapter 6

Friendship and Kinship among Merchants and Veterans in Mali

Richard L. Warms

Introduction

In this contribution, I would like to reflect on the nature of friendship among two different groups in Mali. I worked among merchants in the southwestern Malian city of Sikasso in the mid-1980s and among veterans of the *Tirailleurs sénégalais,* the military regiments conscripted and recruited from France's African possessions during the colonial era, in the city of Bougouni in the mid-1990s. I believe that friendship served substantially different purposes for members of each group and this variety shows that friendship is an essential element of society for both of these groups, but can only be interpreted contextually.

Several threads of scholarship relating to friendship are relevant to the current case. One sees friendship, particularly among children, as part of a process of identity building and enculturation. For example, Dyson, in a study of girls in the Indian Himalayas, notes that friendship is both important and productive. It helped girls 'meet gendered expectations, construct affirming identities, and foster ties of mutuality' (Dyson 2010: 494). But it also reinforced dominant ideas (Dyson 2010; see also Junehui 2011). A second threat, following Bourdieu's influential study of friendships among members of France's upper and middle classes (1984 [1979]), examines the connection between friendship, wealth and power. For example, Ghannam shows how friendship can help some individuals in a low-income neighbourhood in Cairo 'cultivate new "cultural competencies" … that help [them] to operate more easily in middle-class shops, cafés, and neighborhoods' (Ghannam 2011: 795). A third thread connects kinship and friendship essentially seeing these two as inversely related and connected to a rural/urban dichotomy. For example, in a study in the early 1990s, Beggs, Haines and Hurlbert (1996) found that, in Louisiana, rural personal networks are more complex and of greater intensity than urban personal networks, but emphasize kinship and neighbourhood solidarities. Friendship is more often found in urban locations. Communitarian authors hail the growth of friendship in contemporary society. They often see this as supplementing and expanding kin relations and as a characteristic of postindustrial society (Pahl 2000; Spencer and Pahl 2006).

The notion that kinship and friendship should be inversely related seems commonsensical in our own society. We tend to understand ourselves as moving from tight-knit rural communities held together by networks of kin to urban environments held together by voluntary groupings such as unions, clubs and honorary associations. This has been a principal vision of Western society ever since Durkheim (1947 [1893]), Tönnies (1968 [1897]) and Weber (1968 [1921]). Such ideas were extended to Africa with research conducted in the 1960s on voluntary associations by authors such as Little (1965, 1976), Meillassoux (1968) and Gist and Fava (1974). The gist of each of these arguments is that as people leave village communities held together by formal bonds of kinship and other forms of association, and migrate to cities, such bonds tend to be replaced by voluntary and less formal friendship ties. It is not clear, however, that these ideas are actually empirically true in our own society or in the current-day capitalist periphery of West Africa. As other chapters in this volume demonstrate, friendship ties play an important role in many rural settings and in time-honoured notions of what being a member of a particular community means. In modern African cities, I will argue, friendship ties do not have an inverse relationship with kinship ties or other forms of association. Kinship and friendship may reinforce one another. Friendship may lead to kinship and both may be instrumental in navigating the economic and political uncertainties and difficulties of life in modern urban Africa. Friendship is also vital in both enculturation and in establishing economic connections. These points will be illustrated by the differing roles friendship and kinship play for merchants in Sikasso and veterans of the *Tirailleurs sénégalais* in Bougouni.

Friendship among Merchants in Sikasso in the 1980s

In the mid-1980s, I did my doctoral research on merchants in the marketplace at Sikasso in southwestern Mali. My understanding of the West African economic history included the notion of ethnic monopoly of trade. In 'traditional' West Africa, the 'long-distance' trade was conducted by members of specific ethnic groups, particularly Hausa and Dyula who lived as strangers and as minorities in diverse local contexts, often occupying their own area in urban settings. Many of these individuals served as landlords to itinerant traders moving merchandise between the desert, savannah and forest zones of West Africa, particularly salt, kola nut and cattle. The ethnic bonds among such people facilitated trade because ties of kinship, common language and common religion enabled financial arrangements, especially credit, that were essential to trade, and because landlords knew and understood local markets and were able to act as brokers to the merchants.[1] The goal of my research was to find this system of trade, if I could, and to try to figure out what had happened to it if I could not. I had been warned that I would be unlikely to find such a trading system, so I was not terribly surprised when I found virtually no ethnically based trade in Sikasso. I concluded that it had died, a victim of a combination of the specific history of Sikasso (particularly the siege of 1898 and subsequent plundering of the town), French colonial policy and the expansion of capitalist markets in the twentieth century.[2]

The central question of my research then became whether anything had replaced the ethnic system. One possibility was, of course, that the market was simply chaotic, a multitude of buyers and sellers with little relation among them. Another was that it was organized in a more or less simple top-down manner with the most powerful merchants operating as patrons to all others. The reality proved to be somewhere in-between the two. On the one hand, there were a great many independent operators working in the Sikasso market and in the smaller markets in outlying villages. Barriers to low-level involvement in trade were few and many merchants had only scant links to others. On the other hand, there were clearly a number of individuals who were large-scale merchants. These operated the large boutiques surrounding the market and often held permits to import foreign goods. Such large-scale merchants supplied goods, generally on credit, to smaller merchants who operated small market stalls and small shops in the quarters of the town, and travelled to periodic rural markets as well.

This was the general outline of the system; but how did it actually operate? Two factors are critical to answering this question. The first is the weakness of economic institutions in Mali. The second is the general context of friendship and kinship as well as the history of ethnic trade described above. Although there were both commercial and state-run banks operating in Mali, their presence in smaller towns such as Sikasso was extremely limited. Further, they were almost completely unable (and unwilling) to provide financing for all but the largest and best established businessmen. Add to this the fact that the police force and justice system were also extremely weak and two things become immediately apparent: first, there were no official commercial or state channels through which an aspiring merchant could get access to credit; second, there were virtually no legal and reliable means for a creditor to collect 'bad' debt or even hold the debtor to justice. And yet, virtually all commerce, large and small, depends on the extension of credit. This meant that individuals who want either to start in business or to expand an already existing business must gain access to the funds necessary through someone who is wealthy and who will either make them an outright gift or trust them to repay a debt. The first of these should not be understood as a gift given for purely altruistic purposes with no expectation of return. Rather such gifts are given in anticipation of continuing social and economic relationships. The second implies a fixed sum of money and a fixed repayment schedule.

An aspiring merchant may look anywhere for the credit or cash necessary to begin a business: family members, former civil servants who were able to amass wealth, and remittances from relatives or friends who live in the Ivory Coast, Europe or America. I have seen examples of all of these. However, the primary place they look is to other merchants. All large-scale merchants I talked to in Sikasso had loaned merchandise or cash to aspiring merchants, and the majority of small merchants I talked to had received such loans. In general, larger merchants report that loans are given in the form of merchandise (although occasionally cash is transferred) and, as prescribed by Islamic law, loans are given without interest charge. Large merchants agree to provide goods for small merchants at a price that includes a profit for the large merchants (although they claim this profit is small). Small merchants further mark up goods when they sell them. In the case of loans of cash, large merchants hope to increase the strength of a desirable relationship.

The trouble with such loans of goods or cash is that they are not secured and not really recoverable. So, merchants need to be very careful to whom they lend money. When I asked merchants how they determined who to lend to, overwhelmingly they replied that it was an issue of confidence. They loaned to people in whom they had confidence. The next question was how that confidence was built. Here, several elements are involved and friendship is critical.[3]

First, while there did not seem to be any real ethnic element to trade, certain people were at an advantage in securing credit; particularly sons of merchant families and sons of families that were well known and established in Sikasso. Newcomers from rural areas or other towns had greater difficulty securing credit, but it was not impossible for them.

Second, confidence is built slowly. Early loans to merchants are small. Lenders say that if an individual comes back week after week and repays his debt, he can always get a new loan and new loans are likely to be larger than older ones. Merchants say that this weekly dependability is the single most important factor in determining loan availability and size.

Third, as merchants show their dependability, in at least some cases, friendship will become a critical factor. Older loaning merchants wish to strengthen their ties to successful younger merchants. A man who has several aggressive, successful and dependable young traders who receive goods from him on credit stands to reap a substantial financial benefit.

Young merchants who show themselves dependable can go to any of a number of larger merchants. Large merchants are generally friendly with each other; however, they must compete with each other for access to the best younger merchants. The competitive nature of the marketplace and the low profit on most individual items means that merchants are generally unable to attract and hold good clients by offering better deals than their competitors. However, they can try to bind their clients through friendship.

In a sense, friendship presents a dilemma for traders. On the one hand, it is a way for merchants to cement bonds with the most promising (and congenial) of their clients. On the other hand, it may be more difficult to collect a debt from a friend than from an acquaintance. Tilo Grätz (this volume), for example, reports that artisanal gold miners in northern Benin say that they prefer not to give loans to friends because it is morally difficult to demand that a friend return money and it risks ending the friendship.

There are several reasons why Sikasso merchants do choose to make bonds with their clients closer through friendship, and these are not mutually exclusive. The choice might reflect a cultural difference between southern Mali and northern Benin. However, it is more likely explained by two economic factors. First, as noted above, merchants need a means of preventing their best clients from seeking relationships with other merchants. Since it is difficult to do this through economic means, there are few alternatives to bonds of friendship and kinship. Second, relationships between merchants and their clients are not friendships among equals. Wealthy merchants have much more money, power and influence than their clients. In the final analysis, a wealthy merchant can afford to lose a client, even a good one, more than the client can afford to lose the patronage of a wealthy and powerful merchant. This situation is exacerbated by the fact that while several powerful merchants may want the clientage of a promising young merchant, far fewer will be interested after that person has refused to pay a debt. The result is that aspiring merchants are always under very substantial pressure to pay their debts. Word about peoples' reputation travels fast. Someone who fails to repay a debt might find himself unable to find another patron, not only in Sikasso, but throughout much of the rest of Mali as well.[4]

The critical practical element in the formation of friendships for Sikasso merchants is the tea drinking circle or *grin*. In Mali, it is common for wealthier urban men and women to pass their afternoons (and sometimes mornings as well) drinking tea. Such tea drinking is, on the one hand, quite informal: groups are usually single-sex, but men and women may drink together; passers-by may be invited to drink and one may 'drink and run' as well. On the other hand, there is a specific series of steps and a certain formality to the capable execution of these.

Chinese green tea is used. Two small tea pots, a charcoal brazier, one large (33 cl) and several small (shot sized) glasses are required. Tea is poured back and forth between the two pots while sugar is added and a head of foam is built. The same tea leaves are used to make three successive batches of tea; the first being extremely strong and intense, the last quite weak, but extremely sweet. While children sometimes make tea for their elders, men take pride in their ability to produce good, strong, aesthetically pleasing glasses. Aesthetically pleasing tea has good colour, but is really characterized by a thick head of foam. This foam is produced by repeatedly pouring the tea from pot to pot and ultimately from pot to glass from as high as one can. It requires a good eye and steady hand. While, as I mentioned above, people can be given a single glass of tea (and some have specific preferences for one of the three), in general when tea is prepared, mostly all members of the group making it will sit from the assembly of the tea items to the final cup, a process that takes anywhere from sixty to ninety minutes.

While the making of tea is certainly a ritual, it has no religious overtones. It can be done on virtually any occasion and is primarily an act or gesture of friendship. Tea drinking gives merchants (and many others) an extremely practical method of moving individuals from purely commercial relations to relationships based more on friendship. A merchant who wishes to befriend another will repeatedly invite that person to sit for tea. Further, the relatively long time it takes to make and consume the three glasses of tea gives time for relaxation, exchange of ideas and conversation of varying sorts. People may propose and discuss business deals, but they are just as likely to talk about family and friends. Sometimes younger men will play cards. In any event, drinking tea allows for an arena in which friendships may be formed and ideas exchanged. It plays a critical role in building the confidence between merchants and their best clients.

Tea drinking has a spatial element as well. Most Sikasso shops are dominated by a large wooden counter. Merchants sit or stand on one side of the counter, customers and clients, on the other. The counter thus separates the two and reinforces both social distinction and division of labour. Merchants who are sharing tea, however, generally move from behind the counter to sit in a circle, creating an informal and relatively intimate space for conversation. They may sit in front of a shop, or in some cases, in a private area behind the shop. Particularly in the latter case, the spatial element of tea drinking provides dramatic physical reinforcement of the move from formality to friendship.

Tea drinking may be implicated in two additional ways. It provides a forum for discussion that may lead either to the strengthening or diminishing (to know you isn't always to love you) of relationships between merchants and their clients in matters of faith and matters of kin.

Trade in West Africa has long been tied to Islam (Hiskett 1984). Perinbaum, for example, notes that 'one cannot overestimate the moral importance of Islam [to trade]' (1972: 789). Dyula and Hausa merchants were generally members of Muslim communities living among practitioners of traditional African religions. Islam favours the development of trade because its common belief system, and, to a lesser extent, the use of Arabic, tied Muslims together and differentiated them from the members of many traditional religions among which they operated. Of course, in modern-day Mali, these advantages are lost. A century ago, while Islam was very influential, Muslims were a relatively small part of the population (particularly in the southwest, where Sikasso is located). Today, virtually the entire population of the nation identifies itself as Muslim, although many continue to practise certain elements of traditional religion alongside Islam. Almost without exception, merchants identify themselves as Muslims, but simply being a Muslim no longer serves to differentiate them from neighbouring communities. Probably in response to this, in the 1980s, merchants in Sikasso and in other Malian cities were increasingly associating themselves with the 'Wahhabi', Muslims who based their practices on Saudi styles and beliefs rather than on West African ones.[5] This association comprised not only certain specific beliefs about the practice of Islam but visible differences in prayer (praying in an 'arms crossed' position). At that time, it was understood that the Wahhabi were generally wealthier than others and more strict in their observance of Islam. The self-identification of merchants as Wahhabi served to separate them from the general population and provide some of the exclusiveness previously created by Muslim identity alone. Wealthy Sikasso merchants overwhelmingly identify themselves as Wahhabi and younger merchants generally identify increasingly with the Wahhabi group as they gain the confidence of their patrons. Taking tea allows time for the discussion of matters of faith and for merchants to affirm their Islamic identity and move to Wahhabi practice.

In the case of the more prosperous younger merchants, bonds of friendship and religious affinities with older patrons, developed through confidence building and socializing, are often converted into bonds of kinship. A marriage between an aspiring young merchant and a daughter from his patron's family solidifies and formalizes the relationship between patron and protégé. Such bonds make it very difficult for a protégé to escape from his debt to a patron or engage in business dealings unknown to the patron. It reduces the chances that the protégé will move to a different merchant.

It is most desirable for the aspiring merchant to marry a patron's daughter. He will thus become the patron's son-in-law and the familial relationship between them will mirror their patron-protégé relation. In fact, almost half (fourteen of thirty-one) of the important merchants I spoke with in Sikasso had made such a match. Several other young merchants seemed about to make similar matches with their patrons' families (but I do not know if this did, in fact, happen).

Friendship is thus instrumental in the lives of Sikasso merchants. It is partially a product of the cultural background of the region: friendship is, in general, a strong cultural value and there is time and encouragement for people of all sorts to forge fairly close bonds. However, it is also an adaptation to weak governmental and banking institutions: it helps to assure continuity in commercial and financial relationships in a market where credit is hard to obtain and enforcement almost impossible. Merchants tend to convert friendship into kinship and this further reinforces their financial and business dealings. Of course, to say that friendship is instrumental is not to comment at all on its emotional value or the intensity of connection between the individuals involved. I have seen no reason to believe that friendship and kinship relations among merchants are any more or less 'genuine' than such relations among other people.

Friendship among Veterans in Bougouni in the 1990s

In the 1990s, my anthropological research turned from merchants in Sikasso to veterans of the *Tirailleurs sénégalais* living in and around the Malian town of Bougouni, 100 miles south of Bamako. The French conscripted men heavily from the Bougouni area, and some enlisted as well. While numerous men from the Bougouni region fought in World War I, none remained alive when I worked there in the 1990s. The veterans remaining served primarily in Morocco in the 1930s, in World War II and in Vietnam.[6]

Men were normally conscripted to serve three- or four-year terms of service. However, often, at the time of conscription, they were offered an option to enlist. If they did so, they served a longer period, but they were eligible for certain benefits. The primary one of these was a life-long pension that could be gained for twenty years of service or its equivalent (under combat or in difficult locations, extra time credit was given). Some of those who were conscripted were offered opportunities to remain in French military service at the close of their tour of duty and often took these options.

Conscripts who served for four years often returned with nothing. In some cases, even the uniforms they wore and other issued personal equipment was taken from them and they were liberated as one might free a prisoner. More often they were allowed to keep personal items, but were given no lasting benefits, such as a pension or special access to health care. Most of these men returned to their towns and villages and tried to pick up life as they left it off. In many cases, they have tried to forget their experiences as best they could. Such individuals may (or may not) have one or two close friends who were also veterans. However, although they were known to other veterans, particularly veterans who served long enough to be pensioned, they seemed to have relatively few connections to veterans at large. They rarely came into the town of Bougouni and were unlikely to be present at the Maison des Anciens Combattants (MAC; the social club and office for veterans).

Military service led to a degree of life-long alienation for many of these individuals. As one said to me:

> When you come back, you have to follow the ideas of the people in the village. If not, if you try to tell them all about the army and what you have seen, they are never going to understand you. You can explain things and there are those who will just say you are lying. You just let them alone, at least that's the way I've gotten along. (Lassana Samaké, February 1995)

In stories and legends, veterans are often portrayed as drunkards or as somewhat deranged.[7] On the one hand, men such as Lassana Samaké, who I have just quoted, are certainly not the crazies and drunkards of legend. On the other, they are somewhat different from other members of their community. They have had experiences of culture and violence that are difficult for those around them to understand, and this cannot help but affect their lives.

The case of pensioned veterans is more complex. Veterans who served the equivalent of twenty years received life-long pensions from the French government. While from the time of independence until recently, such pensions were very much less than those received by French citizens, they frequently still amounted to a substantial income by local standards.[8] In virtually every case in the Bougouni region, such pensioned veterans who came from rural villages did not return to settle there, but moved to larger cities.

Receiving a pension created an interesting dynamic within veterans' patrilineal and patrilocal families. The head of such families is usually the eldest of a series of brothers. The family head has the right to control family resources including land, labour and any income received by other family members. Military conscription only rarely fell upon eldest sons. First, there is only one eldest, but many younger sons (so the odds favour younger sons). Second, elder sons were generally able to protect themselves – family heads tended to send junior members to war. In many cases, this meant that pensioned veterans returning home found themselves in relatively junior positions within their families. As a result, older family heads demanded (and by tradition were entitled to) control of their pension money.

This situation was exacerbated by the fact that, among the Wassulunke, as among many polygynous groups, there is a sharp distinction between siblings (same father, same mother) and half-siblings (same father, different mothers). Individuals generally share great solidarity with full siblings, but relations with half-siblings can be rivalrous and problematic. The upshot of this is returning pensioned veterans often faced demands for control of their pensions from older half-siblings. Very few pensioned veterans in the Bougouni area put up with such demands for long. Rather than ceding control of their pensions to older brothers and especially older half-brothers, these veterans frequently chose to break with their families and move into town. There are almost no pensioned veterans living in rural communities in the Bougouni area. The only such veterans I was able to find are themselves heads of households.

Veterans were able to make the move into town for several reasons. First, with a pension veterans were men of independent means and did not require financial support from their families. Second, there was, in many cases, an organization there waiting to receive them and to facilitate their transition to life in town. The national veterans' association maintained (and continues to maintain) branches in most cities in Mali (and, indeed, throughout areas of Francophone West Africa where soldiers were conscripted in any quantity). The veterans' organization provided facilities that included a building which served as a meeting place, an emergency shelter and often a bar. Finally, veterans had a ready-made network of friends and acquaintances, consisting of other men with whom they may or may not have served, but with whom, in any event, they shared certain elements of experience. Such ready-made networks not only facilitated veterans' adaptation to urban life; they also provided an easy way for veterans to diminish the importance of kinship bonds.

The continued importance of friendship to veterans is demonstrated by the solidarity they show with regard to personal events and by the role the veterans' association and the MAC continue to play in their lives. If the veterans' association calls a meeting, most of those physically able to attend will be there. If a veteran dies, again, most of those who can attend the funeral will attend. The same is true of other life-cycle events. They may show this solidarity with regard to politics as well.

The MAC continues to provide a focal centre to the veteran community. Scheduled events at the MAC are quite rare, but there are almost always a few people to be found there. Perhaps one third of the veterans living in Bougouni are relatively frequent visitors to the MAC, and it serves as a place where they can come, hang out, talk and relax. The MAC does include a bar. In some MACs I have visited, drinking is common and you could always find people in the bar. In Bougouni, while there are veterans who do drink (and one or two who are, in fact, drunkards), I never saw anyone use the bar. Bougouni is a town where a degree of Islamic propriety is today the norm, and veterans are certainly no exception.

Although the presence of friends certainly made the transition to city life easier and more attractive for veterans, friendship may have been less economically instrumental for them than for Sikasso merchants. Veterans frequently mentioned jobs they had gotten or other benefits they had received because they were veterans. But they rarely mentioned friendship as an important factor in these jobs. It was more often a matter of an official who was a friend of veterans rather than an individual who was a personal friend. This was particularly the case for veterans who served in the 1940s. Between 1947 and 1952, Meker, an idealistic French colonial official with socialist leanings, served as commandant of Bougouni. Meker was known as a friend to veterans and provided many with jobs and housing. He was often mentioned with great fondness by veterans (many of whom reviled other French colonial officials).[9]

Further, the friendship I have seen at the MAC and at the homes of veterans seems to me the comradeship of old men who have known each other for many years. Many are retired from jobs in the civil service or, occasionally, from careers in business. They talk, they do a bit of farming, they manage their often very large families. Perhaps, had I visited twenty years ago, I would have found them talking about collaborations and projects, but they are at the wrong point in their life cycle for that. Further, it is clear that if as younger men veterans had spent their time discussing such economic collaborations and projects these either did not come to fruition or did not play major roles in their lives. No veteran looked back on their extensive economic ties to another veteran, nor did veterans have extensive kin times.

Thus, although veterans in Bougouni undoubtedly form fast friendships, these are usually not instrumental in terms of either career or kinship. Friendships are certainly important, but they are more likely to be forums in which people discuss and relive past experience, share stories, provide emotional support for each other and assurance that life-cycle ceremonies will be well attended, than they are to lead to kinship or economic ties among friends.

Conclusion

In conclusion, I would first like to reflect on the similarities and differences between the groups I have focused upon in this chapter. Both of these groups are clearly the product of social change. The opportunities seized by today's merchants are systematically different than those offered by precolonial trade. The products being sold, in most cases, did not exist (at least not in the same form) in the late nineteenth century. The routes and means by which these move are new, as are the networks of relationships that propel them. Similarly, veterans of the French colonial army are obviously not a group of any great antiquity. They are, in fact, a group tied to a particular era, that of colonialism; change created this group, and in a few years, it will disappear. Thus, these groups present extremely good subjects for the study of social change.

However, a comparative analysis of these two groups suggests differences in the treatment of the moral basis of friendship. For veterans, the key moral obligation of friendship was solidarity, demonstrated through attendance at funerals and life-cycle events, co-operation with programs promoted by the national association of veterans. The moralities in everyday relationships were indeterminate. For merchants, friendship was, in a sense, about a certain type of morality. My argument is that, given the weakness of banking and political institutions, friendship was one of the merchants' best hedges against loss to debtors. Of course this is a very limited type of morality. The fact that a person repays his loans fully and on time and is able to build his confidence level with a patron says nothing about the morality of his dealings with other people and the state.

The merchants and the veterans also differed from each other in the manner in which they managed the relationship between friendship and kinship. Among merchants, friendship supplemented and often led to kinship while, to the best of my knowledge, among veterans, friendship sometimes helped individuals to escape the bonds of kinship, and in some ways did replace them.

For the purposes of this paper, the most important question remains that of the relationship of friendship and kinship in current-day African societies. As I already noted in the introductory section of this paper, many analysts, from the nineteenth century to the present, have seen an evolutionary trend in kinship. Traditional societies (particularly rural societies) are held together by kinship. In the face of modernity, urbanization, increased specialization and the multiplication of roles, friendship comes to replace kinship. Thus, we have 'progressed' from a society dominated by relations of kin to one increasingly dominated by friendship, with the circle of kin becoming more restricted. The data that I have presented above on the relationship between friendship and kinship suggest that this model of the shifting nature of that relationship in connection with growing urbanization and modernization is only transferable to a limited extent across settings. In the towns in which I conducted my research, for example, the model according to which such developments go hand in hand with a decline of the importance of kinship and an increase of that of friendship only found validation for one of the two groups under study, namely, the veterans. As my data also imply, there is a need for a more differentiated understanding of the relationship between friendship and kinship.

Among people in Sikasso and Bougouni, both friendship and kinship have historically been powerful forces. And both are critical means through which people have survived and adapted to the economic, political and technological exigencies of life. Friendship is an extraordinarily adaptable and powerful means of confronting a new social and economic situation: friends help people adapt to the economic and social challenges. It is clear that kin can do these things as well, and that the relationship between kinship and friendship is fluid. Connections between kin may be a catalyst for friendship: a friend of my kinsman may also be my friend. Conversely, friendship may, over time, lead to kinship as people marry into the families of their friends. All of this suggests that the relationship between kinship and friendship is a function of particular historic, economic and social forces. Kinship and friendship are different, but they are certainly not opposed to each other (see also Guichard, this volume). Further, it may be precisely under the conditions described in this chapter and several other contributions to this book, and particularly that of Grätz, that the dynamic relations between kinship and friendship are most important. In the relatively unstable political and economic environment of both West and East Africa, the ability of individuals and families to survive and prosper is tightly linked to their networks of kin and friends. Since governmental and social institutions are often very weak or ineffective, 'getting things done' requires such a network. These trends have probably increased over the past decade. New technology such as cell phones, internet access and social media has enabled Malians to expand their social networks and keep in closer contact with each other, and given them a greater degree of access to international banking and money transfers. At the same time, declining national and regional stability, particularly the military coup of 2012 and the subsequent wars have made national institutions even less dependable and increased the need for wide and effective networks of friends and kin. By comparison, both friendship and kinship might be of reduced importance in the wealthy, technological societies of Europe, North America and Asia. In these places, people may rely more heavily on governmental and other social institutions to assure their economic and social survival. Cell phones and social media allow people to keep connected more than ever before. And such media has become important to people's psychological well-being, and occasionally, to political action. However, having long lists of Facebook friends does not necessarily correspond to having many deep and abiding connections with other people. In fact, the permanence of the electronic record and the size of friend lists may closely limit communication. Despite our electronic networks, relationships with others, both kin and friends, might become comparatively attenuated and, as Weber (1968 [1921]) feared a century ago, bureaucratized.[10]

Notes

1. There are many outstanding resources on long distance trade in Africa; see, for example, Cohen (1965, 1966, 1971), Amselle (1977), Lovejoy (1980) and Launay (1982).
2. For more information about the trade and merchants of Sikasso, see Warms (1987, 1990, 1992, 1994).
3. In *The Problem of Trust,* Seligman (1997) distinguishes *confidence* from *trust*. Seligman sees confidence as the expectation that an individual will fill the role that is assigned to him/her. Trust, on the other hand, occurs when people must fill multiple and often contradictory roles. It is the faith that individuals will maintain their fundamental principles and obligations despite such contradictions. Seligman argues that confidence is characteristic of premodern societies since it is nothing 'but confidence in well-regulated (and heavily sanctioned) role relations of an ascriptive nature' (Seligman 1997: 36). Seligman continues: 'The "trust" that is so often seen to bind members of tribal, peasant or other types of pre-modern societies is not trust at all but confidence in a very particular mode of social organization based on ascriptive categories' (1997: 37). Seligman sees trust as reflecting the philosophy of the Scottish Enlightenment and a particular condition of wealthy, industrialized societies. Whatever utility Seligman's distinction has in the analysis of the condition of modernity in wealthy societies, it seems to me to be based in an overly simplistic understanding of non-Western societies. In African societies (and perhaps everywhere) people must always fill multiple roles. People in all societies must negotiate the often contradictory demands of their many contextualized identities; they are kin-group members, fill economic roles, have religious and ritual roles and today often have bureaucratic roles as well. Further, in current African societies and especially as regards bureaucratic roles, confidence that individuals will fill role expectations may be less common than trust that they will maintain their fundamental principles. The trajectory may be from trust to confidence, rather than as Seligman would have it, from confidence to trust. In this contribution, I use the word 'confidence' to describe Sikasso merchants' attitude because it is the best English translation of the word they themselves used (*confiance* in French and *danaya* in Bambara) rather than to imply a social evolutionary trajectory from confidence (along with the failure of state institutions) to trust in individuals (despite the contradictions caused by strong institutions).
4. I should point out that there is a difference between failure as a result of breach of confidence and failure for reasons of chance. Many merchants reported substantial failures. Shipments were lost due to weather, mechanical failures, the depredations of state authorities or unsuccessful efforts to elude state control. In many of these cases, patron and client agreed that the loss was unavoidable, and, while such a circumstance certainly did

nothing to improve a client's prospects, new loans were often forthcoming. On the other hand, loans that were not repaid without such mitigating circumstances led to a break in the patron-client relationship.
5. There is (and, in the mid-1980s, was) substantial controversy surrounding the use of the word 'Wahhabi'. I retain the word because it was, in the mid-1980s, the word most commonly used by Malians to designate this group of Muslims. Members of the Wahhabi group often disliked the use of the term because it seemed to suggest that they were a group within Islam and followers of a particular holy man, Muhammad ibn Abd al-Wahab, and thus that their beliefs should have a standing similar to that of the followers of other holy men. They preferred to call themselves 'Sunna'. This nomenclature suggests that they follow the proper paths of Islam, rather than any individual interpretation of them. However, this also suggests that those who do not agree with them are incorrect in their religious practice or practise lesser, impure versions of Islam. Hence, the term 'Sunna' is no more acceptable than 'Wahhabi'. For more information on the development of the Wahhabiyya in Mali, see Kaba (1974).
6. Numerous sources provide additional detail about the *Tirailleurs sénégalais*. Among the most important are Echenberg (1991), Lawler (1992), Lunn (1999) and Mann (2006).
7. For some examples, see Diop's short story 'Sarzan' in *Les contes d'Amadou Koumba* (1961) and Diabate's 1979 novel *Le lieutenant de Kouta*.
8. A key grievance of Malian veterans is that the size of their pensions was fixed in 1959, a consequence of the Guinean vote for complete independence from France. By the early 2000s, a veteran who was a French citizen received a pension approximately 10 times greater than a Malian who had done identical service. In 2001, 2006 and again in 2010 the French government moved to rectify the situation. Veterans in the 1990s were quick to point out that France would wait until the vast majority of them died to remedy the injustices related to their pensions … and they proved essentially correct.
9. Interestingly, Meker wrote a memoire of his years in the colonial service and focused substantially on his time in Bougouni. This book is entitled *Le temps colonial* (1980).
10. The argument that bonds of both kinship and friendship in the United States have become attenuated is made forcefully by Putnam in his book *Bowling Alone* (2000) and subsequent works such as *Better Together* (Putnam and Feldstein 2003). Putnam (2000) notes, for example, that in the United States the number of people attending club meetings has already dropped by 58 per cent between the mid-1970s and 1998; according to him, the number of people having regular family dinners has dropped by 33 per cent within the same period of time and the number of those having friends coming over regularly has dropped by 45 per cent.

Chapter 7

'Down-to-Earth'

Friendship and a National Elite Circle in Botswana

Richard Werbner

Introduction

My analysis of friendship as a social process among urban elites[1] carries forward three interests, which bring together shifts in theory and fresh empirical observations. The first is the broad interest that foregrounds the moral in the social, because it is not reducible to power and its many guises or disguises. An alternative approach, relentlessly rehearsing the social as no more than the instrumental or tactical transactions over resources, has become virtually a spent force, after its decades of intellectual dominance, especially in political anthropology. Against that stands the exploration of how actual practice creates and responds to moral passion, to a distinctive ethos, to highly situated values.

A second and related shift is emerging with the revived interest in seminal contributions by anthropologists of the Manchester School to the study of personal relationships.[2] It could be argued that some of the underlying ideas in the school's arguments about social networks now seem outdated. If so, that is in good measure because of the considerable mainstream of network analysis inspired to rethink those arguments, particularly in the landmark work of Barnes (1954), Epstein (1969a, 1969b) and Mitchell (1969, 1974). But once again illuminating are their central concerns with the meanings persons in a network contribute to their relationships, and how these meanings circulate or become realized in gossip. Even further, the revived interest is in the importance in networks that both density and multiplexity have, density being the mutual implication of network members independently with each other, such that they know and meet each other directly and are not merely linked through one person as the focus of the network, and multiplexity being the many-strandedness and diversity of their interconnection.

The third growing interest is in the current problematizing of elites, distinction and the making of civic virtue (Lentz 1994; Fumanti 2003, 2007, in press;

Werbner 2004, 2012; Savage and Williams 2008; Werbner 2010; Yarrow 2011). For this third interest, Epstein's work is perhaps the most relevant in the Manchester network studies. Epstein (1969b) points a way forward in his analysis of the flows of gossip, of their openness and closure among urban elites themselves, and their impact on norms and values of nonelites. To pursue that, my own approach extends the network studies questions to social mobility and the accomplishments through which elites emerge, constitute cliques, generate convivial subjectivities and sustain long-term friendships (see also Jacobson 1973). Raised on that basis are further arguments on the importance of elite friendship for the constituting of openness and public trust in postcolonial state formation.

Elites of the First Postcolonial Generation as Friends

Members of the first postcolonial generation to rise to the decision-making echelon of the civil service in an African state sometimes form urban-based friendships within very distinctive friendship circles, the elite cliques being mainly generated from shared occupation. Over the course of their upwardly mobile careers, from youth to elderhood, from student to top civil servant, and beyond that, upon leaving the civil service, from civil servant to elite politician, leading professional, corporate executive or company director, they look primarily to one another for the friendships they value and invest in the most. Being few in number, they are aware of being very much the vanguard for an expanding salariat. It is usually such a small world for insiders joining or belonging to the top echelon of an emerging postcolonial civil service that they are able to keep close track of their fellows; they make it their business to know each other's movements, successes and failures. A great deal of political and professional gossip circulates among them: it is finely detailed and entails highly coloured knowledge of personal conduct, which they use in defining their friendship circles more or less exclusively.

Some elites in the first postcolonial generation become what I would call 'boon-companions'. Postcolonial elite boon-companions are both highly convivial, often sharing their leisure time with one another, and also mutually supportive in business partnerships, joint entrepreneurship and the risk-taking ventures of their lives.[3] Like many friendships in Africa and elsewhere, boon-companionship tends to be a relation of homophily, of like with like, in many respects and above all, same sex, roughly same generation and professional history (i.e., the civil service). Unlike friendships in isolated dyadic relations, however, these elite boon-companionships thrive or fail in tandem with friendship circles.

In such friendship circles, the ethos, values and purposes come to be heavily influenced by experiences that are formative for the rise of first-generation postcolonial elites. Of course, much depends on the stability and legitimacy of the postcolonial regime itself. Given peaceful, negotiated transfers of power from one administration to the next, the formative experiences are, nevertheless, in unprecedented moments, for it is a matter not merely of rising, often very rapidly, in a new civil service, but of having to inherit, yet reform or somewhat disengage from the ways of the old colonial regime. There are also the fresh dilemmas that a professional or technocrat faces when, as a 'been-to', he or she comes from the shared ordeals of student life, often in the metropolitan academies of former colonial powers, and goes on to deal with strangers in the public, while negotiating ways through the inner corridors of government. Looking back, perhaps after leaving the civil service, and especially when confronted by changes introduced by a second or even third generation of elite successors, first-generation elites readily turn their formative experiences into a highly significant imaginary past of shared beginnings. For all their present differences, there was a time they now recall when they went through so much together, projecting an image of being alike, even equal, in some deeper, or perhaps merely sentimentally felt, sense. All of that – the formative experiences accompanied by fresh dilemmas, the remembered beginnings – is productive of a shared consciousness of special accomplishment and, indeed, of a sense of distinction, setting first-generation elite friendship circles apart.

How far such elite friendship circles reach across ethnic differences varies considerably, from postcolony to postcolony, and over time, even within the same postcolony. Usually, however, being urban based and with a diaspora beyond a rural home area, the elite friendship circles reflect and contribute to ethnic processes that emerge in urban settings, such as the formation of supertribes or the use of old rural-derived labels for more inclusive ethnic categories. If a first-generation elite friendship circle appears to be dominantly or even exclusively from one ethnic group, this tends to be one that draws together strangers with distinct origins perhaps in distant rural areas, but whose ethnicity has been redefined in various ways by their elite positioning. In no simple way is the first-generation elite friendship circle merely an aftereffect of ethnicity. Indeed, perceptions to the contrary – the sense of an opening out to include others as friends across old ethnic boundaries – are often important for first-generation elites in their formation of a circle.

That said, a brief comment is needed about kinship and about straddling town and country. Most first-generation elites from the national decision-making echelon tend to be urban villagers based in the city who straddle town and country by also keeping homes in their villages of origin. It is now well known that in Africa such urban villagers usually take care not to cut themselves off from their kin in the countryside and that they have to exercise much social skill to meet their translocal commitments to kin. How friendship circles affect and respond to straddling is an open question, the answers to which continue to be renegotiated throughout the course of the lives of members of first-generation postcolonial elites.

Elite Friends in Botswana's Capital

In this contribution, I want to explore first-generation elite friendship through an account of an elders' friendship circle formed mainly by Kalanga urban villagers, almost all men, in Botswana's capital city, Gaborone. In other articles, I have discussed the cosmopolitan ethnicity and politics of recognition among Kalanga (Werbner 2002b, 2002c, 2002d, 2008), and in this contribution I mention their ethnic relations only briefly. One might conceptualize the friendship circle as having a core of Kalanga and a periphery of non-Kalanga who, like the Kalanga, are elites long established in Gaborone. But for convenience here, I regard the friendship circle primarily in terms of its core. The men who are closest to one another within the circle correspond to those I refer to as boon-companions. Boon-companionship is not ethnically restricted, and some Kalanga have Tswana boon-companions, but the density of links these Tswana boon-companions have with inner circle Kalanga elders is considerable, and thus they, too, like the Kalanga, are effectively embedded within the same friendship circle.

Included in this circle of leading members of the state and commercial elites are the most prominent of the self-identifying Kalanga in the capital. Kalanga are now regarded as the largest and most assertive of the country's minorities, Tswana being the recognized majority. Friends belonging to this minority elite circle all know each other well, and most are or have been, more or less close friends for decades. Among them are the former chief justice, the former attorney general and later foreign minister, the late minister of finance, former high commissioners, the former managing director of British Petroleum, the long-term chairman of Barclays Bank, directors of this and other financial or investment institutions, the retired head of one of the biggest retail chains who was an assessor on the Industrial Tribunal until his recent death, and the managing directors and important shareholders in some of the capital's largest private enterprises under citizen direction or ownership. All of them have been or still are top civil servants from the decision-making echelon: they all own real estate in the capital. Moreover, holding portfolios of company shares, perhaps most importantly in companies they founded, each has become, in their phrase, 'a man of substance', 'a substantial person', without first, or indeed ever, becoming a successful or top politician, such as a minister, until very recently (except for the one woman among the friends, and the late minister of finance, a brilliant economist and technocrat somewhat above party politics).[4]

Pioneer Graduates and the Egalitarian Ethos

Beginning my Botswana research among Kalanga in 1964, before independence, I easily came to meet and know most of the friends now in the capital's elite circle of Kalanga elders early in their careers and mine, largely through the density of their own network, through the accidents of fieldwork for very different purposes in several parts of the country, and through their early study visits to Britain. Before them, at the end of the colonial protectorate, there were less than a couple of dozen graduates. Even that first postcolonial graduate cadre was quite small. It included a select few from the Lesotho-based predecessor of the University of Botswana and others, such as the founders of the Botswana Student Association in the United Kingdom, whose particularly close bonds with each other continued to be highly significant for the inner circle of friends. The friendship circle was thus mainly founded upon the shared egalitarian experience of peers in their youth. As a consequence of my early and long engagement, I was able to enjoy, during my recent fieldwork, the convivial fellowship of being associated not only with what they poignantly call 'the hard times', but also with the 'times of truly being', in another much-loved and often used phrase, 'down-to-earth and accessible'.

'Down-to-earth and accessible' – in the friends' ethos, the beginning of elite wisdom is knowing oneself to be a man or woman of the people, not removed from the shared earth by rank, position, wealth or power. Nevertheless, when not addressing me by one of my Kalanga nicknames or my clan honorific, 'Nkumbudzi' (Remembrancer), some of the friends took pleasure in calling me 'Professor', to which I responded, as expected, in a mutual recognition of honour and distinction, 'CJ' for the Chief Justice, 'AG' for the Attorney General, and so forth. So, too, when I and my wife Pnina accompanied them or other dignitaries on civic occasions, we were always given rosettes, clearly marked with 'V.I.P.' It is no paradox, therefore, to say that along with the admiration for leadership skills in being 'down-to-earth and accessible', the elite friends, like most of their countrymen and countrywomen, also have a fine sense of hierarchy and status; having an office does matter, though one has to wear it with modesty and, if possible, wit.

If you went on a Saturday night to an extreme corner of the capital's Notwane Club, in front of the glass cases full of winners' glittering trophies, inscribed sports shields and silver loving cups, you might have found many of the inner circle of friends, drinking their rounds and mainly talking about business and politics, besides sports. Their favourite spot was known somewhat jokingly as the 'Top Table', perhaps after a place in the first president's old college, Balliol. But the Notwane Club was not posh, snobbish or expensive, unlike its neighbour immediately up the road, the Golf Club, which attracted expatriates along with a city smart set, including jet-setting academics. Instead, the Notwane Club was popular, with cheap beer, and despite the 'members only' sign, it attracted mixed crowds, members and nonmembers, rich and poor, and many civil servants of different grades. It also had an unwritten rule of free speech.

Open critical argument about issues of the day was, above all, the pride of the 'Top Table'. Members of this inner circle of friends have carried this engagement well beyond the 'Top Table', I should stress. They have helped found and lead a good number of public forums and other racially and ethnically integrated institutions for good governance, civic interests and the critique of public policy (Werbner 2004, 2008). They have counteracted the tendency within government to operate from an inner circle by giving considerable backing to the tendency to strengthen open and informed debate. Such cultural and political work reflects the civic importance of the elite friendship circle, and its contribution to the expansion of the public sphere.

That contribution is advanced, along with other contributions, to elite communication across party lines and personal influence on public policy, an influence linked to a long history of personal relations among the first generation postcolonial elites. I was told that for a former president, himself a member of that generation and once a friend and frequent member of the 'Top Table', a going away party was held as he was about to take up his new office, and the farewell speech for him was full of banter about his banishment from the Club to prison, the State House. The phrase 'Kitchen Cabinet' was used, however, for the casual consultations and substantial arguments about politics and policy issues that the president was well known to continue having with members of the inner circle of friends, on publicly visible visits, when he would drink at their homes. Indeed, since the president made no secret of it, rumours would fly about the inclusion in the 'Kitchen Cabinet' of a senior and very eminent adviser to the main opposition party, himself a retired permanent secretary, sometime managing director and substantial investor. Against pressure from each of their parties, both have refused to give up their long and very close friendship, starting from many years of working together in the civil service, or their pleasure in drinking and talking freely with each other.

Postcolonial Urban Transitions and the Friendship Circle

Two urban transitions have been most important for the central placement and then growth of the friendship circle: first, the founding of the city itself as Botswana's capital, and second, decades later, the diamond boom and the rapid expansion of the city along with vast gains in the value of real estate. The friendship circle was created in the capital in the south by Kalanga originally from very different chiefdoms in the north, where they continue to keep homes. Some of the circle's members had already become friends during their schooldays at a boarding school near Gaborone, but it was in the capital as a small town that the circle began to take its present form. As a country Botswana itself is small, in population if not in territory. The capital Gaborone, the country's one city, has very recently grown at an unprecedented rate. However, immediately after independence in 1966 and in the city's first decades, during the early careers of the present elders, it was a very small town, in every respect. Most of its middle- and upper-echelon civil servants knew one another; spotting people and their origins simply by their car licence plates (in the past, indicating home district and thus, to some extent, tribal origin) was something of a Gaborone guessing game, and its car parks were open books of calling cards for other residents. The circle and its boon-companionships thus formed in a context of small town familiarity and intimacy among people who were especially drawn to know each other well as civil servants, participating in the same round of formal and informal public occasions and identified by their ethnicity as among the upwardly mobile achievers.

As for the second transition, the diamond-led boom and its impact, we need to recognize the unstable, perhaps footloose nature of the special positioning which put some Kalanga in the vanguard of an emerging commercial elite. In the 1980s, top businessmen and eventually businesswomen came from the ranks of the most senior civil servants. Leading the way in this enterprising transfer and thus gaining a valuable head start were Kalanga, some of whom felt not only pulled by their anticipation of the coming diamond-led boom, but also pushed by their sense of a glass ceiling in the civil service, of being blocked from full advancement by majoritarian discrimination. Members of this enterprising minority saw others from the majority safely cocooned within 'the system', but not themselves. In the classical discontented style of minorities 'of uneasy feet', to follow Veblen's characterization (1950), they went further afield, took command of fresh opportunities and got ahead with the next phase of competition and co-operation. They also founded a series of real estate companies, some of which won state allocations of land for skyscrapers and now provide both rents and continuing occasions for their participation in joint affairs.

The inner circle elites have become closely linked in big business. They are the directors or shareholders of a recognizable set of companies, which they formed mainly during the boom of the 1980s. Some have origins in local elites of the past, being the children or close relatives of school teachers and headmasters, minor chiefs or storekeepers, but they are very much aware of themselves as first-generation elites in their own contexts. As they have advanced in their careers, most have shared in making, from the state salariat, the core of what I call the national directorate.

Primarily based in the capital, the national directorate is an interlocking establishment of company directors who wear many hats, sit on many boards and meet regularly on one occasion after another, again and again. There are now some outstanding directors who have made their way only through business, or only through having been politicians, but the one-time top civil servants command many of the posts and still largely lead the national directorate. One might speak of the growth of a directorate-technocrat complex to convey the mutual interpenetration of establishments.

By this directorate-technocrat complex I do not mean to convey a cosy monolith. Quite the contrary, members usually do know their rivals and competitors very well, often from their schooldays, and, if anything, it sharpens their formation and reformation of political factions and related blocs or sides in business. My attention, though, was repeatedly drawn to the exceptional individual who was often much welcomed for being on both sides. 'Business is politics, and politics is business', one of the most influential directors told me in spelling out the connections between state and commercial elites and between political factions and business blocs. Between 2008 and 2011, a dispute over investments linked to the Botswana Stock Exchange brought considerable public attention and media reports on the interlocking business interests of a former president, a former chief justice, former permanent secretaries, former ambassadors and other public figures (Morewagae 2011a, 2011b).

Enduring Boon-Companionship, Trust and Interethnicity

Within this context of network density and the interlocking relations of the directorate-technocrat complex, it is not surprising that certain boon-companionships are long lasting and expansive, although vulnerable to major struggles within the directorate-technocrat complex.

Given present limits, two examples, a pair of Tswana and Kalanga friends and another of Kalanga only, must suffice to illustrate this. The Tswana and Kalanga friends reached the top of the civil service through highly successful postcolonial careers in local posts, and without treading in one another's footsteps. They built their friendship in the capital Gaborone which has remained their base for over forty years; and they and a third friend recently formed the third president's 'Kitchen Cabinet' of trusted intimates. The Tswana friend came to the civil service as a professional; as the son of a head-teacher and prominent activist in South Africa, originally from the south of Botswana, he grew up and was educated in South Africa, taking his degree in chemistry at Fort Hare. At the peak of his career, he became director of personnel for the civil service, then founder of the Botswana Power Corporation and eventually manager of a number of other parastatals. Coming from the other end of Botswana with barely a primary school education and learning very much on the job, the Kalanga friend rose through the ranks in one ministry after another, starting as a clerk and interpreter and eventually serving as permanent secretary in the Ministry of Home Affairs. It was the Kalanga friend who retired from the public service and ventured into the private sector first, becoming a corporate manager for a major company with huge construction projects at the beginning of Botswana's great building boom. But together, and working as business partners, the two friends became substantial investors in real estate and other companies, some of which they themselves founded along with prominent Kalanga and others. As an elder, the Kalanga friend became partially sighted, and the Tswana, as his constant companion, became his driver, putting his own Mercedes at his Kalanga friend's ready disposal

– they became a familiar sight together, especially at their favourite drinking place, the Notwane sports club, where the Tswana friend continued to be an accomplished tennis player even in his old age. Although the Tswana friend took no part in the public debate over minority rights, which has recently become increasingly intense, he remained steadfast in his friendship as his Kalanga boon-companion pursued a life-long campaign in support of the Kalanga language, ethnic equality and diversity in public life. As younger men, they were the vocal leaders, first of the Bechuanaland African Civil Service Association and then of its postcolonial successor, the Botswana Civil Service Association. Over the decades of their very close friendship, they both sustained a strong commitment to inter-ethnic voluntary associations, from the Botswana Society to Botswana's branch of Transparency International, and including their favourite sports club. In good measure, their interethnic boon-companionship thrived on the fact that they contributed to causes in the wider public and civic interest, and won distinction in their efforts to expand critical deliberation in the public sphere.

Comparison to a case of ethnic boon-companionship among Kalanga is illuminating. In this case, the links between the two Kalanga boon-companions were extremely close, from years of one being the civil service deputy of the other, of granting high-level foreign service and local posts to one another in turn, and having lived nearby in great amity. In business, they tended to concentrate more on one company's board than another, as it were dividing the labour between them. Thus, one is a director of Barclays and Stockbrokers Botswana and the other of the Standard Bank and Botswana Power Corporation. In addition, they have jointly planned and invested in a number of projects, from the manufacture of PVC pipes (a somewhat unsuccessful venture) to catering for airlines at Sir Seretse Khama Airport, then very busy due to sanctions against apartheid in South Africa. I want to stress how important their experience at the highest levels of the foreign service has been for their sensitivity to prospects in global markets and international trade, and thus for the long-term success of their partnership with each other and with their non-Kalanga partners who are Indians. Their Indian partners started from opposite ends of the country, and based their major growth in different sectors, one being that of wholesale supplies and the other the motor trade with exclusive import franchises, such as for Toyota and Mercedes. Hence their partnerships, although independent, have developed from one another, and differentiated in ways that were complementary rather than involving competition or rivalry. Although a major struggle over control of a leading investment firm, with 30 per cent ownership of the Botswana Stock Exchange, drew them into what the media called 'a bitter fight over money and shares' (Morewagae 2011b), they were able to reach an agreed out-of-court settlement and continued their co-operation in a major venture known as '21st Century Holdings'.

This example reveals a positive dynamic between intraethnic friendship and interethnic trust: one is not advanced at the expense or to the exclusion of the other, as is sometimes assumed. Trust among Kalanga themselves was the wellspring for extending trust to potentially trustworthy others beyond their own ethnic group. In other words, for these elites, the beneficial and supportive strength of their intraethnic relations was crucial for opening out the same potential in interethnic relations and thus for enhancing their friendship as a cosmopolitan accomplishment. Of course, all of these partnerships thrive within a broader context, immediately in the public sphere sustained by a state that stands out in Africa for being capable, stable and financially creditworthy.[5] Taking that as given, my argument addresses the problem of trust and the selective dynamics in friendship, ethnicity and entrepreneurship (for more analysis in depth, see Werbner 2004, 2008).

Kinship and Friendship

So far, I have said rather little about kinship, the second leg of this volume's standing interest. What I have tried to do is position the first and friendly leg firmly on urban ground within a necessarily all-too-brief history of minority elite formation. It is beyond my present scope to consider elite kinship in its urban and translocal meanings. But, to continue the metaphor, how do the two legs go together?

Although some elders of the friendship circle are related, they are, on the whole, not close kin or affines. Their friendships have not become steps on the way to becoming relatives. None of the children or grandchildren of the friends have married each other, and relatively few of these offspring have become close friends. What is reproduced from generation to generation is not the specific friendship circle, but the capacity to constitute circles appropriate to each generation. The friendship circle and the relations of boon-companionship, while primarily for a founding generation, have nevertheless been embedded in dense networks and multiplex relations: they have thus been enduring, highly stable and not fragile or volatile. The same, it is worth saying, is true of the marriages of the elite friends: none is divorced, and all are married to non-Kalanga, as I have explained elsewhere (Werbner 2002b, 2004, 2008).

The most striking march of kinship together with friendship is in mobilization sets for the public occasions of rites of passage, such as weddings and funerals.[6] For such occasions, along with the relatives, the boon-companions are always prominently mobilized, and usually also many of the inner circle. It is a matter of obligation for them all, friends along with kin, and in this time of AIDS in Botswana, it is a heavy, time-consuming obligation which makes for a great deal of public sociability and intensified social circulation, connecting friends and kin informally. Friends also join kin and family members in domestic space, being entertained and fed at each other's homes, often on weekend *braais* or barbecues, with abundant meat and drink.

By contrast, where friendship most distinctively comes into its own space is in the club and pub. Although some women, including players of club sports, do come to both, the inner-circle friends' wives almost never join their husbands at either; nor do fathers and sons usually drink together. If family matters come up in casual gossip, they are usually marginal to the general flow of conversation. Hence the divide between kinship and friendship is most realized in convivial leisure, which is, however, not divorced from matters of business, politics and sport as favourite topics.

Conclusion

In conclusion, I would argue that in Gaborone for minority elites of the first postcolonial generation, both the urban friendship circle and boon-companionship mesh durably with kinship, and do not displace it, or take any load or emotional charge from it. Compared to kinship, both are more narrowly defined, being specific to the same generation, gender and class, unlike kinship which is reproduced from generation to generation and extends across gender and class. The friendship circle and boon-companionship form a personal sphere which complements that of kinship, while overlapping and in part interpenetrating it. This postcolonial formation was not a response to some supposedly typical transition in urbanization, such as a move from a universe of the personal relations in the countryside to impersonal ones in town. The early urban transition in the friendship circle's formative years at the beginning of the postcolonial era was more a move from one universe of personal relations to another, which if somewhat mixed, was still dominated by personal relations, and even more closely linked to the countryside and the affairs of kin. While the later urban transition during the diamond-led boom came with a vast expansion in the postcolonial state bureaucracy, in impersonal relations, ethnic heterogeneity and host-stranger relations, it also locked the elite friends even more closely into interdependence between their leisure, business, financial and even political affairs. The outcome was a strengthening of their standing as one of the capital's power elites and, I would argue, an enhancement of their capacity to meet their highly valued commitments and obligations of kinship.

It is evident, from my arguments, that the dynamics of elite friendships during postcolonial transformations have to be studied over the long term and from generation to generation (see also Fumanti 2003, in press). In the next stage of analysis, we will need to have a much richer understanding of how elite friendships affect and, in turn are affected by the making not merely of kinship but of elite dynasties (see Pina-Cabral and de Lima 2000). For Botswana, in particular, my own account here stands at a threshold before a major field of exploration now emerging in the anthropology of social mobility, elite sociality and friendship.

Notes

1. I carried out urban research in Gaborone in 1999 with support from the Nuffield Foundation, and in 2000–2002, 2007 with partial support from the Economic and Social Research Council (grants R00239145, RES-000-22-2483), the International Centre for Contemporary Cultural Research and the University of Manchester. For parts of this paper, I draw on Werbner 2002b and 2004.
2. For reviews on this school, see Werbner (1990) and Evens and Handelman (2006).
3. On the significance of conviviality for postcolonial subjectivity, see Nyamnjoh (2002) and Werbner (2002a).
4. At the time of my writing of the first draft of this article, one of the elite friends was standing for parliament, and was viewed as a possible minister in the future. He won his seat, held one prominent ministry, then became a back-bencher and is now deputy minister of finance. The attorney general at the time of my early fieldwork has since held the most senior posts as minister, and served as the foreign minister.
5. See Solway (2002) for a full and illuminating analysis of the importance of public trust and state-backed institutions for the development of interethnic relations and the debate about multiculturalism.
6. For an account of the funeral of a leading member of the elite friendship circle, see Werbner 2008.

Chapter 8

Negotiating Friendship and Kinship in a Context of Violence

The Case of the Tuareg during the Upheaval in Mali from 1990 to 1996

Georg Klute

Introduction

Since Mali gained independence from France in 1960, the Malian Tuareg have been involved repeatedly in armed upheavals. One of these started in 1990, almost simultaneously with an upheaval of Tuareg in neighbouring Niger. Both upheavals lasted until the mid-1990s. The Malian upheaval was formally ended in a ceremonial burning of weapons, known as the 'Flame of Peace' (*Flamme de la Paix* in French), in the Saharan town of Timbuktu in 1996.

 The Tuareg upheavals of the 1990s aimed originally at building up autonomous regions or even a state that would embrace all members of the 'Tuareg nation' (*temust* or *tumast* in Tamasheq). Among Tuareg, ethno-nationalist ideas emerged mainly in Algerian and Libyan exile, where thousands of Malian and Nigerien Tuareg had fled, in search of employment, during a series of droughts in the 1970s and 1980s. Particularly in Libya, some of these migrants were recruited into the army, where they came into contact with members of rebel or 'revolutionary' movements with comparable goals, namely, building up autonomous regions or states of their own. Ideologically, the 'Tuareg nation' was represented as a unit of people sharing common descent, speaking the same language, and, above all, equals in dignity and morals. All quarrels between the Tuareg themselves, i.e., former conflicts between regional and tribal groups, or differences between various classes of the hierarchical traditional society, were to disappear and make room for a national identity in a future Tuareg state. This state should reach ideally even beyond the boundaries inherited from the postcolonial state

(Klute 1995: 55–56). Despite its discourse of national unity, however, the ethno-nationalist movement of Tuareg in Libyan exile first divided into a Nigerien and a Malian part; after having returned to Mali at the end of 1989 and beginning of 1990, the Malian rebel movement soon split up into several factions which opposed one another politically at first, and later also militarily.

This contribution deals mainly with the changing nature of relationships between various Tuareg rebel movements during the 1990s upheaval of Malian Tuareg.[1] Though I will concentrate on the relationship between two Malian rebel movements that would become involved in a fratricidal war in 1994, I will have to refer, for purposes of clarity, to the whole area affected by the Tuareg upheavals in the 1990s, including large parts of the southern Sahara and the northern Sahel, reaching from the Mediterranean shores and the Libyan, Algerian and Chadian Sahara to the northern parts of Niger and Mali. In order to make my arguments more understandable, I will deal not only with events connected directly to the fratricidal war between two Tuareg rebel movements in 1994, but also with the period between 1980, when the first 'revolutionary' organization of exiled Tuareg was founded in Libya, and 1996, when the Tuareg rebellion in northern Mali formally ended.

The following reflections draw on field studies conducted between 1990 and 1998 in southern Algeria, northern Mali, northern Niger and France. Besides relying on 'classical' methods of data collection in anthropological fieldwork, such as observation and interviews, my reflections are based on biographical studies. Between October and December 1996, I collected biographical data of 241 persons in the region of Kidal in northern Mali (a region then inhabited by roughly 35,000 people) with the help of questionnaires that comprised several entries each.[2] The most influential men (and women) of the region, i.e., those whom my informants considered to form the local elite, were selected and questioned: on the one hand, the enquiry addressed tribal chiefs and tribal notables, and, on the other hand, it took into consideration 'intellectuals', i.e., people with high school degrees (or more). The collected data were then entered into a database that is organized in such a way that it is possible to follow various relation-building processes between different persons and members of different political, tribal or descent groups; the entries cover a period ranging from the creation of the first ethno-nationalist organization that prepared the rebellion in Libyan and Algerian exile, to 1996, when that rebellion formally ended.

As I will show below, friendship played an important role particularly among Tuareg migrants during the years of exile that preceded the outbreak of the military upheavals in 1990. Here, friendship fulfilled two functions: first, it served as an ideological tool that was supposed to strengthen the unity of an imagined utopian Tuareg nation. Second, relationships stemming from friendship had the potential to cut across tribal or kinship-based identities and solidarities. Political orientations indeed followed the same *transversal logic*.

Identities were negotiated and reshaped again in the course of and after the military upheaval, which took place in northern Mali between 1990 and 1996. My main thesis is that the *logic of descent* eventually prevailed over any other logic of relation building. This holds true in particular for the year 1994 when two Malian Tuareg rebel movements fought a fratricidal war.

The Ideology of Friendship

Despite the impressive volume of scientific and, especially, popular literature on the Tuareg, so far, only one work has dealt explicitly with friendship (Klute 2011).[3] Relationships among Tuareg, or between Tuareg and other people, are mostly described and analysed in terms of kinship, intertribal, interethnic and political relations, or as ritualized relationships linking, for example, business partners or hosts and guests. Aspects of personal, dyadic relationships are hardly mentioned as if considered less important than political, military or economic aspects.

This state of affairs is surprising in so far as friendship terms and the notion of friendship have become very important and discussed issues in Tuareg society ever since Tuareg migrant workers in Algerian or Libyan exile began to organize themselves politically, several decades ago, in order to obtain cultural and political autonomy. Before the Tuareg started to migrate in great numbers, and before exiled migrant workers organized themselves politically, however, friendship, intimacy or simply politeness among Tuareg, or between Tuareg and members of other ethnic groups, were usually not expressed in terms of friendship, but rather in kinship terms; even friendly interethnic relationships ('joking relationships') were thought to be a kind of vague kinship, a distant form of cross-cousinship. Moreover, it was not unusual for Tuareg to address even strangers in kinship terms ('cross-cousin'), when they wanted to behave in a friendly or simply a polite manner. As in many other preindustrial societies, the Tuareg also expressed relationships of various kinds (political, economic, alliances or even merely personal, dyadic relationships) mainly in kinship terms. The predominance of kinship terms in emic representations of relationships, however, should not lead to the conclusion that kinship was actually the only logic underlying any type of relationship (Grätz, Meier and Pelican 2004: 15–16.). Instead, we should, as always, differentiate between emic notions and analytical terms.

In practice, friendship terms started to replace kinship appellations among Tuareg migrants from 1980 onwards. Before I come to the reasons which caused this change in emic representations of appropriate appellations, let me give a brief description of what I call the 'modern migration movements' of the Tuareg.[4]

The history of modern migrations of the Tuareg dates back to the last years of colonial rule in the 1950s. Hundreds of Tuareg from Mali and Niger migrated to southern Algeria where they were employed in the oil industry, or became mercenaries in the French colonial army. From the middle of the 1950s onwards, the French recruited more and more Tuareg in order to cope with the growing anticolonial, national resistance movement in Algeria (FLN: Front de Libération National; National Liberation Front).

In the following years, the number of Tuareg migrants in Algeria increased. In 1963 and 1964, groups of Tuareg in northern Mali revolted against the Malian government. As they were small in number and poorly armed, the Malian army had no difficulty in suppressing the upheaval rather easily, despite the fact that the Tuareg had a much better knowledge of the terrain and that they were superior individual fighters. Hundreds of Tuareg, including women and children, fled the suppression campaigns of the Malian army. A decade later, when a heavy drought decimated the herds of many Tuareg nomads in northern Mali and Niger, a new wave of thousands of refugees arrived in Algeria, and from there, continued also to Libya. A similar drought occurred in the 1980s; again, thousands of Tuareg from Mali and Niger fled to the neighbouring countries in the north.

Sentiments of common origin and common destiny developed in the milieu of Tuareg migrants in Algeria and Libya. This was partly due to the fact that their Algerian and Libyan hosts treated these migrant workers and their families quite badly as Tuareg from abroad, without differentiating between regional groups, tribal identities or social strata. Tuareg migrants started to address one another as *amidi*, 'friend', and not as 'cross-cousin', etc., as they used to do before. As their Algerian and Libyan hosts thought the (exiled) Tuareg formed a homogenous ethnic group, the exiled Tuareg, too, started to imagine themselves as an ethnic group, united by common traits.

There is virtually no scientific work, based on fieldwork and direct observation, which covers this period of Tuareg exile in Algeria and Libya preceding the beginning of the Tuareg rebellion in 1990. All publications concerning this period are based on data collected retrospectively. As 'revolutionary' movements and violent wars are very dynamic processes, indeed, statements of social actors can undergo dramatic changes in short periods of time. What was said yesterday can be omitted or forgotten today. This is particularly true if one takes into account that the Tuareg still live in a predominantly oral culture, where all statements are actually shaped by circumstance and, as in this case, by the balance of power prevailing at that moment.

In order to overcome these methodological difficulties, I have used the migrants' poetry as a historical source. I have chosen poetry as a historical source for two reasons: first, because poetic texts are, so to say, more resistant to changes than prosaic ones; second, because the Tuareg migrant poets recorded their works on audio cassettes, and in this way, prevented all later modifications. On the whole, I have collected some 200 poems (or songs); from this collection, I have selected a corpus of about 50 pieces according to the following criteria: audibility, possibility to date the creation and possibility to identify the author and the circumstances of the piece's creation. This corpus covers the period from 1978 to 1996. The careful interpretation of the migrants' poetry, combined with other data, has actually contributed to the reconstruction and analysis of the Tuareg upheavals in Niger and Mali.

With regard to emic appellations, the analysis of migrants' poetry reveals several interesting points:

- In my collection of about 200 pieces of Tuareg migrant poetry, geographical names do appear, but no tribal names and no terms indicating membership in a specific social stratum are employed. This omission surely reflects the authors' desire to overcome social or tribal differences within Tuareg society. Such an omission is indeed consistent with the ideology according to which each and every Tuareg should be equal in a future, though still utopian, nation-state, regardless of his/her tribal or social belonging.
- In the corpus of 50 or so poems that I have been able to date with precision, a clear distinction is made between appellations used in referring to Tuareg who migrated and those used in referring to Tuareg who 'stayed home'. Whereas the Tuareg who stayed home are addressed, with few exceptions, in kinship terms, Tuareg migrants are mostly just called 'friend(s)'. In this corpus, the latter appellation is used in a way that fits well with ideological attempts to homogenize rather heterogeneous communities of Tuareg migrants in Algerian or Libyan exile. On the other hand, the fact that Tuareg who stayed home are addressed, with much affection, in kinship terms hints at the political project of the Tuareg migrants: to give up exile, to return home and to fight for political and cultural autonomy.

  However, life in exile seem to have favoured the development of personal relationships and friendships that cut across habitual social or tribal divisions: appellations such as 'friends' (*imidiwen*) clearly had concrete and material foundations.

This first 'revolutionary' organization of Tuareg migrants was founded in Al Khums[5] (ca. 100 km southeast of Tripoli) at the end of August 1980 with the semiofficial support of Libya; it was called Front Populaire de Libération du Sahara Arabe Central (FPLSAC; Popular Front for the Liberation of the Arabic Central Sahara) and included Tuareg from Mali as well as from Niger. The same year, Muammar Gaddafi opened the first military camp for Tuareg in order to offer military training and to recruit them into his famous Islamic Legion.

Apparently, such camps were also places that provided many opportunities for forging new personal relationships. Friendship bonds were formed between Tuareg from Mali and from Niger, between vassals and nobles and even between members of different tribal confederacies which were long since considered sworn enemies at home in Mali or Niger. Personal relationships grew even stronger, when Tuareg mercenaries became comrades in arms. Hundreds of Tuareg migrants fought as Libyan mercenaries in various campaigns in Lebanon or Chad, sent there by the Libyan leader for his ambitious political goals.

In retrospect, i.e., after 1990 and their return to northern Mali, the ex-migrants underlined the significance of friendship bonds as a basis for cohesion within the 'revolutionary' movement by saying that, in Libyan or Algerian exile, even close kin sometimes became personal enemies and started hating each other. In part, these narratives are local expressions of the experience of migration and exile as transitional situations, changing even traditional representations of the foundations of personal relationships (see also Meier 2004).

As already noted, factors such as social status and tribal affiliation lost much of their significance as barriers to friendship among Tuareg during the years spent in exile. In fact, many Tuareg of different social and tribal origins developed genuine affection for one another while living abroad. On the other hand, this tendency had a political dimension and a similar ideological background as the use of the appellation *Kal Lamiger*. The latter appellation – a poetic neologism composed of the Tuareg word *Kal* ('people of') and the terms 'Mali' and 'Niger' – began to be applied by migrants to all Tuareg in the 1980s. Both its creation and its use were expressions of the wish to overcome the various divisions among the Tuareg – even state boundaries – in order to erect a common Tuareg nation-state. As late as 1992, when I did fieldwork in southern Algeria, it was impossible to ask for tribal names or the social status of persons because this was considered as detrimental to the national cause.

However, the project of a common nation-state began to crumble in 1987, when the united resistance movement of exiled Tuareg, the FPSAC, first split. One day after the death of Seyni Kountché, Niger's dictator and general-president, the Malian Tuareg, and only the Malian Tuareg, founded a new clandestine resistance movement. The Tuareg of Niger completely withdrew from the project that promoted a common nation-state of all Tuareg. The Nigerien Tuareg hoped for democratic change in their home country after Seyni Kountché's death. They, therefore, voted against the plan of a military and necessarily violent upheaval and opted for a peaceful political struggle. After that, the common military or political project of the Tuareg from Mali and Niger ceased to exist, despite the fact that later Malian and Nigerien rebel movements kept contact, and despite the fact that some rebels fought on an individual basis, and occasionally on the other side of the border.

From Friends to Enemies

In late 1989 and early 1990, around 20,000 Tuareg migrants were sent back from neighbouring Algeria and Libya to Mali and Niger. Among them and their followers were a few hundred who had been mercenaries for a number of years in Libya's Islamic Legion; some had fought in campaigns for the Libyan leader, as I mentioned earlier. These people had organized clandestine associations of Tuareg migrants in exile. The return of the migrants to their home countries coincided with the beginning of the Tuareg rebellion of the 1990s.

The military upheaval in Mali had three phases. The first phase, which was marked by a successful struggle against the Malian army, ended with the Treaties of Tamanrasset in January 1991.

This struggle began when the Malian army threw returnees from Algeria and Libya into refugee camps. Since the Malian secret service knew of the existence of the Tuareg migrants' clandestine organizations, it took advantage of the situation in the camps to arrest some of their inhabitants. At the end of June 1990 a group of armed rebels attacked the town of Menaka in northeastern Mali and freed those who had been arrested. This successful military operation was the signal for further military attacks. The rebels, who had organized themselves the same year as the Mouvement Populaire pour la Libération de l'Azawad (MPLA; Popular Movement for the Liberation of Azawad),[6] achieved surprising military success against the Malian army in the second half of 1990. During this phase no more than about 200 experienced Tuareg fighters executed all military operations. The rebels forced the Malian government to deploy at least two thirds of the Malian army, i.e., 4,000 out of 6,000 men, in the north. The rebels countered this with a typical guerrilla campaign. The civilian population were the main victims of the army's search and destroy missions which they employed to capture the mobile rebels. The harsh behaviour of the army, in turn, caused the population to take the rebels' side, and increasing numbers joined the MPLA (see also Klute and von Trotha 2004).

The Tuareg rebels also benefited from the changed global political situation at the beginning of the 1990s and the serious crisis of the military regime in Mali, which was due to fall in March 1991. In order to rid itself of one of the conflicts, the Malian government signed a peace treaty under the mediation of Algeria in January 1991. In the Treaties of Tamanrasset, as the peace agreement was known from then on, the signatories agreed to grant special status to the north of Mali, plus to economic concessions, which was practically equivalent to autonomy for the Tuareg.

During the first phase of the military upheaval, the poets of the rebels continued to address those Tuareg who had not joined the armed rebellion yet, in kinship terms. Apparently, affective appellations, such as kinship terms, were supposed to convince those Tuareg who had stayed at home to join the armed struggle and to become members of the imagined, though still utopian, Tuareg nation-state. The rebels, on the other hand, were still called 'friends', 'my friends', etc., but more and more martial appellations were used too, such as 'wild beasts', 'fighters' or 'martyrs'.

Implementing the Tamanrasset Treaties proved almost hopeless. Moreover, the success of the fight against Mali had unleashed neotribal, social and political dynamics among the Tuareg which would become the driving forces for the second phase of the rebellion: the splintering of the rebel movement.

In spite of the agreements of Tamanrasset, some rebel groups continued their attacks in the spring of 1991. Soon afterwards, the united rebel movement (MPLA) split into first two and later three politico-military movements that acted independently, both militarily and politically. The divisions among these rebel movements – which, notably, included the Front Populaire de Libération de l'Azawad (FPLA; Popular Front for the Liberation of Azawad, founded in spring 1991) and the Armée Révolutionnaire de Libération de l'Azawad (ARLA; Revolutionary Army for the Liberation of Azawad, founded in autumn 1991) – did not just reflect diverging political orientations. As I have shown in an earlier publication (Klute 1995), these divisions also reflected relations of hostility and alliance among tribes or confederations of tribes that had first emerged, in these specific constellations, during the colonial conquest at the beginning of the twentieth century. In the face of the French colonial army, Tuareg groups essentially had three options: to resist (as most groups did), to collaborate or to wait and see what the French conquerors were like and how they would act.

What is of importance here, however, is the fact that the leaders of the three movements had known one another personally for a long time: they had all been in Libyan exile; they had all lived in the same military camps; they had all received the same military training; and they had all fought in the same military campaigns in Syria, Lebanon and Chad. Equally important as their shared experience in exile, however, is the fact that they were of about the same age. This also holds true for most members of the three armed militias. Friends of the same age group had become political enemies and, as I will show later, military enemies as well.

There was not only an internal differentiation within the rebel movement, but also a differentiation among the opponents of the rebels. In reaction to Tuareg raids against the settlements along the Niger River, a militia of the 'black' Songhay was mobilized against the 'white' Malians in a *chasse aux Blancs*. With the support of certain elements in the army, it carried out pogroms against the Tuareg and Moors. These pogroms resulted in many Tuareg and Moors fleeing en masse, first to Mauritania, but also to Burkina Faso, Niger or Algeria; the number of war refugees reached 100,000.

However, the political situation in Mali changed radically after the fall of the military regime in March 1991. After many months of talks, mediators from France and Mauritania helped the warring parties conclude the *Pacte National* in April 1992. In this treaty, which marked the end of the second phase of the rebellion, the new transitory government of Mali was able, politically speaking, to get its way in many respects: the idea of federalism was dropped, together with the idea of an Azawad region, a region which, once again, was referred to, mainly, as the 'North of Mali', as had been the case before the outbreak of the upheaval. The Malian government also agreed to incorporate a great number of rebels into its armed forces and public service.

The strongest rebel movement, the FPLA, though, refused to sign the pact. Accordingly, the situation in Mali showed little change. The dissidents continued their attacks. In addition, armed bands of former rebels, operating beyond the control of the larger rebel movements, increased their actions. The young men acted on their own accord and preferred to rob travellers and transports of any kind, especially those of the international aid organizations.[7] The few overland roads and important tracks were only passable under military escort.

Nevertheless, there was still hope of peace. In the second half of 1992, the French helped the Malian government to form the first military units made up of both army and former rebel personnel. These units which the French called *patrouilles mixtes* ('mixed patrols'), deployed in the north, were to guarantee public safety. By the beginning of 1993, the regular Malian army had absorbed more than 600 rebels. Official plans provided for a further 3,000 fighters. State administration was slowly gaining ground in the northern regions again. International donor organizations made significant financial means available for the promotion of peace. The newly elected democratic president Alpha Oumar Konaré convinced the northern population of his peaceful intentions. In the summer of 1993, all rebel movements adhered to the National Pact.

This did not bring about peace, however. Instead, the rebellion entered its third and bloodiest phase. Its major characteristics were a renewed and ongoing dissolution of administrative structures of the central government in the northern region, and ethnic strife between 'white' and 'black' Malians, particularly in 1994.

In May 1994 the foundation of the Mouvement Patriotique Ganda Koy (MPGK; Patriotic Movement Ganda Koy), often simply referred to as Ganda Koy (literally, 'Masters of the Land' in Songhay), was announced. It was a militia in which former Songhay members of the army came together to fight the Tuareg and openly to perpetrate the expulsion of Arab and Tuareg nomads. After a unit of the regular army, consisting of integrated former rebels, was ambushed by members of the Ganda Koy militia, three of the four Tuareg rebel movements – among them the FPLA and ARLA – left the National Pact and started their attacks again. Once again, tens of thousands fled, as the rebel attacks started a new cycle of reprisals and pogroms.

Particularly during the phase of ethnic strife in the Tuareg rebellion, interethnic and even intraethnic friendships became very problematic, indeed. Of course, personal interethnic relationships of various kinds, including interethnic friendships, did exist in prewar times. In the context of this armed conflict, however, ethnic differences became so strongly politicized that it became dangerous openly to declare friendship with members of other ethnic groups.[8] Interethnic friends could not – at least in the Malian case – prevent violence against their counterparts or help in conflict resolutions, as some earlier scholars supposed (e.g., Mühlmann 1940).

One informant put it as follows:

> And these pogroms have been blind. They did not save anybody. They were directed against an ethnic group, against the Tuareg, against the Moors. Good relationships were of no use. Marriage was of no use. Mixing was of no use. And what happened? Everybody was forced. Either you are on this side or the other. Neutrality did not exist any more; one could not be neutral. You had to choose sides, and some choices were inevitable. There were people who did not have any choice, because, if you are light-skinned, even if you wanted to choose the side of the government, you could not ... This has forced everybody to one side.[9]

Yet, a few people indeed refused to 'choose sides'. These people were not actually sanctioned by killing, as in many other contemporary small wars, but by avoidance, and, more importantly, through the disapproval of women. In fact, some Tuareg women left their husbands to follow rebel lovers, if they felt that their spouses adopted an in-between position.

However, the year 1994 was marked not only by ethnic strife. At the beginning of that year, a new conflict broke out between Tuareg rebel movements. This conflict led to a fratricidal war between two movements, both of which had their military base in the region of Kidal and recruited the majority of their fighters in that region. The first movement, the Mouvement Populaire de l'Azawad (MPA; Popular Movement of Azawad),[10] had a very small social basis, though. At the beginning of the war, its members consisted almost exclusively of women and men from one of the leading noble tribes in the Kidal region. The second movement, ARLA, by contrast, was a heterogeneous coalition of all those who wanted to end the dominance of the regional group of leading noble tribes; it recruited members of noble and vassal strata alike.

At the very beginning of the war, in late February 1994, ARLA committed two strategic errors, which in retrospect decided the outcome of the war, though fighting would continue for another ten months. The first error was an ambush, in which the second commander-in-chief of the MPA was killed while in pursuit of bandits. The killed man was one of those officers who had been highly decorated by the Libyans for their service in the Islamic Legion in Libya and Chad. He was, in accordance with the agreement of the National Pact of 1992, a colonel in the Malian army and was a member of the Supervisory Commission of the Agreements of the National Pact. At the beginning of 1994, with the so-called 'mixed brigades', he hunted down bandits, who were in part fighters of ARLA. The latter, however, believed that the sole purpose of these supposed 'bandit hunts' was to crush ARLA, so that the colonel's brigade would be the only militia in northern Mali. Nevertheless, the fact that the colonel was of slave origin was of crucial importance. What appeared to be a heavy loss was in fact a great opportunity, for it allowed the MPA – i.e., the movement led by nobles – to make up its numerical disadvantage and to enrol Tuareg of slave origins into its ranks.

To convince former slaves to rally to their movement, the nobles stressed that they had asked ARLA to hand over the murderers immediately and to compensate the family of the victim. Pursuing the colonel's murderer, the nobles of the MPA argued, proved that they were ready to protect the 'weak members' of their society against violence. Another argument put forward to persuade former slaves to join the MPA involved friendship. It was emphasized that the leader of this movement (a man of noble origin) and his (murdered) second in command (a man of slave origin) had been close friends. This friendship was said to be of greater value than the republican, egalitarian and antinoble discourse of ARLA. At the same time, friendship was said to transcend social origins. All these arguments were well received by the former slaves of the region, who then adhered to the nobles' movement, the MPA, in great numbers.

The second major error was kidnapping the head of the noble tribe who called the tune in the MPA. The kidnappers threatened to kill their victim and all 'feudal oppressors'. Incidentally, the very day the kidnapping took place a group of 60 fighters from ARLA was trapped in an ambush and would be released only in exchange for the kidnapped. This move inflicted three wounds upon ARLA from which it never recovered. One was military, the other was moral and social and the third was political. ARLA revealed its military inferiority when its victory turned into a humiliating defeat; its boldness turned out to be an ill-considered act of impudence which, instead of challenging the claim to leadership of the nobles, simply confirmed it. After it had alienated all vassals or former slaves by the murder of the second commander-in-chief, it now lost the support of all the other noble tribes of the region. All (noble) groups turned away from ARLA, allying themselves with the MPA, for the MPA had proved that it was capable of giving their members that which is at the heart of 'good leadership': protection of the weak, law and order.

The biographical data I collected among the local elite in the Kidal region shows that the stratum divide during the fratricidal war in 1994 was very clear: not a single person from the stratum of former slaves had joined ARLA, or the vassal movement; instead, most (80 per cent) were members of the nobles' militia. The same holds true regarding the stratum of the nobles. In fact, no one from the leading noble tribes had joined the vassal movement. As already suggested, nearly all members of the other noble tribes had left ARLA after the kidnapping of the noble tribe's head mentioned in the preceding paragraph. Most had joined the MPA; some had left the armed fight altogether. From the middle of 1994 onwards, only people of vassal origin were members of ARLA.

At the end of 1994, civilian populations of northern Mali were becoming so war-weary that 'traditional' leaders and spokesmen of the rebel movements initiated reconciliatory meetings between various ethnic groups of northern Mali. These culminated in a solemn peace ceremony in March 1996 in Timbuktu, *La Flamme de la Paix,* which sealed a peace that however fragile, lasted about a decade. The peace agreements of the National Pact of 1992 were taken up again and made allowance for Ganda Koy, the Songhay militia, which then adhered to the pact. The second Tuareg rebellion in postcolonial Mali had ended.

The Logic of Descent Prevails

At the end of 1994, i.e., at the end of the fratricidal war between two rebel Tuareg movements in northern Mali, the only militia in the Kidal region was the MPA, the nobles' militia. The nobles had won the war; they still had weapons, even if only unofficially. They now forbade all fighters of ARLA to enter the region for five years. They also threatened to shoot immediately any armed person they came across. Moreover, they demanded that stolen goods be returned.

As is well known, a military victory does not mean that the war wounds are healed and that sentiments of hate and vengeance are suddenly forgotten. The return of the nobles' uncontested power, however, was not the result of mere opportunism on the part of the defeated vassals. The nobles won their position by clever moves of reconciliation, which aimed at the reintegration of the vassals into the local society. They sought to achieve these goals through a marriage and through the rewriting of local history.

The marriage was no less than the marriage of the military leader of the nobles' movement. The bride was the former wife of the man who used to be the groom's best friend and comrade in arms, but, above all, she was from a vassal tribe, and all three, the bride and the two men, shared a common, long-standing past. They were together in Libyan exile where the two men were recruited by the Islamic Legion. If one was noble and the other one vassal, it did not prevent them from fighting together with the Legion in Lebanon and preparing the upheaval in Mali. At the beginning of 1990 the two men secretly returned to Niger; they fought together in the very first Tuareg attack in Mali. Both men were friends and excellent and courageous fighters. So the eventual break between the friends was particularly dramatic at the beginning of the war between 'brothers': close friends had become arch-enemies.

Everyone in the Kidal region was sure about the political nature of this union. There were those who simply declared the bride to be the spoils of war – the vassals could not even keep their women. Others looked on the marriage as a sign of reconciliation. The union with the former wife of the vassals' best fighter meant that the vassals belonged once again to the local community. On the other hand, the marriage also clearly demonstrated that friendship no longer served as a solid foundation upon which to build political relations or to achieve political objectives. Instead, friendship had been replaced by kinship bonds.

The second measure of reconciliation aimed more broadly at establishing a new basis for the political reintegration of vassals into the local society. For this purpose, the nobles made use of the strong legitimizing resources of history.[11] They simply set about rewriting local history. By doing so, they tried to make up a new tradition: the tradition of a fundamental unity due to consanguinity and the care of the strong for the weak.

The strategy used was as follows: the nobles delegated a man of noble origin to reestablish the affiliation of the vassals, through their genealogies, with the community of the Kidal region. This man had the right profile for the job. He is a fluent multilingual speaker and has learned the art of persuading audiences during his exile in Libya. There, his job was to persuade the Tuareg in Libyan exile to join the Islamic Legion. In the tradition of an Arab scholar, he reconstructed the genealogy of each of the families from each of the groups living in the Kidal region and recorded it in school notebooks. He believed, with a few exceptions, to be able to trace all families back to five forefathers who were related to one another. For him, the genealogical data that he had collected gave a new historical outlook explaining the relationship between nobles and vassals in the region. Most importantly, he concluded that the existence of vassals was a myth; there were no vassals in the region. In his view, the label 'vassal' had just established itself in those groups which, over the years, had become weak, politically and militarily, and which had been forced to submit to the supremacy of strong families. According to his reconstruction of history, however, all Tuareg were actually interrelated by kinship and consanguinity. In a society in which kinship is one of the foremost principles, this conclusion was of crucial importance for restoring peace: the label 'vassal' is not a primordial, but a secondary, less significant social distinction.

With his school notebooks and genealogical evidence in hand, the man toured the Kidal region for several weeks in 1995 with the aim of convincing the vassals of their true origins. A summary of his message is as follows: the vassals may exercise no violence against the nobles; the nobles are related to the vassals; and people are not violent towards members of their own family.

In the end, however, the attempt to impose the old ruling ideology of a basic cohesion between the rulers and the ruled, couched here in terms of kinship and consanguinity, was unsuccessful. During the most recent violent events in northern Mali, the two men mentioned earlier in this section, who had been friends and comrades in arms in Libyan exile and during the first half of the Tuareg upheaval against the Malian government from 1990 to 1996, did indeed fight against each other in 2012, just as they had in the fratricidal war of 1994.

In October 2010, a group of young Malian Tuareg founded the Mouvement National de l'Azawad (MNA; National Movement of Azawad).[12] The movement's political demands for the autonomy of northern Mali, however, were ignored by the Malian government, and two of its leaders were arrested. After the defeat of the Gaddafi regime in August 2011, many Malian Tuareg, among them several thousand who had been recently enrolled in the Libyan armed forces, returned to Mali, bringing with them light and heavy arms. While some returnees demanded (and received) integration into the Malian army, others joined members of the MNA in forming the Mouvement National pour la Libération de l'Azawad (MNLA; National Movement for the Liberation of Azawad).

On 17 January 2012, the MNLA started attacks in northern Mali and succeeded, in two and a half months, in conquering all towns and villages in the north and in defeating completely the Malian army. On 6 April, the movement declared the independence of Northern Mali, announcing the erection of a new state called 'Azawad'. This success had been facilitated by a putsch of army officers in Mali's capital, Bamako. Not only did the putsch oust President Amadou Toumani Touré but it also broke down chains of command. As a consequence, logistical support failed to reach army units fighting in the north.

Other factors contributing to the rebels' success were the military alliances that the MNLA concluded with armed groups of Islamist orientation in Northern Mali, in particular with Ansâr ud Dîn ('Supporters of the Faith'). Ansâr ud Dîn came together at the end of 2011 at the instigation of the former leader of the MPA, i.e., the man of noble origin whose marriage was discussed briefly at the beginning of this section. According to some of my informants, this man founded Ansâr ud Dîn because he had not been selected in October of that year for the position of general secretary of the MNLA. After the rejection of his candidacy, he created his own militia, taking members of the MNLA who belonged to his tribal group with him. Apparently, tribal solidarity and kinship ties supplanted political convictions.

Ansâr ud Dîn combines two sorts of claims: the 'old' claim of the Malian Tuareg for autonomy and the claim to organize society in an Islamic mode, namely, according to sharia law (Klute 2013). The latter claim is not really supported by the MNLA, which, as mentioned above, nevertheless concluded alliances with Ansâr ud Dîn and other groups of Islamist orientation. The fact that these alliances had been formed for pragmatic purposes only became obvious in the summer and autumn of 2012, when groups of Islamist orientation, including Ansâr ud Dîn, drove the MNLA, first from all the cities and towns in northern Mali and then completely out of the country.

The ex-friend of the Ansâr ud Dîn leader and former officer in the ARLA movement has had a different career. After the end of the 1990–1996 upheaval, he was integrated into the Malian army, where he became a high-ranking officer. At the beginning of 2012, he fought on the Malian side against the MNLA and

Ansâr ud Dîn. He and his unit, however, were defeated and even had to flee Mali to neighbouring Niger. They returned to Mali in January 2013, after the international coalition of African states under French leadership intervened militarily in Mali, driving Ansâr ud Dîn and other Islamist groups to the extreme north of the country.

Conclusion

As I have shown in this contribution, friendship was an important issue for Tuareg before the beginning of the Tuareg upheavals in 1990 in northern Mali and northern Niger. Along with national, regional, tribal and social-stratificational identities, friendship bonds were much discussed, negotiated and renegotiated during the time of exile of Tuareg migrants. In order to overcome regional, tribal or social divisions of 'traditional' Tuareg society, members of clandestine Tuareg resistance movements avoided habitual appellations which were supposed to evoke tribal, social or regional identities; instead, they addressed one another as 'friend' because friendship bonds were thought to strengthen the unity of an imagined, but still utopian Tuareg nation.

After thousands of migrants were sent home at the end of 1989 and the beginning of 1990, some groups of Tuareg in northern Mali started a rebellion which would last until 1996. Though the rebels were first surprisingly successful, the united movement soon split up into various factions, opposing one another politically and later also militarily. In particular, during a phase of ethnic strife in 1994, when the Songhay militia Ganda Koy called for ethnic cleansing of all 'white' Malians, northern Mali was forced into an ethnic divide. As a result, interethnic friendships that had been forged long before the beginning of the rebellion increasingly broke down, and almost everybody was obliged to give up all those relationships and ties of friendship that cut across ethnic boundaries.

The same year, a fratricidal war between two Tuareg rebel movements broke out in northern Mali. This violent intraethnic conflict, and the intraethnic divisions that the conflict brought to the fore, negatively affected those friendship bonds among Tuareg that had cut across tribal and social boundaries.

The winning side of the fratricidal war in northern Mali, a group of tribes of noble Tuareg, undertook measures of reconciliation in order to reintegrate the defeated into the local society. These measures included attempts at overcoming former (tribal or social) divisions that were not based on friendship, as had been the case during Tuareg exile, but on kinship and consanguinity.

However, there is no doubt that friendship is not only a relational term but a political term as well. In much the same way as kinship, consanguinity or descent, it may be used to legitimize political relationships, alliances or hostile relationships.

In the context of violent conflicts, I would argue, friendship bonds that cut across identities perceived to be primordial by the respective warring parties are rather difficult to maintain. In the case of the Tuareg rebellion of 1990–1996 at least, social actors increasingly built relationships on tribal affiliation and consanguinity, i.e., on relationships that they considered to be more stable and more trustworthy than mere friendship.

Interestingly, the recent violent events in northern Mali have set off dynamics that indeed confirm my findings. Since 2012, as in 1994, both interethnic and intraethnic friendship bonds have, as a rule, been strongly affected by the ongoing conflict, and many of these bonds have been supplanted by relationships that the conflicting parties regard as more primordial and, thus, more trustworthy than friendship. The MNLA, however, still includes Tuareg of various tribal origins and social strata, whereas Ansâr ud Dîn recruits most of its members from one particular tribal group (with noble status). The latter fact again points to the importance that actors in northern Mali ascribe to 'primordial' ties.

Notes

1. This chapter represents an updated and a more comprehensive version of an earlier publication (Klute 2011).
2. These questionnaires contained the following entries: informant's name, father's name/mother's name, age, class (including remarks on class affiliation), lineage of informant, lineage/mother, lineage/father, regions of origin, region of current residence, country of current residence, social origin, school qualification, professional qualification, professional career, professional occupation, member of Tuareg exile movement: yes/no (place, time, circumstances, tasks, motivations, remarks), member of Tuareg rebel movements 1–4 (time, tasks, remarks), personal comments on the interview conducted while collecting the completed questionnaire.
3. Apparently, little has changed since Leupen (1978) and Chaker (1988) compiled bibliographies on the Tuareg, neither of which contains among titles or key words any entry concerning 'friendship'.
4. For more details, see Klute (1991, 1994, 2001) and Boesen and Klute (2004).
5. Libyan transcription of 'Khoms'.
6. 'Azawad' is the name given to the region to the north of Timbuktu. The word is also used, by extension, to refer to the wider region of northern Mali, which the Tuareg consider to be their territory.
7. The international aid organizations were favoured targets because of their four-wheel drive vehicles which were, on the whole, comparatively new. Under desert conditions, these vehicles are highly valued equipment. With mounted machine guns they provide a highly effective combination of mobility and fire power (Klute 2009).
8. For an interesting study on identity construction and processes of inclusion and exclusion in contexts of conflict, see Schlee (2008).
9. Iswadan ag Saghid, Kidal, November 1996, my translation.
10. After the Tamanrasset peace agreements of January 1991, the MPLA changed its name to MPA, indicating, thereby, that the Azawad region had, by then, been liberated.
11. For a discussion of the use of the region's Islamic history as legitimizing resource, see Klute (2003).
12. For more details on the foundation of the MNA, see Morgan (2012).

Afterword

Friendship in a World of Force and Power

Stephen P. Reyna

Introduction

In the Introduction to this volume it is noted that friendship relations can be seen as constituting a 'social capital'. Given that 'capital' was Bourdieu's (1986 [1983]) term for power, this amounts to recognition that friendship concerns social power. Equally stimulating here is the first chapter by Martine Guichard, which draws attention to 'veiling' and 'emotional economy' as useful concepts for the investigation of friendship. Although Guichard does not clearly theorize about friendship in terms of power, her approach contributes to an understanding of friendship in such terms, i.e., an understanding that is at the core of this essay.[1] Here, I present a 'string being theory' (hereafter 'SBT') account of friendship which treats friendship as an aspect of force with the ability to cause any number of powers. As such, friendship is viewed as a way that individuals manage to string events together, giving everyday life its order. Evidence supporting this argument comes from ethnographic sources in this volume and elsewhere. The notion of 'emotional economy', as defined by Guichard, is used to explain the veiling of power involving friendship in high places in the United States. The argument making this case has three parts. The first part presents the general approach. The second part applies it to friendship. The third part grounds it in ethnographic information. Finally, the findings of the third section are employed to make proposals concerning debates about the relative importance of friendship and kinship in different social fields, and about whether friendship is helpfully conceptualized in utilitarian or nonutilitarian terms.

The Approach

> What is the world? ... a play of forces. (Nietzsche, *The Will to Power*)

This section first specifies the ontology that defines what is to be explained in the perspective of SBT (Reyna 2001, 2002, 2003) and, then, presents generalizations accounting for why the world is, in some Nietzschesque sense, 'a play of forces'. Let us begin by introducing two ontological favourites for modelling social reality since the nineteenth century.

Methodological individualism – exemplified in a variety of rational action theories – is the first of these. It proposes that the irreducible atom of social reality is individuals, so that it is these actors that theory needs to explain. Structural functionalism has been a second ontological framework, especially in works stimulated by Durkheim (1966 [1895]) or Parsons (1951). It supposes that what is out there are not individuals, but actors relating with others; which means that the irreducible reality in need of theory is not individual atoms, but social elements. These ontologies can be synthesized into a third. Certainly, there are individuals, but equally certainly, actors are deployed in social relations. SBT rests upon the ontological claim that social reality is a monism composed of conjoined spaces: interior space (I space), structures of the brain that perform the functions of the mind, and exterior space (E space), different social relations. This is a monism because brains are in actors and actors are in social relations.[2] SBT explains what happens in this monism. What happens is that things get done. Social *being* is social *doing*. 'Doing' is stringing events out over time. Five generalizations adduced below help to explain social doing. The crucial thing that gets done is events. These are deployed in strings.

A 'string' is direct observation at low levels of abstraction and high levels of particularity of social events as they occur over time. Abstract and general representations of strings are 'logics', statements high in generality of abstract classes of strings. Logics are identified *spatio-temporally* and in terms of their *powers*. Spatio-temporal identification abstractly signifies where in space and when in time the empirical referents of logics occur. The power of a logic is the outcome of a particular spatio-temporal sequences. Exxon-Mobil may be said to have the world on a string of gasoline sales if it sells $1 trillion of gasoline globally in 2002 to make a $200 million-dollar profit, and, then, uses some of this to sell $1.2 trillion of gasoline the next year to make even more profit. This string exhibits a logic whose power is capital accumulation, and whose spatio-temporal order is represented by Marx's (1909 [1867]) famous 'M-C-M'.[3]

Logics include 'logical possibilities', i.e., alternatives of the same logic. Armies and navies are different logical possibilities of violent logics. Individual and social strings and logics should be distinguished. 'Individual strings and logics' involve what persons have done with their life over time. 'Social strings and logics' involve what an institution, understood in a Malinowskian fashion (Malinowski 1939), or combination of such groups, have done over time.

Some logics are simple; others are complex depending upon the numbers, the lengths and the knotting of their strings. The 'number' of strings in a logic is how many strings operate when it achieves its powers. The 'length' of a string refers to the number of events in it. 'Knotting' is the connection of one string with another. Simple logics have few, short strings, with little knotting. Strings knotted in particular manners are 'webs'. Next we are introduced to a dynamic duo.

Strings occur in 'fields', the spaces and times in which institutions, and the strings that they produce, operate. Every enduring group has its strings. The stringing together of events by institutions involves force and power. This dyad is understood in a Hobbesian manner in SBT, which means that the two are analysed as the operation of causation in the fields of social life.[4] 'Force' is capacities within individuals or groups that allow them to be antecedent events that cause subsequent ones. Force, so understood, is distinguished from violence, one of its manifestations. Force is *any* ability to cause something. Violence is a *particular* force. Power is the effects of force, i.e., subsequent outcomes in social events. Hence, no force, no causes; and, if no causes, no effects or powers. Force and power are a 'dynamic duo' that literally make events happen, raising the question: how it is that force has the power to make events and, then, to make connections between events, thereby making strings?

This question will be answered in two steps. First, it will be explained how force and power create events and, second, how events are connected. A 'force resource' is something material, including the actors themselves, which changes over space and time to get something done. There are four such resources: instruments, actors, culture and authority. The latter two resources choreograph the two former ones. Instruments are tools – monies and raw materials, etc. – inanimate things that people use to make things happen. Actors are people who perform practical or discursive action. 'Practical' action is the use of the body, often with tools, to get something done. Labour is economic practical action. 'Discursive' action is the use of the body to speak or write.

'Culture', learned and shared (at least by some) knowledge, tells people *what is* and *what to do about it*. 'Choreography' is about arranging of the timing and utilization of resources, by specifying what resources are to be employed, how, and in what temporal sequence. 'Perceptual' culture identifies what is to be used when the events of strings are to occur. 'Procedural' culture identifies how and in what temporal order resources are to be used. Procedural cultural choreography may be distinguished in terms of the numbers and types of force resources to be organized. 'Authority' is formally sanctioned rights and responsibilities vis-à-vis instruments, actions and cultural information. A 'sanctioned' resource is one that has other resources added to it to augment the force of which it is a component. Actors, usually through inheritance, law or administrative decree, acquire authoritative resources. The police or military sanction these. Police and soldiers specialize in violence. So here, authority is sanctioned by violence. A 'formally' sanctioned resource is one made explicit by written law or policy that has been formulated by some procedure (a vote or administrative decision).

Utilization of resources is an 'exercise of force'. Such exercises might be anything that has an outcome. Remember an event is 'anything' that has an outcome.

In SBT *anything* is an exercise of force that has an outcome, i.e., causes power. Events themselves are structures with two parts. The first part is its force; the second part is the power caused by the exercise of its force. This is a 'force/power' dyad. (A word is in order here as to how events can be symbolized. Events in a sequence will be designated as 'E' followed by a number indicating their place in the sequence. A string with three events will be 'E_1, E_2 and E_3'.) The occurrence of such a dyad is an event. 'Plays of force' are situations in fields where exercises of force in one string, or strings, have powers in other strings which have had their own exercises of force. Having grasped how events are constituted, it is time to consider how force has the power to connect events. A notion of reflexivity is now introduced.

In SBT reflexivity is important because it connects events.[5] Specifically, 'reflexivity' is neurological processes of actors whereby they observe antecedent events to interpret what they are and, then, select actions based upon their desires that choreograph force resources to make subsequent events. Desire is part of the operation of different parts of the brain in a cultural neurohermeneutic system (hereafter 'CNHS') and is the *intentions* and *emotions* of perceptual and procedural culture and/or authority *stored* in the neural networks of actors' brains.[6] Desire tells you how you should feel about an antecedent event and what to do about it – with it recognized that you feel good about doing what your culture and authority intends you to do, and bad about doing what is culturally or authoritatively taboo.

Intentions, and the procedural culture or authority shaping them, may be more specific or general and more obligatory or optional. A 'specific' intention is one that precisely specifies particular choreographing of force resources. The intentions of doing a heart operation are extremely specific. A 'general' intention is one that specifies a broad range of choreography of force resources. The intention of 'nurturing' is quite general. 'Obligatory' intentions are ones that must be obeyed. 'Optional' intentions are those that may or may not be choreographed. Regardless of the type of intentions in humans, their desires tend to be quirky.[7]

To recapitulate: certain things are elemental. One elemental thing is that to live you have to do. When you do, you exercise force to achieve power, based upon your reflexivity, thereby stringing events together. Living in the world is exercising force to achieve power. In this sense, then, Nietzsche was correct. The world *is* 'a play of forces' to achieve powers and in such a world it helps to have more force to have more power. Friendship will turn out to be a way of augmenting force. It is time to apply this SBT approach to friendship.

The Theory

First, let us specify friendship's ontological status. A concept's 'ontological status' is where in the world its empirical referents are to be looked for. Friendship can be observed in two places. The first place is in the realm of culture. The second one is in fields of power. Let us visit these two places. In the perceptual cultural realm, friendship is a word – *friend* (English), *rafiq* (Chadian Arabic), *kapam* (Barma in Chad) or *ami* (French). The attributes that classify a person as a friend vary with population, time and social position. A contemporary French *ami* is different from a Chadian *rafiq*; an AD 800 English friend is different from her Victorian counterpart; a female Barma *kapam* differs from a male Barma *kapam*; as do friends who are rich from those who are poor. Some version of friendship is found in an enormous number of known societies; so many that friendship, like kinship, appears effectively a cultural universal.

Procedural cultural rules are associated with those perceived as friends. Friends, in varying amounts and kinds, provide each other with force resources. They do so generally following expansive procedural cultural rules involving some form of reciprocity (Sahlins 1972). For example, among the Barma, who were the ethnic group that dominated the precolonial state of Bagirmi, and with whom I lived along the banks of the Chari River, a *kapam* is someone who is supposed to aid you *noko ojo* (a lot). Consider the case of Al-Hadj Ahmet. It was planting season, just before the rains in 1970. Ahmet was a fine farmer, a bit of a go-getter, who sometimes took chances. One of these was the planting of a field of flood recession sorghum by the side of the river. This was risky. There might be heavy rainfall and, if so, the river could rise and drown the plants; or there might be drought and, if so, there would not be enough moisture for the plants. Working alone Ahmet got the field cleared and planted, and the young seedlings were doing quite fine. Unfortunately, not everything went right. Disaster struck in the form of two amorous hippopotamuses. They rose from the river one night, ambled into Ahmet's field, conducted a loud and long mating, and destroyed most of the plants in the field.

Ahmet now became the butt of a number of jokes and the source of not a few new proverbs like 'Don't plant where the hippos do it'. Ahmet was in a real bind. The rains were just beginning. Everybody was busy clearing or planting their own fields. He could not even get a younger brother (*mudj mbassa*) to help. Then Musa Ngollo stepped in and worked with Ahmet to put in a new field – this time of millet, well away from the river. Musa and Ahmet were not relatives to each other (*tosimge*). Rather, they were *kapamge* (friends) and, when I asked Musa why he assisted Ahmet, he replied, '*shokul hanna kapamge*' (things of friends). Musa's laconic statement was an articulation of a procedural cultural rule that didn't really need to be articulated (except to educate young ethnographers) – friends help friends.

Aristotle, in *Nichomachean Ethics* (1976), began a tradition that distinguished between friendships based upon utility from those based upon other qualities. This tradition continues in the present with some scholars, especially Silver (1989, 1990, 1997), arguing that modern Western friendship became nonutilitarian starting in the eighteenth century.[8] However, consider that American 'friends' owe each other 'trust'. Someone you can trust is 'loyal' to you. A loyal person is expected to do what their friend desires. If your friend desires 'help', you give help. Help could be labour, money and tools. Of course, these are force resources. This means that over time friends supply at least a portion of each other's force, thereby augmenting the amount of force available to them. The Barma and American examples allow specification of friendship's social ontological status. It exists socially when ethnographers identify groups in strings involving reciprocity in force resources, whose members assert they are doing so because they are friends.

Five generalizations systemize the preceding discussion. The first generalization is the most general and relates friendship to power. It asserts:

(1) Friendship is logic based upon actors reciprocally exchanging force resources in their individual strings to enhance their powers in social fields.

The second generalization explains how power is enhanced. It brings force into the picture and states:

(2) Friendship enhances actors' power by increasing the force available to them, so that exercises of force in their force/power dyads are greater, causing more substantial outcomes, i.e., more powers.

The third generalization explains how friendship works to increase force by adding force resources, asserting:

(3) An actor's force is increased either by: (a) insuring that force resources conferring force are available with greater reliability; (b) augmenting existing force resources; or (c) adding new force resources.

The 'reliability' of a force resource is the certainty of its supply. You can rely on your friends to help you out. Among the Barma, neighbours and kin were supposed to help in harvesting. When the time came to help, neighbours might have had more important things to do. Even kin could be sick. But you could count on your *kapamge*, especially if you had helped them in the past. The augmenting of existing force resources is adding new force resources to already existing ones. Mariyam was an Abu Krider Arab woman, another Chadian group among whom I conducted fieldwork. One time when I was there, her husband's uncle and family visited. Abu Krider procedural culture obliged Mariyam to feed these important affines. However, she was low on food and needed extra millet to feed them. It was a number of days until the next market. Her *rafiq*, Hadidja, gave her the needed millet. Mariyam combined her own with Hadidja's cereal and had a filling meal to present to her relatives. The adding of new force resources is just that: sometimes you have to have something, and sometimes you do not have it, so you get it from a friend. Other things being equal, a person with only two friends has fewer people to rely upon than one with a network of many friends. If Mariyam had only Hadidja for a *rafiq*, there would be far fewer people to supplement her millet supply than if she had fifteen *rufgan* (sing. *rafiq*).

Guichard shows (this volume) how different forms of kinship influence friendship. These differences are part of the context in which friendship is found. Context is known to be a significant factor in friendship (Adams and Allan 1998a). The two following generalizations concern the institutional context prevailing in fields and how this may influence friendship. 'Institutional context' denotes the sorts of institutions prevalent in fields operating in particular places and times. Context is relevant to friendship because most force resources are concentrated in institutions. So actors wanting power need to acquire access to force resource-providing institutions; or, in their absence, develop alternative ways of finding access to them. Two sorts of institutional contexts seem especially relevant: those of nonmodern versus modern institutions. Of course, important institutions in non-Western contexts are those of kinship and age groups; while in Western contexts they are capitalist enterprises, government hierarchies and universalistic religions. Two generalizations may be derived from the preceding. The first is:

(4) Where the context is such that force resource-providing institutions exist in a field, friendship can incorporate actors into those institutions, or institutions into fields, providing them with additional force resources, thereby enhancing their powers.

The next generalization concerns fields where, for some reason, the context is such that force resource-providing institutions are absent. This would comprise situations in non-Western fields where actors find themselves without relatives or age mates. It would involve situations in Western fields, where actors are in places without either business or government. In such betwixt and between niches,

(5) Where the prevalent force resource-providing institutions are absent in a field, friendship itself may provide actors access to force resources, thereby enhancing their power.

The preceding five generalizations might be thought of as opening speculation about an SBT of friendship because each of the generalizations details how through friendship actors may acquire increased power in the individual strings of their lives. This theory is presently heavy on speculation. The following section offers some validation.

Validating the Theory

Elsewhere (Reyna 2004), I have offered suggestions concerning validation. One of these is that theories are never completely validated, so that it is known that they are absolutely true. However, they can become truer and truer the more they have been validated against other, competing theories. What follows in this section is a preliminary step in validation, provision of sufficient evidence to warrant the plausibility of SBT speculations about friendship. This analysis is of eight cases of friendship in African and U.S. contexts. Each case might be imagined as a different logical possibility of friendship. The goal of the analysis is to ascertain the degree to which the evidence in the cases is consistent with that required if generalizations three through five are true. The information concerning the United States is included in order to compare non-Western with Western contexts.

Non-Western Institutional Context/Kin Institutions Present

Tiv (Nigeria)

Consider friendship as reported by Paul and Laura Bohannan in *Tiv Economy* (1968). They reported that Tiv had 'best friends' (*hur-or*). Friends, as was the case with the Barotse (Zambia), were involved in generalized reciprocity (Bohannan and Bohannan 1968: 142). This reciprocity was important in the domestic mode of production. Specifically, the Bohannans said: 'The basic work group is connected with family structure and limited by residence, but for special tasks ... best friends can be called in' (1968: 75–76). The tasks that are 'special' are labour intensive. They are activities like weeding, harvesting or threshing. Such chores are time dependent. They need to be performed quickly or the amount produced is compromised. Normally, the labour of the family is insufficient to perform the chores in a timely manner.

From the perspective of SBT, 'best friends' are labour, the economic form of practical action. Tiv families normally have a supply of labour. But this is limited to a small number of co-residential family members. The alliance between 'best friends' allows them to help each other, especially when there is some extra demand for workers, such as at harvesting. This is evidence supportive of generalization #3 which shows how Tiv could augment productive force at times when the string of events involved in farming required them. In addition, it is evidence consistent with generalization #4. In fields where families are prevalent, Tiv 'best friends' supply these institutions with additional labour, when needed, allowing the strings involved in the farming logic to increase farming output, i.e., agricultural power.

However, the friendship the Bohannans describe for the Tiv was quite widespread among African horticultural peoples[9] whose farming systems are occasionally characterized as exhibiting risk-aversive production strategies. Certainly, horticulture as practised in the African environmental context, as is the case with most rain-fed farming throughout the world, is risky business. Equally certainly, as Kerr documents (1995), African savannah horticultural systems feature a number of risk-mitigation practices. Friendship qualifies as one of these because friends provide each other with labour, seeds or tools in times of need. From the optic of SBT, risk mitigation is about maintaining powers when these appear threatened. There is always a risk that something may reduce the force resources needed to perform horticulture. However, friendship replaces the lost force, maintaining horticultural productive powers.

Maasai (Kenya and Tanzania)

Paul Spencer, this volume, discusses East African Maasai friendship (*shorisho*). He writes, in part, of past pastoral fields in which families were present and important in livestock production. A friend (*ol-chore*) is 'a trusted exchange partner'; a person who could be 'asked for help in the past, perhaps to restock his depleted herd'. A man gives some animals to a friend in need. The animals in the pastoral economy, such as was that of the Maasai, are the crucial force resource, so this is evidence supportive of generalization #3. Further, if the man receiving the animals were married, the restocking of the herd would augment the productive force of the man and his family's pastoral economy, increasing its productive outcomes when these had been reduced by the destocking.

Guichard, this volume, explains that the sort of friendship described by Spencer for the Maasai was, and is, found in many pastoral populations. She interprets such friendship as 'risk-minimizing' strategy, echoing what was said about friendship among farmers. Guichard's insight is perceptive, but it needs to be noted that the risks she is concerned with have implications for force and power among herders. Herding is risky because the major force resource, animals, is easily lost to disease, drought, poor pasture and the like. Stock losses result in force resource decline that, in turn, result in diminished productive powers. Friendship in risky environments replaces the destocked animals, adding force-increasing productive powers.

Mossi and Fulbe (Burkina Faso)

Mark Breusers, this volume, investigates friendship in interethnic fields in Burkina Faso. His discussion of friendship is nuanced and reflects, among other things, on the significance of host-guest arrangements for the development of friendships between Mossi, who are largely farmers, and Fulbe herders on transhumance. These arrangements include grazing relationships, whereby 'a herdsman gains access to crop residues, pastures, and water', while 'the host's field is fertilized'. According to Breusers, not all grazing relationships involve friendship, though they 'may evolve into' it. From the standpoint of SBT, the existence of grazing relationships is evidence supportive of both generalizations #3 and #4. Crop residues, pasture and water are pastoral force resources. Fertilization from manure is a farming force resource. The fact that securing these resources is notably heightened through friendship is evidence supportive of the third generalization. Further, the Mossi family is part of the institutional context of Fulbe herders and, as just noted, a force resource-providing institution. The grazing relationship incorporates Fulbe actors into this institution giving them access to some of its force resources, which is evidence supportive of the fourth generalization.

Non-Western Institutional Context/Kin Institutions Absent

Barotse (Zambia)
Gluckman's Barotse ethnography is rich, and he, like the Bohannans, is one of the few social anthropologists who mention friendship. In *The Ideas in Barotse Jurisprudence* (1965) he said:

> A noteworthy fact of Barotse life is the tendency to expand isolated transactions between strangers into multiplex associations that resemble kin relationships ... For example, Barotse barter goods with one another. Many people with small surpluses of products of specialized skills or particular environments travel through the country seeking to trade with others who have goods they lack ... But once a couple has made several barter exchanges of this kind, they consider they have entered into a pact of friendship (*bulikani,* literally 'the quality of being equals'). Thereafter they do not barter item for item, but they are under a general obligation to help each other and to outdo each other in generosity, rather than to seek a good bargain. They thus obtain hospitality, protection, and an additional home in an area they lack kin. (Gluckman 1965: 173–74)

A crucial point reported by Gluckman was that Barotse itinerant traders moved into fields where their own kin institutions were absent. Some of these traders shared 'friendship', giving each other 'generosity', which included, among other things, 'goods'. At one level of the analysis, such gift exchange is generalized reciprocity. However, from the vantage of SBT, where the emphasis is upon force and power, a friend's gift is a force resource – perhaps food or an implement – needed to continue commerce. Its reception by the trader is an observation consistent with the third generalization. Friendship increases an actor's force by adding a particular force resource. Additionally, the information in Gluckman's text is supportive of generalization #5 because friendship provides Barotse traders with force resources when their own kin institutions, which would normally provide them, are absent. Otherwise put, *bulikani* appears to have allowed traders to string out the events in their trading logics in fields with unpromising institutional contexts.

Gold Miners (Benin)

Grätz, this volume, analyses friendship in fields where the usual kin institutions are absent. His concern is with the men who leave their home villages and migrate to the mining camps of the Atakora Mountains in northern Benin. Here, there are generally few relatives and modern mining institutions are equally absent. Social life is rather improvised and friendship seems to be a chief way of choreographing the improvisation. This is especially true with regard to mining. As one of Grätz's informants put it: 'Among the gold miners I had many friends ... Some of them, I knew before, but in the mining fields we started working and staying together' (Grätz 2002b). Consequently, the actual mining enterprises were small teams, basically of friends. They are quite egalitarian, though they generally have a leader, a person with more experience in both the actual mining operations and the marketing of gold. In the absence of both kin groups and modern mining firms, friendship teams become the mining institution. Two force resources are provided by friends. The first is labour; the second is the procedural culture of the actual operations; and the provision of both force resources is evidence warranting generalization #3. Further, it should be clear from the preceding that friendship operating in the absence of kin or any other mining institutions provides the forces that give the mining its productive powers, observations consistent with generalization #5. Let us leave Africa and travel to contemplate friendship in modern institutional contexts in imperial, and imperious, America.

Western Institutional Context/Industrial Institutions Absent

Norman Street (Brooklyn)

America is a bipolar sort of place. The term 'bipolar' refers to manic-depressive disorders. On the one hand, there are the poor neighbourhoods in urban centres, which offer developing-world living at its most economically 'depressed'. On the other hand, there are the wealthy's fortified estates, where men collect 'trophy wives' and trophy wives collect 'boy toys', plus a lot of other stuff, in a 'manic' fury of consumption. Susser, in *Norman Street* (1982), studied the Greenpoint-Williamsburg neighbourhood of Brooklyn during a time of fiscal crisis for New York in the 1970s. This was a largely 'industrial white working-class community' (Susser 1982: vii) – lower class, though by no means the poorest of the poor. Of course, as Bob Dylan sang during those years, 'the times, they are a changing'. Deindustrialization was in full swing. A key institution of modernity, industry, tended to disappear, and with it went decently remunerated employment opportunities.

Susser describes a neighbourhood whose basic institution was the household. This was occupied by family kin groups, often smaller than their African counterpart, often lacking the ideal nuclear family organization fashionable in the culture of white privilege. Norman Street families were often fractured, in the sense that some critical family member – a mother or father – was not there due to the exigencies of poverty exacerbated by deindustrialization. Two sorts of households were found close to each other: those of people who were kin, and those of people who were unrelated by kinship. People in these latter sorts of households were 'neighbours'. Some neighbours 'took up' with each other and became good 'friends'. Adopting a metaphor made famous by Fortes (1949) in the African context, the community of Greenpoint-Williamsburg was a 'web of kinship' *and* friendship.

Further, just as in Africa, co-resident households – both those related by friendship and those related by kinship – provided each other with 'support' that involved 'cooperation' (Susser 1982: 144). This meant that the 'poor working class ... assisted one another in a variety of areas, including small financial loans and the sharing of laundry, cooking, shopping, and baby-sitting. Individuals and families moved from one household to another in response to changes in their economic or family situations' (1982: 159). Susser reports that this co-operation involves 'reciprocal relationships' (1982: 159), which brings us back to generalized reciprocity. Susser further insisted that the 'formation of local kinship and friendship ties' were important 'for economic survival' (1982: viii). From the vantage of SBT the support that households acquire from friends comes in the form of two force resources, which exist in the households, but which are severely limited due to their poverty. These resources are instruments (everything from pots and pans to money) and practical action (in the form of labour to help out with household chores). The observation that these force resources are added to households is consistent with generalization #3. Additionally, Susser's data is supportive of generalization #5 because friendship provides Norman Street families with additional force resources to, in U.S. slang, 'keep the family going'. This is extending the string of family events, giving the family additional power to 'keep going' in a context where the force resources needed to do this are so scarce due to the decline of industrial institutions of modernity.[10]

Contemporary Institutional Context/ Government and Industrial Institutions Present

George W. Bush

Let us become acquainted with President George W. Bush and one of his 'good ole buddies', an acquaintance that will lead to Guichard's concern for emotional economy and veiling. Even before Bush became president, as the son of a wealthy and presidential father, he frequented fields whose institutional context was rich in government agencies and businesses, in which he participated at the highest levels. The press reported that Bush appeared to have become involved in financial irregularities at Harken Energy during the time he was a director at this Texas oil company (1986–1993). Donahue, while researching this story, revealed that Bush involved Harken in the affairs of a friend from Colombia in South America. Donahue reported:

> George W. Bush went to work for Harken Energy in 1986 … Harken gave Bush $2 million in stock options, a $122,000 consulting job, and a seat on its board of directors.
>
> While Bush was working for Harken, Rodrigo Villamizar, an old friend Bush had met at a fraternity party in 1972, became director of Colombia's bureau of Mines and Minerals, the ministry that oversees the sale of oil concessions by the state oil company, Ecopetrol. According to a December 2001 report in *Counterpunch,* Bush had helped Villamizar out in the '70's by getting him first a job with the Texas state senate's Economic Development Committee, and then a seat on the state Public Utilities Commission. Toward the end of Bush's tenure at Harken, Villamizar returned the favor by granting Harken a series of oil contracts in Colombia.
>
> The bulk of the oil contracts were in the Magdalena Valley where military officers, drug traffickers, and cattle ranchers had come together to form right wing paramilitary groups that fought guerrillas, assassinated union leaders and human rights activists, and terrorized peasants in order to force them off coveted land. Most of the oil companies doing business in the region either tacitly accepted or actively sought out the protection of these death squads. A 1996 Human Rights Watch report documents the fact that the Colombian military armed and assisted these groups and, under the guidance of the CIA, integrated them into its intelligence networks. The close cooperation between the military and the paramilitaries continues today …
>
> No one is alleging that President Bush personally ordered paramilitaries to kill peasants and intimidate union leaders in order to improve Harken's bottom line. But at the same time, given his close ties to Villamizar, and the fact that his father was President at the time, it is highly unlikely that Bush was ignorant of the human rights issues involved in oil drilling in Colombia Valley. (2002: 1–2)

Donahue's account is of an instance of a transnational friendship operating between two privileged kin groups. The Bush family, by U.S. standards, is 'old money'. It has been rich since well back into the nineteenth century. However, in the case of Bush that wealth has depended upon, at least in part, high position in oil companies such as Harken Energy. The family of Rodrigo Villamizar, while not as rich as that of Bush, is part of Colombia's ruling elite, which sends its children to exclusive private schools where they can establish transnational 'friendships' that help their families. Foreign students in search of affluent American friends start at the high school level and continue through the undergraduate level in university. Rodrigo was a product of this system and attended Yale University. Bush also attended Yale where, at a fraternity, he made a buddy of Rodrigo. Bush and Rodrigo then went to Texas where – like Tiv, Tallensi, Baroste or Brooklyn friends – they started helping each other with gifts. Only, by Tiv, Tallensi, Barotse or Brooklyn standards, the gifts were pretty titanic.

It is time to bring in the concept of 'emotional economy', which is 'a disposition to distribute goods and services on the basis of *actual* feelings experienced towards other people' (Guichard, this volume). Bush and his Colombian friend were involved in such an economy. They liked each other and were disposed to distribute goods and services to each other. In SBT terms, this means that they provided force resources to each other. Bush first gave Rodrigo a job with the Texas state senate, and then one with the Texas Public Utilities Commission in the 1970s. Later, after Rodrigo returned to Colombia and had become director of the Bureau of Mines, he gave to his amigo contracts for Harken to work in Colombia's oil rich Magdalena Valley. This is a generalized reciprocity (Sahlins 1972), based upon an emotional economy of high-paying jobs and oil contracts, and, as a result, Bush and Rodrigo found their force resources augmented.

The evidence is equally consistent with generalization #4. Bush gets Rodrigo a job in Texas government. The job provides income. The income is the essential force resource in the exercises of force performed in Rodrigo's family that allowed them to have the powers to string out events as befits a rich family. Rodrigo does not directly give Bush anything. What happened instead was that an institution, Harken, because of the oil contract, was authorized to integrate itself into a field, that of the Magdalena Valley oil producers, where it could pursue revenues, some of which were paid to Bush as consultant and director fees. It is quite sad that death squads butchered the poor so that Harken and Bush could augment force resources. Members of the Bush and Villamizar families would be the first to deplore this situation. However, regardless of such sentiments, in both Rodrigo and Bush's cases, friendship incorporated them in institutions in Western, modern fields, in ways that augmented their force resources and powers, evidence consistent with generalization #4.

Let us return to emotional economy and the veiling of friendship. The gifts flowing in the Bush/Villamizar emotional economy are in violation of U.S. and Colombian procedural culture and authority. Contracts should be awarded on the basis of merit, not emotion, in both societies. Thus, the Bush/Villamizar emotional economy, derived from their friendship, violates U.S. and Colombian culture and authority. Put bluntly, the 'good ole buddies' friendship is corrupt and, as Guichard's research predicts, needs to be veiled. It is time to return to Africa, with a sense of déjà vu.

Kalanga National Elite (Botswana)

Richard Werbner, this volume, investigates some of Botswana's national elite. His analysis is of double interest: first because it offers observations of the sort of actors whom others have accused of causing the criminalization of the African state (Bayart, Ellis and Hibou 1999), and second because it presents a situation in an African context that is reminiscent of Bush and his friend. Botswana following independence (1966) enjoyed an economic boom, especially in the 1980s, that revolved around its diamonds. A number of modern transnational corporations, such as British Petroleum or Barclays Bank, invested in the new nation at this time. Werbner studies what he calls 'boon-companions' or friendship circles that began prior to independence among the Kalanga, a minority ethnic group long established in Gaborone, Botswana's capital. These friendships, often formed in educational institutions, have continued as friends took civil service positions in the government and prospered. As the years passed after independence, the friendship circles became 'locked … even more closely … between their leisure, business, financial, and even political affairs. The outcome was a strengthening of their standing as one of the capital's power elites'. They are especially 'closely linked in big business' as directors and/or shareholders. What is the nature of this linkage? Here, Werbner is quite blunt: friendship circles are 'mutually supportive in business partnerships, joint partnerships, and the risk-taking ventures of their lives'. Otherwise put, friends help friends do business. This is, in the words of the old Yankees baseball player, Yogi Berra, 'déjà vu all over again' because it was exactly the sort of relationship that has just been described for Bush and Rodrigo. It is equally evidence in support of the third and the fourth generalizations.

The evidence from the eight logical possibilities of friendship supports generalizations #3 through #5. However, eight nonrandomly selected cases are a tiny sample. Thus, an SBT of friendship might be validated in a very few instances. Such speculation is worthy of further consideration in the form of further validation. Let us conclude the argument, which leads us back to Nietzsche.

Conclusion

> The means of the craving for power have changed, but the same volcano is still glowing … (Nietzsche, *The Gay Science*)

We shall get to Nietzsche's 'volcano' in a moment, after addressing two issues that have occupied imaginations in the study of friendship. The first issue concerns the supposedly nonutilitarian nature of friendship in Western modern society argued by Silver (1989, 1990, 1997). Concepts are laminates of explicit and implicit meaning; and the term *utilitarian* is no exception. Something that is utilitarian is explicitly 'useful', 'practical', 'functional' and, implicitly, with regard to human relationships, not particularly desirable. A utilitarian friend is a conniver interested in what s/he can 'get' out of the relationship. So the Silver view of friendship constructs a duality that implicitly denigrates utilitarian, non-Western, nonmodern friendship.

The findings of this chapter are not especially supportive of the Silver position because of evidence that friendship in fields of power in modern capitalist society is utilitarian. Bush and Rodrigo's relationship is typical of many friendships among the wealthy. Indeed, friendship appears to be a major way that the affluent acquire force resources which allow them to continue the power of acquiring wealth. Friendship in this SBT optic is a logic giving the affluent the power of maintaining their class position. Meanwhile, among the poor in Brooklyn, abandoned by modern industrial institutions, people do have to be practical to confront poverty, and one of the few ways they have of doing this is by creating friendships and, then, using them to acquire force resources. They are thereby acquiring the power, not to maintain elevated class position, but more modestly to make do in a grim institutional context. Admittedly, the evidence of two cases is fragmentary, but I share with Grätz in this volume the hunch that nonutilitarian friendship 'is a romantic Western ideal'. However, perhaps there is more to it than just romance. Certainly, friends help each other out among privileged elites, be they in Washington or Gaborone, but by obscuring the practical benefits of their interactions the affluent hide the reality that they are rich not because of their hard work, but because of their 'boon-companions'. This suggests future research where analysis of nonutilitarian cultures of friendship should appraise the degree to which such cultures are a false consciousness.

The second issue to be addressed concerns the relative significance of kinship and friendship. Make no mistake about it: kin-based institutions in Africa were, and are, important in rural populations less touched by modern institutions because the bulk of force resources were vested in them. You desired land (with 'land' understood broadly here as raw materials), you got it from your kin. You wanted labour, you got it from your kin. Procedural culture, a third force resource, came with conventions for allocating what kin got what land and labour. However, friendship certainly existed in these fields of kinship; so the question is: what was the role of friendship? Perhaps some insight into this question can be gained by considering the dilemma of Abdul Qader, a Barma gentleman living in two realms. On the one hand, he was a Western-educated person holding a middle-level position in a business. On the other hand, he was a Barma *deb ngollo* (big man), with a web of kinship that spread far and wide throughout Chad. Once Abdul Qader and I travelled from N'Djamena, the capital of Chad, to a provincial town where he had both relatives (because his grandfather had founded the Barma neighbourhood in the town) and friends (because he had gone to high school there). We were only going to be in the town for a few days and I wondered who Abdul Qader would see more of.

It turned out we saw only friends for the vast bulk of time. These were relaxed gatherings – food eaten, small gifts exchanged and remembrance of the past, especially of the glory of their football team. Only in the last little bit of time before we were to return to N'Djamena did we see the relatives. This was a big, formal meal, with certain things done specified by *hada* (cultural rules). As the meal was ending, the relatives began to place certain demands upon Abdul Qader about coming to N'Djamena and staying with him and, when they were there helping them to find jobs, get educated or fix certain matters with the bureaucracy. To each demand, Abdul Quader responded in the affirmative. He had to or he would not be a *deb ngollo*. Yes, he would do this. Yes he would do that, yes, yes, yes! As we drove away, a harried and tired Abdul Qadir said in French, 'Mes amis, je peux choisir de les aider; avec mes parents, je dois aider. Peut-être pour mes parents N'Djamena est trop loin … pour qu'ils viennent vraiment me voir.' This vignette suggests, at least for the Barma, that a crucial difference between kinship and friendship is the role of compulsion. Kinsfolk are 'obligated' to each other.

Other contributors to this volume appear to reach a similar conclusion. Spencer suggests that there is less obligation attached to friendship when he states that it is 'often ambivalent and essentially fragile'. There is not a great deal of obligation in 'ambivalent' and 'fragile' relationships. Guichard speaks of kinship as opposed to friendship being 'based on principles that are more firmly agreed on'; generally, the 'more firmly agreed' upon a principle is, the greater the obligation attached to it. Grätz's informants exhibit an annoyance at the obligatory aspect of kinship. For example, one young miner acknowledged: 'In case I work together with my brother … or with my father, it may be that after all, he demands a higher portion of the yields, and I cannot refuse this'. With kinsfolk, the young miner 'cannot refuse'; while with friends, as another informant expressed it, 'you will find an understanding'.

The preceding suggests that the procedural culture of friendship is less and that of kinship is more obligatory in its choreographing of force resources. When the bulk of force resources were concentrated in kin institutions, such societies were, or are, aptly called 'kin-based', as in rural African societies. This means that the procedural culture of force resource-inheritance distributed land, labour and instruments to the kin of an actor who had just died. Similarly, the procedural culture of resource allocation distributed land, labour and instruments between kin during different stages of the life-cycle of an actor. Male kin were owed different force resources when they were juniors, adults and elders. The same was true of female kin. When this was the case, the obligatory procedural cultures choreographing kin institutions' force resources explicitly allocated these resources, making possible the powers exhibited in kin-based pastoral or horticultural logics. Where is friendship in these fields of kinship? One way of imagining it is as supplemental logic augmenting enterprising actors' powers in these fields. Friends may activate optional procedural cultures that give them access to force resources on the basis of friendship that they would not otherwise acquire through kinship. Most importantly, they may receive labour, tools or business opportunities. For example, the more friends a Barma farmer has, the more people he can call upon to help augment the work of his relatives with the weeds when these are threatening to choke his crop. The more Mossi friends a Fulbe herder has, the more people whose fields he can call upon to graze his animals in as the pastures dry up during the dry season. So with more force, their strings generate more power. Now it is on to Nietzsche.

Ordinary life, doing, is stringing events together. Events are strung together by exercising force resources to effect different powers. 'Craving for power' is the desiring it. Force resources are the 'means of craving'. Cravings are choreographed by procedural culture into different logics with their different logical possibilities. Friendship is an individual logic that makes powers because reciprocal procedural cultures choreograph acquisition of force resources by friends. If you are poor and want enough, friendship can help you acquire the power of enough, as is illustrated by the logical possibilities discussed for Norman Street, the Tiv, Barotse, Maasai, Mossi, Fulbe and the gold miners of Benin. If you are rich and want more, friendship can help acquire the power of more, as is illustrated by Bush and the national elite in Botswana.

Notes

1. Even recent publications on friendship such as those compiled by Desai and Killick (2010) or written by Hruschka (2010) do not indicate a growing recognition in anthropology of the utility of studying friendship as an instance of power.
2. Elsewhere (Reyna 2002), I have shown why a monistic approach is desirable. The general argument is that since Descartes (1960 [1637]) a number of social theories have tended towards dualisms characterized by disconnected subjective and objective realms. However, to some scholars – Bourdieu and myself included – these realms seem parts of a common whole. The problem is how to conceptualize this commonality. In Bourdieu, the subjective is the *habitus* and the objective is fields of capital. However, I show that the reality of the habitus is unspecified (Reyna 2002: 29–35), and a monism is unsatisfactorily conceptualized if one of its main components is unknown. In SBT, I-space corresponds to the subjective, and is the actuality of certain parts of the brain, while E-space corresponds to the objective, and includes social relations of power. This is a monism: I-space structures are in actors and actors are in social relations of power. The terms 'subjective' and 'objective' are replaced by I-space and E-space because of the former pair of terms' association with Cartesian dualism. Additionally, the subjective has had an aura of ineffability.
3. The equation in the text reads: 'a sum of money (M) used to purchase a commodity (C), when that commodity is sold, leads to an increased sum of money (M)'.
4. Hobbes (1971: 69) argued that power was a form of causality. This view was important in the American behavioural political science, especially with Dahl, who asserted, 'power relations can be viewed as causal relations' (1986: 38).
5. See Lynch (2000) for a review of the reflexivity literature.

6. The idea of a CNHS (Reyna 2002, 2006) represents both the most important structure in I-space and a rethinking of the nature of culture. I-space is all biological structures within actors' bodies. The CNHS is the set of structures within the brain that represents realities in E-space and in the areas of I-space other than the CNHS. The CNHS works by having perceptual and procedural culture imbedded within its neural networks. Sensations of E-space are classified as particular messages of perceptual culture. Perceptual and procedural cultural representations are associated with different emotions. Particular instances of perceptual culture have their procedural cultural instructions: perceive a sensation to be a 'lion', proceed by treating it carefully and feel less fearful when one does so.
7. Let me clarify the quirkiness of desire. Individuals have basic, positional and individual cultural understandings (Reyna 2002). 'Basic' culture involves broadly shared understandings in a population. Pretty much every English speaker understands what a 'man' is. 'Positional' culture is less broadly shared since it refers to understandings held by those in the same social position. 'Position' is similarities in class, gender and race, etc. Rich and poor can both tell a policeman when they see him. However, the rich view him more as an 'officer of the law'; while the poor tend to classify him as a 'pig', or worse. 'Individual' culture is positional and basic understandings influenced by individuals' experiences. George H.W. Bush, the father, had never been a drunkard, had practised combat, had not been treated by his father as a mediocrity and had not experienced 9/11 during his presidency. George W. Bush, the son, had been a drinker, had shirked combat, had been treated as a mediocrity by his father and had experienced 9/11 while president. Bush father and son shared the same basic and positional cultures being rich, male and presidents. They had varying individual cultures and, it turned out, very different desires about how to treat Iraq's ruler. Thus, it seems the strings of social life involve a quirky, and individual, causality.
8. Silver states that the modern friendship 'ethic ... is constituted by sentiment and affect rather than calculation and utility' (1997: 67). Silver's friendship 'ethic' is in SBT terms a culture of friendship. There is reason to be sceptical about the existence of this culture because of Silver's evidence for it. His evidence comes from eighteenth-century philosophers' philosophies of friendship. These philosophers include Hume, Smith, Ferguson, Defoe, Dr. Johnson, etc. (see especially Silver 1997: 49–67). However, there is *no* data from people actually living at the time concerning their friendship culture. Thus, Silver presents eighteenth-century philosophers' ideas of what constituted friendship in the absence of evidence of what eighteenth-century friends actually thought about the matter.
9. Tallensi friendship operated in manners similar to those described in the text for the Tiv. Fortes said: 'It is a common thing for Tallensi [Ghana], especially men to have friends ... in other clans than their own, and nowadays in neighboring tribes. Friends visit one another ... , help one another somehow, and give one another gifts' (1949: 337). 'Help', among other things, was agricultural or other forms of labour.
10. Two classic studies of U.S. poverty further report that friendship involves the provision of force resources needed to string along the events of individuals or families. Stack, discussing friendship among 'black' welfare mothers in the Midwest, has one of her informants report the procedural culture as: 'When I have a friend and I need something, I don't ask, they automatically tell me that they are going to give it to me' (Stack 1974: 57). Liebow studied friendship among poor 'black' men in Washington, DC. Here, the procedural culture was that friends should give and receive 'goods and services in the name of friendship' (Liebow 1967: 163).

Bibliography

Adams, R., and G.A. Allan (eds). 1998a. *Placing Friendship in Context.* Cambridge: Cambridge University Press.

———. 1998b. 'Contextualising Friendship', in R. Adams and G.A. Allan (eds), *Placing Friendship in Context.* Cambridge: Cambridge University Press, pp. 1–17.

Aguilar, M.I. 2011. 'From Age-Sets to Friendship Networks in Contemporary Sociology: The Continuity of *soda* among the Boorana of East Africa', *Sociology Mind* 1(1): 16–25.

Allan, G.A. 1979. *A Sociology of Friendship and Kinship.* London: George Allen & Unwin.

———. 1989. *Friendship: Developing a Sociological Perspective.* Boulder: Westview Press.

———. 1996. *Kinship and Friendship in Modern Britain.* Oxford: Oxford University Press.

Almagor, U. 1978. *Pastoral Partners: Affinity and Bond Partnership among the Dassanetch of Southwest Ethiopia.* Manchester: Manchester University Press.

Amborn, H. 2009. 'Mobility, Knowledge and Power: Craftsmen in the Borderland', in G. Schlee and E.E. Watson (eds), *Changing Identifications and Alliances in North-East Africa. Volume I: Ethiopia and Kenya.* New York, Oxford: Berghahn Books (Series 'Integration and Conflict Studies'), pp. 113–31.

Amselle, J.-L. 1977. *Négociants de la Savanne.* Paris: Anthropos.

Arhin, K. 1978. 'Gold-Mining and Trading among the Ashanti of Ghana', *Journal de la Société des Africanistes* 48(1): 89–100.

Aristotle. 1976. *Nichomachean Ethics.* Oxford: Oxford University Press.

Bâ, A.H. 1991. *Amkoullel l'enfant peul. Mémoires.* Arles: Actes Sud.

Badini, A. 1996. 'Les relations de parenté à plaisanterie: élément des mécanismes de régulation sociale et principe de résolution des conflits sociaux au Burkina Faso', in R. Otayek, F.M. Sawadogo and J.-P. Guingané (eds), *Le Burkina entre révolution et démocratie (1983–1993).* Paris: Karthala, pp. 101–16.

Bako-Arifari, N. 2002. 'Friendship and Political Networks in Benin', 18th Biennial Conference of the VAD (Vereinigung für Afrikawissenschaften in Deutschland [African Studies Association in Germany]), Hamburg, Germany, 25 May 2002.

Barcellos Rezende, C. 1999. 'Building Affinity through Friendship', in S. Bell and S. Coleman (eds), *The Anthropology of Friendship.* Oxford: Berg Publishers, pp. 79–97.

Barnes, J. 1954. 'Class and Committees in a Norwegian Island Parish', *Human Relations* 7(1): 39–58.

Bassi, M. 1993. *Report on the Peace Making Ceremony Held in Arbore, Ethiopia, 6–9 March 1993*. Addis Ababa: SNV-Ethiopia. Retrieved June 2011 from http://ora.ox.ac.uk/objects/uuid%3Ae2d08fbd-5c7f-486c-9839-5a17eb80d2b9/datastreams/ATTACHMENT01.

Bayart, J.-F., S. Ellis and B. Hibou. 1999. *Criminalization of the State in Africa*. Bloomington: Indiana University Press.

Beer, B. 1998. 'Freundschaft als Thema der Ethnologie', *Zeitschrift für Ethnologie* 123: 191–213.

———. 2001. 'Anthropology of Friendship', in N.J. Smelser and P.B. Baltes (eds), *International Encyclopedia of the Social and Behavioral Sciences*. Oxford: Elsevier Science Ltd, pp. 5807–8.

Beggs, J.J., V.A. Haines and J.S. Hurlbert. 1996. 'Revisiting the Rural-Urban Contrast: Personal Networks in Metropolitan and Non-Metropolitan Settings', *Rural Sociology* 61(2): 306–25.

Bell, S., and S. Coleman (eds). 1999a. *The Anthropology of Friendship*. Oxford: Berg Publishers.

———. 1999b. 'The Anthropology of Friendship: Enduring Themes and Futures Possibilities', in S. Bell and S. Coleman (eds), *The Anthropology of Friendship*. Oxford: Berg Publishers, pp. 1–19.

Bellagamba, A. 2000. 'A Matter of Trust. Political Identities and Interpersonal Relationships along the River Gambia', *Paideuma* 46: 37–61.

Boddy, J. 2007. 'Allianz und Endogamie im Nordsudan: Implikationen für Identitätsbildung', in J.F.K. Schmidt, M. Guichard, P. Schuster and F. Trillmich (eds), *Freundschaft und Verwandtschaft: Zur Unterscheidung und Verflechtung zweier Beziehungssysteme*. Konstanz: UVK Verlagsgesellschaft, pp. 291–311.

———. 2009. 'Endogamy and Alliance in Northern Sudan', in G. Schlee and E.E. Watson (eds), *Changing Identifications and Alliances in North-East Africa. Volume II: Sudan, Uganda and the Ethiopia-Sudan Borderlands*. New York, Oxford: Berghahn Books (Series 'Integration and Conflict Studies'), pp. 103–35.

Boesen, E., and G. Klute. 2004. 'Direkt von der Wüste in die Stadt. Moderne Migration von Nomaden aus dem Sahara-Sahelraum', *Das Parlament* (Beilage 'Aus Politik und Zeitgeschichte') 10, 1 March 2004.

Bohannan, L., and P. Bohannan. 1968. *Tiv Economy*. Evanston: Northwestern University Press.

Bohannan, P. 1959. 'Some Principles of Exchange and Investment among the Tiv', *American Anthropologist* 57: 60–70.

Boissevain, J. 1974. *Friends of Friends. Networks, Manipulators and Coalitions*. Oxford: Basil Blackwell.

Bonnet, D. 1988. *Corps biologique, corps social. Procréation et maladies de l'enfant en pays mossi, Burkina Faso.* Paris: ORSTOM.

Bourdieu, P. 1984 [1979]. *Distinction: A Social Critique of the Judgement of Taste* (trans. R. Nice). London: Routledge and Kegan Paul.

———. 1986 [1983]. 'The Forms of Capital', in J. Richardson (ed.), *Handbook of Theory and Research for the Sociology of Education.* New York: Greenwood Press, pp. 241–58.

Brain, R. 1976. *Friends and Lovers.* New York: Basic Books.

Breusers, M. 2002. 'The Teeth and the Tongue are Always Together, but It Happens that the Teeth Bite the Tongue': Fulbe's Social and Political Integration in Moaga Society and Their Access to Natural Resources. A Case Study from Burkina Faso', workshop 'The Landed and the Landless? Strategies of Territorial Integration and Dissociation in Africa', Halle/Saale, 27–29 May 2002. Halle/Saale: Max Planck Institute for Social Anthropology.

———. 2012. '"Every Name Has its Path": Imagining and Achieving Fulbe Entanglement in a Moose Community', *Africa* 82(3): 457–78.

———. 2013. 'Mossi-Fulbe Borderlands: Towards a History of Interconnectedness', in S. Van Wolputte (ed.), *Borderlands and Frontiers in Africa.* Münster: LIT Verlag, pp. 55–89.

Breusers, M., S. Nederlof and T. van Rheenen. 1998. 'Conflict or Symbiosis? Disentangling Farmer-Herdsman Relations: The Mossi and Fulbe of the Central Plateau, Burkina Faso', *Journal of Modern African Studies* 36(3): 357–80.

Bruijn, M.E. de. 2000. 'Rapports interethniques et identité: l'exemple des pasteurs peuls et des cultivateurs hummbeebe au Mali central', in Y. Diallo and G. Schlee (eds), *L'ethnicité peule dans des contextes nouveaux: la dynamique des frontières.* Paris: Karthala, pp. 15–36.

Byrne, D., and G.L. Clore. 1970. 'A Reinforcement Model of Evaluative Responses', *Personality: An International Journal* 1: 103–28.

Campbell, J.K. 1964. *Honour, Family and Patronage: A Study of Institutions and Moral Values in a Greek Mountain Community.* Oxford: Clarendon Press.

Carbonnel, J.-P. 1991. 'L'orpaillage au Burkina Faso et au Mali', in E. Le Bris, E. Le Roy and P. Mathieu (eds), *L'appropriation de la terre en Afrique noire.* Paris: Karthala, pp. 122–30.

Carrier, J.G. 1999. 'People Who Can Be Friends: Selves and Social Relationships', in S. Bell and S. Coleman (eds), *The Anthropology of Friendship.* Oxford: Berg Publishers, pp. 21–38.

Carsten, J. 1997. *The Heat of the Hearth: The Process of Kinship in a Malay Fishing Community.* Oxford: Clarendon Press.

———. 2000 (ed.). *Cultures of Relatedness: New Approaches to the Study of Kinship.* Cambridge: Cambridge University Press.

Chaker, S. 1988. *Etudes touarègues. Bilan des recherches en sciences sociales.* Aix-en-Provence: Edisud.

Chauveau, J.-P. 1978. 'Contribution à la géographie historique de l'or en pays baule (Côte d'Ivoire)', *Journal des Africanistes* 48(1): 15–70.

———. 2006. 'How Does an Institution Evolve? Land, Politics, Intergenerational Relations and the Institution of the *tutorat* amongst Autochthones and Immigrants (Gban Region, Côte d'Ivoire)', in R. Kuba and C. Lentz (eds), *Land and the Politics of Belonging in West Africa*. Leiden: Brill, pp. 213–40.

Cohen, A. 1965. 'The Social Organisation of Credit in a West African Cattle Market', *Africa* 35(1): 8–20.

———. 1966. 'Politics of the Kola Trade', *Africa* 36(1): 18–35.

———. 1971. 'Cultural Strategies in the Organisation of Trading Diasporas', in C. Meillassoux (ed.), *The Development of Indigenous Trade and Markets in West Africa*. London: Longman Group Ltd, pp. 266–81.

Cohen, Y.A. 1961. 'Patterns of Friendship', in Y.A. Cohen (ed.), *Social Structure and Personality: A Casebook*. New York: Holt, Rinehart and Winston, pp. 351–86.

Dahl, R. 1986. 'Power as the Control of Behavior', in S. Lukes (ed.), *Power*. New York: New York University Press, pp. 37–58.

De Boeck, F. 1998. 'Domesticating Diamonds and Dollars: Identity, Expenditure and Sharing in Southwestern Zaire (1984–1997)', *Development and Change* 29(4): 777–810.

De Sousberghe, L. 1986. *Don et contre-don de la vie: structures élémentaires de parenté et union préférentielle*. Sankt Augustin: Anthropos Institute.

Desai, A., and E. Killick (eds.). 2010. *The Ways of Friendship: Anthropological Perspectives*. New York, Oxford: Berghahn Books.

Descartes, R. 1960 [1637]. *Discourse on Method and Meditations* (trans. L.J. Lafleur). New York: *Macmillan*.

Descharmes, B., E.A. Heuser, C. Krüger and T. Loy (eds.). 2011. *Varieties of Friendship: Interdisciplinary Perspectives on Social Relationships*. Göttingen: V&R unipress.

Devere, H. 2007. 'Cross-Cultural Understandings in the Language and Politics of Friendship', *Canadian Social Science* 3(6): 14–29.

Diabate, M.M. 1979. *Le lieutenant de Kouta*. Paris: Hatier.

Diallo, Y. 2000. 'Les Peuls et les Sénoufo de la savane ivoirienne: quelques modalités de leurs relations', in Y. Diallo and G. Schlee (eds), *L'ethnicité peule dans des contextes nouveaux: la dynamique des frontières*. Paris: Karthala, pp. 65–91.

———. 2006. 'Joking Relationships in Western Burkina Faso', *Zeitschrift für Ethnologie* 131(2): 183–96.

———. 2008. *Nomades des espaces interstitiels: pastoralisme, identité, migrations (Burkina Faso – Côte d'Ivoire)*. Köln: Rüdiger Köppe Verlag.

Dijk, H. van. 1994. 'Livestock Transfer and Social Security in Fulbe Society in the Hayre, Central Mali', *Focaal: European Journal of Anthropology* 22–23: 97–12.

Dim Delobsom, A.A. 1932. *L'empire du Mogho-Naba. Coutumes des Mossi de la Haute-Volta*. Paris: Domat-Montchrestien.

Diop, B. 1961. *Les contes d'Amadou Koumba*. Paris: Présence Africaine.

Donahue, S. 2002. 'The Other Harken Energy Scandal', *Counterpunch*, 12–14 July 2002. Web version: http://www.counterpunch.org/donahue0712.html (last accessed November 2009).

Du Bois, C. 1974. 'The Gratuitous Act: An Introduction to the Comparative Study of Friendship Patterns', in E. Leyton (ed.), *The Compact: Selected Dimensions of Friendship*. St. Johns: Memorial University of Newfoundland, Institute of Social and Economic Research (Newfoundland Social and Economic Papers No. 3), pp. 15–32.

Du Boulay, J. 1976. 'Lies, Mockery and Family Integrity', in J.G. Peristiany (ed.), *Mediterranean Family Structures*. Cambridge: Cambridge University Press, pp. 389–406.

Dumett, R.E. 1999. *El Dorado in West Africa: The Gold-Mining Frontier, African Labour and Colonial Capitalism in the Gold Coast, 1875–1900*. Athens: Ohio University Press.

Durkheim, E. 1947 [1893]. *The Division of Labor in Society* (trans. G. Simpson). New York: Free Press.

———. 1966 [1895]. *The Rules of the Sociological Method* (trans. S. Solovay and J. Mueller). New York: Free Press.

Dyson, J. 2010. 'Friendship in Practice: Girls' Work in the Indian Himalayas', *American Ethnologist* 37(3): 482–98.

Echenberg, M. 1991. *Colonial Conscripts*. Portsmouth, NH: Heinemann.

Eisenstadt, S.N. 1956. 'Ritualized Personal Relations. Blood Brotherhood, Best Friends, Compadre, etc.: Some Comparative Hypotheses and Suggestions', *Man* 56: 90–95.

———. 1974. 'Friendship and the Structure of Trust and Solidarity in Society', in E. Leyton (ed.), *The Compact: Selected Dimensions of Friendship*. St. Johns: Memorial University of Newfoundland, Institute of Social and Economic Research (Newfoundland Social and Economic Papers No. 3), pp. 138–45.

Eisenstadt, S.N., and L. Roninger. 1999. *Patrons, Clients and Friends: Interpersonal Relations and the Structure of Trust in Society*. Cambridge: Cambridge University Press.

Epstein, A.L. 1969a. 'The Network and Urban Social Organisation', in J.C. Mitchell (ed.), *Social Networks in Urban Situations. Analysis of Personal Relationships in Central African Towns*. Manchester: Manchester University Press, pp. 77–116.

———. 1969b. 'Gossip, Norms and Social Networks', in J.C. Mitchell (ed.), *Social Networks in Urban Situations. Analysis of Personal Relationships in Central African Towns*. Manchester: Manchester University Press, pp. 117–27.

Eve, M. 2002. 'Is Friendship a Sociological Topic?', *Archives Européennes de Sociologie* 43(3): 386–409.
Evens, T.M.S, and D. Handelman (eds). 2006. *The Manchester School: Practice and Ethnographic Praxis in Anthropology.* New York, Oxford: Berghahn Books.
Firth, R. 1957. *Man and Culture: An Evaluation of the Work of Malinowski.* London: Routledge and Kegan Paul.
Fischer, C.S. 1982. 'What Do We Mean by 'Friend'? An Inductive Study', *Social Networks* 3(4): 287–306.
Fortes, M. 1949. *The Web of Kinship among the Tallensi: The Second Part of an Analysis of the Social Structure of a Trans-Volta Tribe.* Oxford: Oxford University Press.
———. 1969. *Kinship and the Social Order: The Legacy of Lewis Henri Morgan.* London: Routledge and Kegan Paul.
Freud, S. 1931 [1910]. *Totem and Taboo: Resemblances between Psychic Lives of Savages and Neurotics.* New York: New Republic.
Fumanti, M. 2003. 'Youth, Elites and Distinction in a Northern Namibian Town', Ph.D. dissertation. Manchester: University of Manchester, Department of Social Anthropology.
———. 2007. 'Burying E.S.: Educated Elites, Subjectivity and Distinction in Rundu, Namibia', *Journal of Southern African Studies* 33(3): 469–83.
———. in press. *The Politics of Distinction: Youth, Elites and the Moral Public Space in Northern Namibia.* Canon Pyon, Herefordshire: Sean Kingston Publishing.
Gareis, E. 1995. *Intercultural Friendship: A Qualitative Study.* Lanham: University Press of America.
Garrard, T.F. 1980. *Akan Weights and the Gold Trade.* London: Longman Group Ltd.
Gebre, A. 1997. 'Arbore Inter-Tribal Relations: An Historical Account', in R. Hogg (ed.), *Pastoralists, Ethnicity and the State in Ethiopia.* London: Haan Publishing, pp. 143–67.
Ghannam, F. 2011. 'Mobility, Liminality, and Embodiment in Urban Egypt', *American Ethnologist* 38(4): 790–800.
Gilmore, D.C. 1975. 'Friendship in Fuenmayor: Patterns of Integration in an Atomistic Society', *Ethnology* 14(4): 311–24.
———. 1998. *Carnival and Culture: Sex, Symbol and Status in Spain.* New Haven: Yale University Press.
Girke, F. 2010. 'Bondfriendship in the Cultural Neighborhood. Dynamic Ties and their Public Appreciation in South Omo', in E.C. Gabbert and S. Thubauville (eds), *To Live with Others. Essays on Cultural Neighborhood in Southern Ethiopia.* Köln: Rüdiger Köppe Verlag, pp. 67–98.
Gist, N., and S. Fava. 1974. *Urban Society.* New York: Crowell.

Gluckman, M. 1965. *The Ideas in Barotse Jurisprudence*. New Haven: Yale University Press.

Grätz, T. 2002a. 'Gold-Mining Communities in Northern Benin as Semi-Autonomous Social Fields', *Working Paper* No. 36. Halle/Saale: Max Planck Institute for Social Anthropology.

———. 2002b. 'Friendship and Social Integration among Gold-Miners in West Africa', workshop 'Friendship, Descent and Alliance. New Perspectives on Social Integration and Dissociation in Changing African Societies', Halle/Saale, 16–18 December 2002. Halle/Saale: Max Planck Institute for Social Anthropology.

———. 2003a. 'Gold-Mining and Risk Management: A Case Study from Northern Benin', *Ethnos* 68(2): 192–208.

———. 2003b. 'Les chercheurs d'or et la construction d'identités de migrants en Afrique de l'Ouest', *Politique africaine* 91: 155–69.

———. 2004a. 'Friendship Ties among Young Artisanal Gold-Miners in Northern Benin (West Africa)', *Afrika spectrum* 39(1): 95–117.

———. 2004b. 'Gold Trading Networks and the Creation of Trust: A Case Study from Northern Benin', *Africa* 74(2): 146–72.

———. 2009. 'Moralities, Risks and Rules in Artisanal Gold Mining in West Africa. The Example of Northern Benin', *Resources Policy* 34(1–2): 12–17.

———. 2010. *Goldgräber in Westafrika*. Berlin: Dietrich Reimer Verlag.

———. 2011a. 'Social-Anthropological Perspectives on Friendship in Africa', in B. Descharmes, E.A. Heuser, C. Krüger and T. Loy (eds), *Varieties of Friendship: Interdisciplinary Perspectives on Social Relationships*. Göttingen: V&R unipress, pp. 355–75.

———. 2011b. 'Orpaillage, droits d'usage et conflits sur les ressources. Etudes de cas au Bénin et au Mali', in E. Jul-Larsen, P.-J. Laurent, P.-Y. Le Meur and E. Léonard (eds), *Une anthropologie entre pouvoirs et histoire. Conversations autour de l'œuvre de Jean-Pierre Chauveau*. Paris: Karthala, pp. 303–24.

———. 2013. 'The "Frontier" Revisited: Gold Mining Camps and Mining Communities in West Africa', *Working Paper* No. 10. Berlin: Centre of Modern Oriental Studies.

Grätz, T., B. Meier and M. Pelican. 2004. 'Freundschaftsprozesse in Afrika aus sozial-anthropologischer Perspektive. Eine Einführung', *Afrika spectrum* 39(1): 9–39.

Granovetter, M. 1973. 'The Strength of Weak Ties', *American Journal of Sociology* 78(6): 1360–80.

———. 1983. 'The Strength of Weak Ties: A Network Theory Revisited', *Sociological Theory* 1: 201–33.

Griaule, M. 1948. 'L'alliance cathartique', *Africa* 28(4): 242–59.

Guichard, M. 2000. '"Something to Hide?" Reflections on Interethnic Relationships and Friendship Ties with Regard to the Fulbe of Northern Benin and

Northern Cameroon', Lecture given at the Max Planck Institute for Social Anthropology, Halle/Saale, 5 December 2000.

———. 2002. 'Überlegungen zu interethnischen Freundschaften bei den Fulbe Nordbenins und Nordkameruns', 18th Biennial Conference of the VAD (Vereinigung für Afrikawissenschaften in Deutschland [African Studies Association in Germany]), Hamburg, Germany, 25 May 2002.

———. 2007a. 'Freundschaft und Verwandtschaft: Zur Unterscheidung und Relevanz zweier Beziehungssysteme. Eine vergleichende Studie mit besonderer Berücksichtigung der Fulbe-Gesellschaft Nordkameruns', in *Max Planck Institute for Social Anthropology Report/Bericht 2007 – Abteilung I: Integration und Konflikt*. Halle/Saale: Max Planck Institute for Social Anthropology, pp. 116–20.

———. 2007b. 'Hoch bewertet und oft unterschätzt: Theoretische und empirische Einblicke in Freundschaftsbeziehungen aus sozialanthropologischer Perspektive', in J.F.K. Schmidt, M. Guichard, P. Schuster and F. Trillmich (eds), *Freundschaft und Verwandtschaft: Zur Unterscheidung und Verflechtung zweier Beziehungssysteme*. Konstanz: UVK Verlagsgesellschaft, pp. 313–42.

Guichard, M., P. Heady and W.G. Tadesse. 2003. 'Friendship, Kinship and the Bases of Social Organisation', in *Max Planck Institute for Social Anthropology Report 2002–2003*. Halle/Saale: Max Planck Institute for Social Anthropology, pp. 7–17.

Gulliver, P.H. 1955. *The Family Herds: A Study of Two Pastoral Tribes in East Africa, the Jie and Turkana*. London: Routledge and Kegan Paul.

———. 1971. *Neighbours and Networks: The Idiom of Kinship in Social Action among the Ndendeuli of Tanzania*. Berkeley: University of California Press.

Hagberg, S. 2006. 'The Politics of Joking Relationships in Burkina Faso', *Zeitschrift für Ethnologie* 131(2): 197–214.

Hallpike, C.R. 1972. *The Konso of Ethiopia: A Study of the Values of a Cushitic People*. Oxford: Clarendon Press.

Hayward, R. 2003. 'Arbore. Arbore Language', in S. Uhlig (ed.), *Encyclopedia Aethiopica*, Vol. 1, A–C. Wiesbaden: Harrassowitz Verlag, pp. 317–18.

Hentschel, T., F. Hruschka and M. Priester. 2003. *Artisanal and Small-Scale Mining: Challenges and Opportunities*. Retrieved January 2014 from http://www.commdev.org/userfiles/files/1044_file_artisanal.pdf. London: International Institute for Environment and Development & World Business Council for Sustainable Development.

Héritier-Augé, F. 1994. 'Identité de substance et parenté de lait dans le monde arabe', in P. Bonte (ed.), *Epouser au plus proche. Inceste, prohibitions et stratégies matrimoniales autour de la Méditerranée*. Paris: Editions de l'Ecole des Hautes Etudes en Sciences Sociales (EHESS), pp. 149–64.

Héritier-Augé, F., and E. Copet-Rougier (eds). 1990. *Les complexités de l'alliance. Les systèmes semi-complexes*. Paris: Editions des Archives Contemporaines.

Hill, L., and P. McCarthy. 2004. 'On Friendship and *necessitudo* in Adam Smith', *History of the Human Sciences* 17(1): 1–16.
Hilson, G.M. (ed.) 2006. *Small-Scale Mining, Rural Subsistence and Poverty in West Africa*. Rugby: Practical Action Publishing.
Hiskett, M. 1984. *The Development of Islam in West Africa*. London: Longman Group Ltd.
Hobbes, T. 1971. 'Of Power', in J.R. Champlin (ed.), *Power*. New York: Atherton Press, pp. 69–77.
Homans, G.C. 1961. *Social Behaviour: Its Elementary Forms*. London: Routledge and Kegan Paul.
Houis, M. 1963. *Les noms individuels chez les Mosi*. Dakar: IFAN.
Hruschka, D.J. 2010. *Friendship: Development, Ecology and Evolution of a Relationship*. Los Angeles: University of California Press.
Izard, M. 1970. *Introduction à l'histoire des royaumes mossi*, Vol. 1–2. Paris, Ouagadougou: CNRS/CVRS (Recherches Voltaïques No. 12–13).
———. 1982. 'La politique extérieure d'un royaume africain: le Yatenga au XIXe siècle', *Cahiers d'Etudes africaines* 23(3–4): 363–85.
———. 1992. *L'odyssée du pouvoir. Un royaume africain: Etat, société, destin individuel*. Paris: Editions de l'Ecole des Hautes Etudes en Sciences Sociales (EHESS).
———. 2003. *Moogo: l'émergence d'un espace étatique ouest-africain au XVIe siècle*. Paris: Karthala.
Jacobson, D. 1973. *Itinerant Townsmen: Friendship and Social Order in Urban Uganda*. Menlo Park: Cummings.
Junehui, A. 2011. '"You're My Friend Today, but Not Tomorrow": Learning to Be Friends among Young U.S. Middle-Class Children', *American Ethnologist* 38(2): 294–306.
Kaba, L. 1974. *The Wahhabiyya: Islamic Reform and Politics in French West Africa*. Evanston: Northwestern University Press.
Kennedy, R. 1986. 'Women's Friendships on Crete: A Psychological Perspective', in J. Dubisch (ed.), *Gender and Power in Rural Greece*. Princeton: Princeton University Press, pp. 121–38.
Kerr, A. 1995. *Farming Systems in the African Savanna: A Continent in Crisis*. Ottawa: International Development Research Centre.
Khatib-Chahidi, J. 1993. 'Milk Kinship in Shi'ite Islamic Iran', in V.A. Maher (ed.), *The Anthropology of Breast-Feeding: Natural Law or Social Construct*. Oxford: Berg Publishers, pp. 109–32.
Kiethega, J.-B. 1983. *L'or de la Volta Noire*. Paris: Karthala.
Killick, E. 2010. '*Ayompari, Compadre, Amigo*: Forms of Fellowship in Peruvian Amazonia', in A. Desai and E. Killick (eds), *The Ways of Friendship: Anthropological Perspectives*. New York, Oxford: Berghahn Books, pp. 46–68.

Killick, E., and A. Desai. 2010. 'Valuing Friendship', in A. Desai, and E. Killick (eds), *The Ways of Friendship: Anthropological Perspectives*. New York, Oxford: Berghahn Books, pp. 1–19.

Klute, G. 1991. 'Die Revolte der Ishumagh', in T. Scheffler (ed.), *Ethnizität und Gewalt*. Hamburg: Deutsches Orient-Institut, pp. 134–49.

———. 1994. 'Flucht, Karawane, Razzia. Formen der Arbeitsmigration bei den Tuareg', in M. Laubscher and B. Turner (eds), *Systematische Ethnologie. Völkerkundetagung 1991, München*. München: Edition anacon, pp. 197–216.

———. 1995. 'Hostilités et alliances. Archéologie de la dissidence des Touaregs au Mali', *Cahiers d'Etudes africaines* 137, 35(1): 55–71.

———. 2001. 'Die Rebellionen der Tuareg in Mali und Niger', Habilitation thesis. Siegen: University of Siegen, Department of Sociology.

———. 2003. 'L'islamisation du Sahara (re)mise en scène. Les idéologies légitimatrices dans la guerre fratricide des Touareg maliens', in L. Marfaing and S. Wippel (eds), *Les relations transsahariennes à l'époque contemporaine. Un espace en constante mutation*. Paris: Karthala, pp. 361–78.

———. 2009. 'The Technique of Modern Chariots: About Speed and Mobility in Contemporary Small Wars in the Sahara', in J.B. Gewald, S. Luning and K. van Walraven (eds), *The Speed of Change. Motor Vehicles and People in Africa, 1890–2000*. Leiden: Brill, pp. 191–211.

———. 2011. 'From Friends to Enemies: Negotiating Nationalism, Tribal Identities, and Kinship in the Fratricidal War of the Malian Tuareg', *L'Année du Maghreb* VII (Thematic issue 'Sahara en mouvement: protestations sociales et 'révolutions'. Le Maghreb à la croisée des chemins', co-ordinated by D. Casajus): 163–75.

———. 2013. 'Post-Gaddafi Repercussions, Global Islam or Local Logics? Anthropological Perspectives on the Recent Events in Northern Mali', in L. Koechlin and T. Förster (eds), *Mali – Impressions of the Current Crisis/Mali – impressions de la crise actuelle* (Basel Papers on Political Transformations No. 5). Basel: University of Basel, Institute of Social Anthropology, pp. 7–13.

Klute, G., and T. von Trotha. 2004. 'Roads to Peace. From Small War to Parastatal Peace in the North of Mali', in M.-C. Foblets and T. von Trotha (eds), *Healing the Wounds. Essays on the Reconstruction of Societies after War*. Oxford: Oñati Institute for the Sociology of Law (Oñati International Series in Law and Society), pp. 109–43.

Labouret, H. 1929. 'La parenté à plaisanterie en Afrique occidentale', *Africa* 2: 244–54.

Lallemand, S. 1977. *Une famille mossi*. Paris, Ouagadougou: CNRS/CVRS (Recherches Voltaïques 17).

Launay, R. 1982. *Traders Without Trade*. Cambridge: Cambridge University Press.

Lawler, N. 1992. *Soldiers of Misfortune*. Athens, Ohio: University of Ohio Press.

Leach, E. R. 1970. *Lévi-Strauss*. London: Fontana/Collins.
Lentz, C. 1994. 'Home, Death and Leadership: Discourses of an Educated Elite from North-Western Ghana', *Social Anthropology* 2(2): 149–69.
Leupen, A.H.A. 1978. *Bibliographie des populations touarègues*. Leiden: African Studies Centre.
Lévi-Strauss, C. 1969 [1949]. *The Elementary Structures of Kinship*. London: Eyre and Spottiswoode.
Leyton, E. 1974. 'Irish Friends and 'Friends': The Nexus of Friendship, Kinship and Class in Aughnaboy', in E. Leyton (ed.), *The Compact: Selected Dimensions of Friendship*. St. Johns: Memorial University of Newfoundland, Institute of Social and Economic Research (Newfoundland Social and Economic Papers No. 3), pp. 93–104.
Liebow, E. 1967. *Tally's Corner: A Study of Negro Streetcorner Men*. Boston: Little, Brown and Company.
Little, K. 1965. *West African Urbanization: A Study of Voluntary Associations in Social Change*. Cambridge: Cambridge University.
———. 1967. 'Voluntary Associations in Urban Life: A Case Study of Differential Adaptation', in M. Freedman (ed.), *Social Organization: Essays Presented to Raymond Firth*. London: Frank Cass and Company, pp. 153–65.
Loizos, P., and E. Papataxiarchis. 1991. 'Introduction: Gender and Kinship in Marriage and Alternative Context', in P. Loizos and E. Papataxiarchis (eds), *Contested Identities: Gender and Kinship in Modern Greece*. Princeton: Princeton University Press, pp. 3–25.
Lovejoy, P. 1980. *Caravans of Kola*. Zaria: Amadou Bello University Press.
Luning, S. n.d. 'The Gender of the Joke: Wives and Female Husbands in Maane, Burkina Faso', unpublished manuscript. Leiden.
———. 2006. 'Artisanal Gold Mining in Burkina Faso: Permits, Poverty and Perceptions of the Poor in Sanmatenga, the "Land of Gold"', in G. Hilson (ed.), *Small-Scale Mining, Rural Subsistence and Poverty in West Africa*. Rugby: Practical Action Publishing, pp. 135–47.
———. 2008. 'Gold Mining in Sanmatenga, Burkina Faso: Governing Sites, Appropriating Wealth', in J. Abbink and A. van Dokkum (eds), *Dilemmas of Development: Conflicts of Interest and their Resolutions in Modernizing Africa*. Leiden: African Studies Centre, pp. 195–211.
———. 2010. 'Beyond the Pale of Property: Gold Miners Meddling with Mountains in Burkina Faso', in C. Panella (ed.), *Worlds of Debts: Interdisciplinary Perspectives on Gold Mining in West Africa*. Amsterdam: Rozenberg, pp. 25–48.
Lunn, J. 1999. *Memories of the Maelstrom*. Portsmouth, NH: Heinemann.
Lynch, M. 2000. 'Against Reflexivity as an Academic Virtue and Source of Privileged Knowledge', *Theory, Culture & Society* 17(3): 26–54.

Malinowski, B. 1939. 'The Group and the Individual in Functional Analysis', *American Journal of Sociology* 44: 938–64.

Mann, G. 2006. *Native Sons: West African Veterans and France in the Twentieth Century.* Durham: Duke University Press.

Marchal, J.-Y. 1983. *Yatenga (Nord Haute-Volta): la dynamique d'un espace soudano-sahélien.* Paris: ORSTOM.

Martinelli, B. 1999. 'Logiques masculines et féminines de l'amitié chez les Moose du Burkina Faso', in G. Ravis-Giordani (ed.), *Amitiés. Anthropologie et histoire.* Aix-en-Provence: Publications de l'Université de Provence, pp. 355–85.

Marx, K. 1909 [1867]. *Capital,* Vol. 1. New York: Modern Library.

Mauss, M. 1969 [1928]. 'Parenté à plaisanteries', in M. Mauss, *Oeuvres,* Vol. 3. Paris: Editions de Minuit, pp. 109–24.

———. 1990 [1923–1924]. *The Gift. The Form and Function of Exchange in Archaic Societies.* New York: W.W. Norton.

Meier, B. 2004. 'Nähe und Distanz: Freundschaften bei nordghanaischen Migranten in Accra/Tema', *Afrika spectrum* 39(1): 41–62.

Meillassoux, C. 1968. *Urbanization of an African Community: Voluntary Associations in Bamako.* Seattle: University of Washington Press.

Meker, M. 1980. *Le temps colonial.* Dakar: Nouvelles Editions Africaines.

Merker, M. 1904. *Die Masai: ethnographische Monographie eines afrikanischen Semitenvolkes.* Berlin: Dietrich Reimer Verlag.

Mitchell, J.C. 1969. 'The Concept and Use of Social Networks', in J.C. Mitchell (ed.), *Social Networks in Urban Situations. Analysis of Personal Relationships in Central African Towns.* Manchester: Manchester University Press, pp. 1–50.

———. 1974. 'Social Networks', *Annual Review of Anthropology* 3: 279–99.

Mizen, P., and Y. Osofu-Kusi. 2010. 'Asking, Giving, Receiving: Friendship as Survival Strategy among Accra's Street Children', *Childhood* 17(4): 441–54.

Morewagae, I. 2011a. 'Big Shots Seek Out-of-Court Settlement', *Mmegi Online* 28(179) 29 November 2011. Retrieved 30 January 2013 from http://www.mmegi.bw/index.php?sid=1&aid=296&dir=2011/November/Tuesday29.

———. 2011b. 'Big Shots' Wrangle Ends – At Last?', *Mmegi Online* 28(180), 30 November 2011. Retrieved 30 January 2013 from http://www.mmegi.bw/index.php?sid=1&aid=329&dir=2011/November/Wednesday30.

Morgan, A. 2012. 'The Causes of the Uprising in Northern Mali', *Think Africa Press,* 6 February 2012. Retrieved January 2013 from http://thinkafricapress.com/mali/causes-uprising-northern-mali-tuareg.

Morris, L. 1984. 'Patterns of Social Activity and Post-Redundancy Labour-Market Experience'. *Sociology* 18(3): 339–52.

Mühlmann, W.E. 1940. *Krieg und Frieden. Ein Leitfaden der politischen Ethnologie. Mit Berücksichtigung völkerkundlichen und geschichtlichen Stoffes.* Heidelberg: Carl Winter's Universitätsbuchhandlung.

Nardi, P.M. 1992. '"Seamless Souls": An Introduction to Men's Friendships', in P.M. Nardi (ed.), *Men's Friendships*. Newbury Park: SAGE, pp. 1–14.

Nietzsche, F. 1967 [1901]. *The Will to Power*. New York: Random House.

———. 1974 [1882]. *The Gay Science*. New York: Random House.

Nyamnjoh, F. 2002. '"A Child Is One Person's Only in the Womb": Domestication, Agency and Subjectivity in the Cameroonian Grassfields', in R. Werbner (ed.), *Postcolonial Subjectivities in Africa*. London: Zed Books, pp. 111–38.

Obeid, M. 2010. 'Friendship, Kinship and Sociality in a Lebanese Town', in A. Desai and E. Killick (eds), *The Ways of Friendship: Anthropological Perspectives*. New York, Oxford: Berghahn Books, pp. 93–113.

O'Connor, P. 1992. *Friendships between Women: A Critical Review*. New York: Guilford Press.

Ogembo, J. 2002. 'Friendship and Kinship in the Vicissitudes of Daily Life in Gusii', workshop 'Friendship, Descent and Alliance. New Perspectives on Social Integration and Dissociation in Changing African Societies', Halle/Saale, 16–18 December 2002. Halle/Saale: Max Planck Institute for Social Anthropology.

Pahl, R. 2000. *On Friendship*. Cambridge: Polity Press.

Paine, R. 1969. 'In Search of Friendship: An Exploratory Analysis in "Middle-Class" Culture', *Man* 4: 505–24.

———. 1974. 'Anthropological Approaches to Friendship', in E. Leyton (ed.), *The Compact: Selected Dimensions of Friendship*. St. Johns: Memorial University of Newfoundland, Institute of Social and Economic Research (Newfoundland Social and Economic Papers No. 3), pp. 1–14.

Panella, C. (ed.). 2010. *Worlds of Debts: Interdisciplinary Perspectives on Gold Mining in West Africa*. Amsterdam: Rozenberg Publishers.

Parkes, P. 2004. 'Milk Kinship in Southeast Europe. Alternative Social Structures and Foster Relations in the Caucasus and the Balkans', *Social Anthropology* 12(3): 341–58.

———. 2005. 'Milk Kinship in Islam. Substance, Structure, History', *Social Anthropology* 13(3): 307–29.

Parsons, T. 1951. *The Social System*. New York: Free Press.

Pankhurst, A. 2006. 'A Peace Ceremony at Arbore', in I. Strecker (ed.), *The Perils of Face: Essays on Cultural Contact, Respect and Self-Esteem in Southern Ethiopia*. Berlin: LIT Verlag (Mainzer Beiträge zur Afrika-Forschung 10), pp. 247–67.

Paulme, D. 1939. 'Parenté à plaisanterie et alliance par le sang en Afrique occidentale', *Africa* 12(4): 433–44.

Pelican, M. 2004. 'Frauen- und Männerfreundschaften im Kameruner Grasland: Ein komparativer Ansatz', *Afrika spectrum* 39(1): 63–93.

———. 2012. 'Friendship among Pastoral Fulbe in Northwest Cameroon', *African Study Monographs* 33(3): 165–88.

Perinbaum, B.M. 1972. 'Trade and Society in the Western Sahara and the Western Sudan: An Overview', *Bulletin de l'IFAN* (Series B) 34: 778–801.

Pillet-Schwartz, A.-M. 1993. *Système de production, identité ethnique et qualité de survie dans l'ancien Liptako. Genèse d'une région sahélienne.* Paris: CNRS.

Pina-Cabral, J. de, and A.P. de Lima. 2000. *Elites, Choice, Leadership and Succession.* Oxford: Berg Publishers.

Piot, C.D. 1991. 'Of Persons and Things: Some Reflections on African Spheres of Exchange', *Man* 26(3): 405–24.

Pitt-Rivers, J. 1973. 'The Kith and the Kin', in J. Goody (ed.), *The Character of Kinship.* Cambridge: Cambridge University Press, pp. 89–105.

Pritchett, J.A. 2007. *Friends for Life, Friends for Death. Cohorts and Consciousness among the Lunda-Ndembu.* Charlottesville: University of Virginia Press.

Putnam, R. 2000. *Bowling Alone: The Collapse and Revival of the American Community.* New York: Simon & Schuster.

Putnam, R., and L. Feldstein. 2003. *Better Together: Restoring the American Community.* New York: Simon & Schuster.

Radcliffe-Brown, A.R. 1940. 'On Joking Relationship', *Africa* 13(3): 195–210.

———. 1949. 'A Further Note on Joking Relationship', *Africa* 19(2): 133–40.

Ramsøy, O. 1968. 'Friendship', in D. Sills (ed.), *International Encyclopedia of the Social Sciences.* New York: Crowell Collier and Macmillan, Vol. 6, pp. 12–17.

Ravis-Giordani, G. (ed.). 1999a. *Amitiés – Anthropologie et histoire.* Aix-en-Provence: Publications de l'Université de Provence.

———. 1999b. 'Le pain, le pouvoir et la grâce', in G. Ravis-Giordani (ed.), *Amitiés – Anthropologie et histoire.* Aix-en-Provence: Publications de l'Université de Provence, pp. 77–98.

Reed-Danahay, D. 1999. 'Friendship, Kinship and the Life Course in Rural Auvergne', in S. Bell and S. Coleman (eds), *The Anthropology of Friendship.* Oxford: Berg Publishers, pp. 137–54.

Rein, G.K. 1919. *Abessinien. Eine Landeskunde nach Reisen und Studien in den Jahren 1907–1913.* Berlin: Dietrich Reimer Verlag.

Reina, R.E. 1959. 'Two Patterns of Friendship in a Guatemalan Community', *American Anthropologist* 61: 44–50.

Reyna, S.P. 2001. 'Force, Power, and String Being?', *Working Paper* No. 20. Halle/Saale: Max Planck Institute for Social Anthropology.

———. 2002. *Connections: Brain, Mind, and Culture in a Social Anthropology.* London: Routledge.

———. 2003. 'Force, Power, and the Problem of Order: An Anthropological Approach', *Sociologus* 3(2): 199–223.

———. 2004. 'Hard Truth and Validation: What Zeus Understood', *Working Paper* No. 65. Halle/Saale: Max Planck Institute for Social Anthropology.

———. 2006. 'What Is Interpretation? A Cultural Neurohermeneutic Account', *Focaal: European Journal of Anthropology* 48: 131–43.
Riesman, P. 1974. *Société et liberté chez les Peul Djelgôbé de Haute-Volta. Essai d'anthropologie introspective.* Paris, La Haye: Mouton.
Rodgers, G. 2010. 'Friendship, Distance and Kinship-Talk amongst Mozambican Refugees in South Africa', in A. Desai and E. Killick (eds), *The Ways of Friendship: Anthropological Perspectives.* New York, Oxford: Berghahn Books, pp. 69–92.
Rogers, S.C., and S. Salamon. 1983. 'Inheritance and Social Organization among Family Farmers', *American Ethnologist* 10(3): 529–50.
Rusbult, C.E. 1980. 'Satisfaction and Commitment in Friendships', *Representative Research in Social Psychology* 11: 96–105.
Sagawa, T. 2010. 'Local Potential for Peace. Trans-Ethnic Cross-Cutting Ties among the Daasanech and their Neighbours', in E.C. Gabbert and S. Thubauville (eds), *To Live with Others. Essays on Cultural Neighborhood in Southern Ethiopia.* Köln: Rüdiger Köppe Verlag, pp. 99–127.
Sahlins, M. 1972. *Stone Age Economics.* Chicago: Aldine.
Santos, G.S. 2010. 'On "Same-Year Siblings" in Rural South China', in A. Desai and E. Killick (eds), *The Ways of Friendship: Anthropological Perspectives.* New York, Oxford: Berghahn Books, pp. 21–45.
Santos-Granero, F. 2007. 'Of Fear and Friendship: Amazonian Sociality beyond Kinship and Affinity', *Journal of the Royal Anthropological Institute* 13(1): 1–18.
Savage, M., and K. Williams. 2008. *Remembering Elites.* Oxford: Blackwell (Sociological Review Monograph Series).
Schlee, G. 1984. 'Intra- und interethnische Beziehungsnetze nordkenianischer Wanderhirten', *Paideuma* 30: 69–80.
———. 1989. 'The Orientation of Progress: Conflicting Aims and Strategies of Pastoral Nomads and Development Agents in East Africa – A Problem Survey', in E. Linnebuhr (ed.), *Transition and Continuity of Identity in East Africa and Beyond – In memoriam David Miller.* Bayreuth: Bayreuth University, pp. 397–450.
———. 2008. *How Enemies Are Made. Towards a Theory of Ethnic and Religious Conflicts.* New York, Oxford: Berghahn Books (Series 'Integration and Conflict Studies').
———. 2012. 'Multiple Rights in Animals: An East African Overview', in A.M. Khazanov and G. Schlee (eds), *Who Owns the Stock? Collective and Multiple Property Rights in Animals.* New York, Oxford: Berghahn Books (Series 'Integration and Conflict Studies'), pp. 247–94.
Schmidt, J.F.K., M. Guichard, P. Schuster and F. Trillmich (eds). 2007. *Freundschaft und Verwandtschaft: Zur Unterscheidung und Verflechtung zweier Beziehungssysteme.* Konstanz: UVK Verlagsgesellschaft.

Schneider, K. 1990. 'Das Gold der Lobi. Aspekte historischer und ethnologischer Interpretation', *Paideuma* 36: 277–90.
Scholz, V., and U. Schultz. 1994. *Wir wollen Turkana-Frauen bleiben*. Münster: LIT Verlag.
Schuster, P., R. Stichweh, J. Schmidt, F. Trillmich, M. Guichard and G. Schlee. 2003. 'Freundschaft und Verwandtschaft als Gegenstand interdisziplinärer Forschung. Einleitung zum Themenschwerpunkt', *Sozialersinn: Zeitschrift für hermeneutische Sozialforschung* 1: 3–20.
Scott, J.C. 1976. *The Moral Economy of the Peasant: Rebellion and Subsistence in Southeast Asia*. New Haven: Yale University Press.
Seligman, A. 1997. *The Problem of Trust*. Princeton: Princeton University Press.
Silver, A. 1989. 'Friendship and Trust as Moral Ideals: An Historical Approach', *Archives Européennes de Sociologie* 30(2): 274–97.
———. 1990. 'Friendship in Commercial Society', *American Journal of Sociology* 95(6): 1474–1504.
———. 1997. '"Two Different Sorts of Commerce" – Friendship and Strangership in Civil Society', in J. Weintraub and K. Kumar (eds), *Public and Private in Thought and Practice: Perspectives on a Grand Dichotomy*. Chicago: University of Chicago Press, pp. 43–74.
Simmel, G. 1950. 'The Dyad and the Triad', in K.H. Wolff. (ed. and trans.), *The Sociology of Georg Simmel*. Glencoe: Free Press, pp. 139–45.
Sindzingre, N. 1985. 'Amis, parents, alliés: les formes de l'amitié chez les Senufo (Côte d'Ivoire)', *Culture, Canadian Ethnology Society* 5(2): 69–77.
Skinner, E.P. 1970. 'Processes of Political Incorporation in Mossi Society', in R. Cohen and J. Middleton (eds), *From Tribe to Nation in Africa. Studies in Incorporation Processes*. Scranton: Chandler, pp. 175–200.
Smith, A. 2002 [1759]. *The Theory of Moral Sentiments* (ed. by K. Haakonssen). Cambridge: Cambridge University Press.
Sobania, N.W. 1991. 'Feasts, Famines and Friends: Nineteenth Century Exchange and Ethnicity in the Eastern Lake Turkana Region', in J.G. Galaty and P. Bonte (eds), *Herders, Warriors, and Traders: Pastoralism in Africa*. Boulder: Westview Press, pp. 118–42.
Solway, J. 2002. 'Navigating the 'Neutral State': Minority Rights in Botswana', *Journal of Southern African Studies* 28(4): 711–30.
Some, B.B. 1971. 'Quelques composantes de la personne humaine chez deux populations de souche dagomba: les Mossi et les Dagara', *Notes et Documents Voltaïques* 5(1): 16–24.
Spencer, L., and R. Pahl. 2006. *Rethinking Friendship: Hidden Solidarities Today*. Princeton: Princeton University Press.
Spencer, P. 1965. *The Samburu: A Study of Gerontocracy*. London: Routledge and Kegan Paul.

———. 1988. *The Maasai of Matapato: A Study of Rituals of Rebellion*. Manchester: Manchester University Press.

Stack, C.B. 1974. *All Our Kin: Strategies for Survival in a Black Community*. New York: Harper and Row.

Stewart, F.H. 1977. *Fundamentals of Age-Group Systems*. New York: Academic Press.

Stone, L. 1997. *Kinship and Gender: An Introduction*. Boulder: Westview Press.

Strathern, M. 1984. 'Subject or Object? Women and the Circulation of Valuables in Highlands New Guinea', in R. Hirschon (ed.), *Women and Property – Women as Property*. London: Croom Helm, pp. 158–75.

Strecker, I., and A. Pankhurst. 2004. *Bury the Spear!* Göttingen: IWF Wissen und Medien GmbH (DVD video).

Susser, I. 1982. *Norman Street: Poverty and Politics in an Urban Neighborhood*. New York: Oxford University Press.

Tadesse, W.G. 1999. 'Warfare and Fertility: A Study of the Hor (Arbore) of Southern Ethiopia', Ph.D. dissertation. London: University of London, London School of Economics and Political Science, Department of Anthropology.

———. 2000. 'Entering Cattle Gates: Trade, Bond Friendship and Group Interdependence', *Northeast African Studies* (New Series) 7(3): 119–62.

Tamari, T. 2006. 'Joking Pacts in Sudanic West Africa: A Political and Historical Perspective', *Zeitschrift für Ethnologie* 131(2): 215–43.

Tauxier, L. 1917. *Le noir du Yatenga*. Paris: Larose.

Thibaut, J.W., and H.H. Kelley. 1959. *The Social Psychology of Groups*. New York: Wiley.

Thompson, E.P. 1991. *Customs in Common: Studies in Traditional Popular Culture*. London: Merlin Press Ltd.

Thubauville, S. 2010. 'Amity through Intermarriage. Some Outcomes of a Workshop on Intermarriage between the Maale, Aari and Banna People of Southern Ethiopia', in E.C. Gabbert and S. Thubauville (eds), *To Live with Others. Essays on Cultural Neighborhood in Southern Ethiopia*. Köln: Rüdiger Köppe Verlag, pp. 252–66.

Tönnies, F. 1968 [1887]. *Community and Society* (ed. and trans. G. Roth and C. Wittich). New York: Bedminster Press.

Turner, F.J. 1935 [1893]. *The Significance of the Frontier in American History*. New York: Henry Holt.

Tylor, E.B. 1889. 'On the Method of Investigating the Development of Institutions; Applied to the Laws of Marriage and Descent', *Journal of the Royal Anthropological Institute* 18: 245–69.

Ueno, K., and R.G. Adams. 2007. 'Friendship', in M. Flood, J.K. Gardiner, B. Pease and K. Pringle (eds), *International Encyclopedia of Men and Masculinities*. London: Routledge, pp. 216–20.

Uhl, S. 1991. 'Forbidden Friends: Cultural Veils of Female Friendship in Andalusia', *American Ethnologist* 18(1): 90–105.

Veblen, T. 1950 [1919]. 'The Intellectual Pre-Eminence of Jews in Modern Europe', in M. Lerner (ed.), *The Portable Veblen*. New York: Viking.

Vernier, B. 2006. 'Du bon usage de la parenté construite avec des humeurs corporelles (sang et lait) et quelques autres moyens', *European Journal of Turkish Studies* 4 (Thematic issue 'The Social Practices of Kinship. A Comparative Perspective'). Retrieved February 2013 from http://ejts.revues.org/623.

Vwakyanakazi, M. 1992. 'Creuseurs d'or et crise socio-économique au Nord-Kivu en République du Zaïre', *Africa* (Roma) 47(3): 375–91.

Walker, K. 1994. 'Men, Women, and Friendship: What They Say, What They Do', *Gender and Society* 8(2): 246–64.

Waller, R. 1985. 'Ecology, Migration, and Expansion in East Africa', *African Affairs* 84(336): 347–70.

Warms, R.L. 1987. 'Continuity and Change in Patterns of Trade in Southern Mali', Ph.D. dissertation. Syracuse University. Ann Arbor: University Microfilms International.

———. 1990. 'Who Are the Traders? Ethnic Identity and Trade in Southwestern Mali', *Ethnic Groups: An International Periodical of Ethnic Studies* 8(1): 57–72.

———. 1992. 'Merchants, Muslims, and Wahhābiyya: The Elaboration of Islamic Identity in Sikasso, Mali', *Canadian Journal of African Studies* 26(3): 485–507.

———. 1994. 'Commerce and Community: Paths to Success for Malian Merchants', *African Studies Review* 37(2): 97–120.

Watson, E.E., and L. Regassa. 2001. 'Konso: Living on the Edge', in D. Freeman and A. Pankhurst (eds), *Living on the Edge: Marginalised Minorities of Craftworkers and Hunters in Southern Ethiopia*. Addis Ababa: Addis Ababa University (Department of Sociology and Social Administration), pp. 246–64.

Weber, M. 1968 [1921]. *Economy and Society* (ed. and trans. G. Roth and C. Wittich). New York: Bedminster Press.

Werbner, P. 2010. 'Many Gateways to the Gateway City: Elites, Class and Policy Networking in the London African Diaspora', *African Diaspora* 3: 131–58.

Werbner, R. 1990. 'South-Central Africa: The Manchester School and After', in R. Fardon (ed.), *Localizing Strategies: Regional Traditions of Ethnography*. Edinburgh: Scottish Academic Press, pp. 152–81.

———. 2002a. 'Introduction. Postcolonial Subjectivities: The Personal, the Political and the Moral', in R. Werbner (ed.), *Postcolonial Subjectivities in Africa*. London: Zed Books, pp. 1–21.

———. 2002b. 'Citizenship and the Politics of Recognition', in I. Mazonde (ed.), *Minorities in the Millennium*. Gaborone: Lightbooks for the University of Botswana and the International Centre for Contemporary Cultural Research, 117–35.

———. 2002c. 'Introduction: Challenging Minorities, Difference and Tribal Citizenship in Botswana', *Journal of Southern African Studies* 28(4): 671–84.

———. 2002d. 'Cosmopolitan Ethnicity: Entrepreneurship and the Nation. Minority Elites in Botswana', *Journal of Southern African Studies* 28(4): 731–53.

———. 2004. *Reasonable Radicals and Citizenship in Botswana*. Bloomington: Indiana University Press.

———. 2008. 'Responding to Rooted Cosmopolitanism: Patriots, Ethnics and the Public Good in Botswana', in P. Werbner (ed.), *Anthropology and the New Cosmopolitanism: Rooted, Feminist and Vernacular Perspectives*. Oxford: Berg Publishers, pp. 173–96.

———. 2012. 'Africa's New Public Cosmopolitans', in G. Delanty (ed.), *Handbook of Cosmopolitan Studies*. London: Routledge, pp. 477–90.

Werthmann, K. 1997. *Nachbarinnen: Die Alltagswelt muslimischer Frauen in einer Großstadt*. Frankfurt am Main: Brandes & Apsel.

———. 2000. 'Gold Rush in West Africa. The Appropriation of 'Natural' Resources: Non-Industrial Gold-Mining in Southwestern Burkina Faso', *Sociologus* 50(1): 90–104.

———. 2003a. 'The President of the Gold-Diggers: Sources of Power in a Gold Mine in Burkina Faso', *Ethnos* 68(1): 95–111.

———. 2003b. 'Cowries, Gold and "Bitter Money": Gold-Mining and Notions of Ill-Gotten Wealth in Burkina Faso', *Paideuma* 49: 105–24.

———. 2008. '"Frivolous Squandering". Consumption and Redistribution in Mining Camps', in J. Abbink and A. van Dokkum (eds), *Dilemmas of Development: Conflicts of Interest and Their Resolutions in Modernizing Africa*. Leiden: African Studies Centre, pp. 60–76.

———. 2009. *Bitteres Gold. Bergbau, Land und Geld in Burkina Faso*. Köln: Rüdiger Köppe Verlag.

———. 2010. 'Following the Hills: Gold Mining Camps as Heterotopias', in U. Freitag and A. von Oppen (eds), *Translocality. The Study of Globalising Processes from a Southern Perspective*. Leiden: Brill, pp. 111–32.

Werthmann, K., and T. Grätz (eds.). 2013. *Mining Frontiers in Africa: Anthropological and Historical Perspectives*. Köln: Rüdiger Köppe Verlag.

Weston, K. 1991. *Families We Choose: Lesbians, Gays, Kinship*. New York: Columbia University Press.

White, C. 1990. 'Changing Animal Ownership and Access to Land among the Wodaabe (Fulani) of Central Niger', in P. Baxter and R. Hogg (eds), *Property, Poverty and People: Changing Rights in Property and Problems of Pastoral Development*. Manchester: University of Manchester, Department of Social Anthropology and International Development Centre, pp. 240–51.

Wolf, E.R. 1966. 'Kinship, Friendship and Patron-Client Relations in Complex Societies', in M. Banton (ed.), *The Social Anthropology of Complex Societies*. London: Tavistock Publications, pp. 1–22.

Wright, P.H. 1982. 'Men's Friendships, Women's Friendships and the Alleged Inferiority of the Latter', *Sex Roles* 8(1): 1–20.

Yaro, Y. 1996. 'Les jeunes chercheurs d'or d'Essakan: l'Eldorado burkinabé', in B. Schlemmer (ed.), *L'enfant exploité. Oppression, mise au travail et prolétarisation*. Paris: Karthala/ORSTOM, pp. 135–49.

Yarrow, T. 2011. *Development beyond Politics: Aid, Activism and NGOs in Ghana*. New York: Palgrave Macmillan.

Contributors

Mark Breusers is lecturer and researcher at the Institute for Anthropological Research in Africa, Catholic University of Leuven, where he teaches courses in economic anthropology and on cultures and development. He has conducted research in Benin and Burkina Faso on indigenous knowledge, rural livelihoods, land tenure, mobility and farmer-herdsman relations. He also works as a food security project manager with Caritas International in Brussels.

Tilo Grätz (Dr. phil. habil.) is an associate professor at the Institute of Social and Cultural Anthropology, Free University Berlin. He has been a postdoctoral fellow at the Max Planck Institute for Social Anthropology in Halle/Saale. He has conducted research in West Africa and Central Europe on topics ranging from migration, media and local-level politics to informal economies and friendship relations. Recent publications: *Mining Frontiers in Africa* (2013, ed. with K. Werthmann), *Domesticating Vigilantism in Africa* (2011, ed. with T.G. Kirsch), *Mobility, Transnationalism and Contemporary African Societies* (2010, ed.), *Goldgräber in Westafrika* (2010).

Martine Guichard is a senior researcher at the Max Planck Institute for Social Anthropology in Halle/Saale. She has conducted research in Benin and Cameroon on local political cultures, ethnicity, friendship and kinship. Her publications include a book presenting the results of a multidisciplinary project on friendship and kinship, *Freundschaft und Verwandtschaft: Zur Unterscheidung und Verflechtung zweier Beziehungssysteme* (2007, ed. with J.F.K. Schmidt, P. Schuster and F. Trillmich).

Georg Klute is Professor of African Anthropology at the University of Bayreuth. He is chairman of the African Studies Association in Germany (VAD) and member of the executive board of the Africa Borderlands Research Network (ABORNE). His topics of interest range from the state in Africa, para-sovereignty, violent conflicts, ethnicity, Islam and nomadism to development studies and research on monetarization and work in preindustrial societies. His publications include *The Problem of Violence: Local Conflict Settlement in Contemporary Africa* (2011, ed. with B. Embaló), and *Beside the State: Emergent Powers in Contemporary Africa* (2008, ed. with A. Bellagamba).

Stephen P. Reyna is currently an associate researcher at the Max Planck Institute for Social Anthropology in Halle/Saale. Additionally, he is an Honorary Professor at the Humanitarian and Conflict Response Institute of the University of Manchester and Professor Emeritus in Anthropology at the University of New Hampshire. He is interested in social and cultural theory, conflict, and Africa, and has numerous publications dealing with these topics, including *Crude Domination: An Anthropology of Oil* (2012, ed. with A. Behrends and G. Schlee); *Connections: Brain, Mind and Culture in a Social Anthropology* (2002) and *Wars without End* (1990). He was the founding and first editor of the journal *Anthropological Theory*.

Paul Spencer was a member of staff at the School of Oriental and African Studies from 1971 until his retirement, when he became honorary director of the International African Institute. He is now Emeritus Professor of African Anthropology at the University of London. He has undertaken fieldwork among the Samburu and Maasai of Kenya as a social anthropologist, and he has published five books on the area.

Wolde Gossa Tadesse is Program Officer for the African Rift Valley at the Christensen Fund of California. He has been a researcher at the Max Planck Institute of Social Anthropology in Halle/Saale (2000–2003) and holds a Ph.D. from the London School of Economics and Political Science. He has conducted research in Ethiopia and his publications include a two-volume book entitled *Property and Equality* (2006, ed. with T. Widlock).

Richard L. Warms is Professor of Anthropology at Texas State University–San Marcos. He is co-author of *Anthropological Theory: An Introductory History* (now in its 5th edition), *Cultural Anthropology* (now in its 11th edition) and *Culture Counts: A Concise Introduction to Cultural Anthropology*. He is, with R.J. McGee, co-editor of *Theory in Social and Cultural Anthropology: An Encyclopedia* (2013). He has written numerous articles on both merchants and veterans of the *Tirailleurs sénégalais,* the subject of his essay in this volume.

Richard Werbner is Professor Emeritus in African Anthropology, Honorary Research Professor in Visual Anthropology, the University of Manchester. Sometime Glaxo-Smith Kline Senior Fellow (National Humanities Center), Overseas Professor (National Museum of Ethnology, Osaka) and Senior Fellow (Smithsonian Institution), he gave distinguished lectures in 2012 for the American Anthropological Association and the Royal African Society. His books include *Holy Hustlers, Schism and Prophecy* (2011), *Reasonable Radicals and Citizenship in Botswana* (2004), and *Tears of the Dead* (1991) for which he won the Amaury Talbot Prize of the Royal Anthropological Institute. The RAI distributes his two film series, *The Quest for Well-Being in Botswana* and *Forum Follies*.

Index

A
Abu Krider, 166–67
abujal, 60
affection, 36
affines, 26–28, 142, 166
    prescribed patterns of interaction between, 21, 25, 39
age, 1, 5, 23, 25, 26, 29, 41n10, 43, 45, 47, 48, 51–53, 59, 60, 64, 68, 77, 86, 103, 105, 113, 115n4, 141, 152, 160n2
age-grade relations, 102, 114
age mates, 7, 43, 45–49, 51, 167
age organization, 53, 59, 64, 68
age-peers, 43, 44, 47, 49
age-set, 7, 43, 46–52, 60, 107
age system, 43–45, 48, 49–53, 59
Algeria, 145–152
Allan, Graham, 19–20
alliance, 1, 7, 8, 9, 11, 15n10, 39, 40n1, 78, 90, 147, 152, 158, 159, 168
    semicomplex systems of marriage alliances, 8, 15n11
    theory, 7, 42, 49–53
    See also friendship: and political alliance building; marriage
altruism, 49
ambivalence, 3, 34, 39, 42, 45, 111–13, 177
America, 121, 130, 171. *See also* United States
Americans, 24, 35, 171–72
amity, 21, 41n5, 70, 104, 109, 141
Ansâr ud Dîn, 158–60
Aristotle, 165
Armée Révolutionnaire de Libération de l'Azawad (ARLA), 152–56, 158. *See also* rebel movement

army, 11, 126, 145, 153
    French colonial, 129, 147, 152
    Malian, 148, 151, 153, 154, 158
ascendancy (Pullo), 88, 89, 90, 91, 95n21
Atakora, 99, 103, 107, 108, 171
autonomy, 12, 22
    political, 147, 149, 151, 158
avoidance, 7, 26, 50, 52–53, 154
    of conflict, 28

B
baami, 60, 61, 72nn3,4, 73n6
Barma, 165–66, 176–78
Barotse, 168, 170, 174, 178
belayDo, 29
Benin, 10, 31, 33, 36, 41n14, 97–116, 123, 171, 178
betrayal, 29, 36, 58, 104, 108
blood-brotherhood, 2
Bohannan, Laura; Bohannan, Paul, 36, 168, 170
bond-friendship, 9–10, 57–59, 61–72, 73n11. *See also jala*
bonding, 45
boon-companionship, 11, 134–138, 139, 140–43
Boran, 58, 59, 62, 65–68, 70, 73nn5,8,13
Botswana, 11–12, 23, 133–144, 175
Bougouni, 11, 119, 120, 125–29, 130, 132n9
Bourdieu, Pierre, 119, 161, 178n2
bride-wealth, 26, 49, 63, 65
    fixed or open, 26
brothers, 13, 23, 26, 27, 45, 48, 50, 61, 80, 84, 85, 92, 94n7, 98, 110, 115n11, 127, 156
bulikani, 170

Burkina Faso, 8, 37, 74–96, 99, 109, 115n5, 152, 170–71
Bush, George W. (former U.S. president), 172–74, 175, 176, 178, 179n7. *See also* friendship: elite: in the United States

C

calculation, 4, 35, 179n8
Cameroon, 8, 29, 31, 33, 37, 41n14, 78
Campbell, John K., 20, 28–29, 31–32, 35
caravan routes, 61–62
cash economy, 60
cattle entrustment, 8, 79, 81–85, 89, 92, 93, 115n13
Chad, 150, 152, 154, 165–66, 176–77
civil servants, 70, 121, 136, 137, 139–40
civil service, 128, 134–35, 138–41, 175
clan, 2, 7, 29, 48–51, 59, 61, 62, 115n11, 137, 179n9
clanship, 7, 48, 49, 52
class (social), 1, 4–5, 12, 13, 23–24, 25, 53, 119, 143, 145, 160n2, 162, 176, 179n7
    upper (*see* elites)
    working, 171, 172; and friendship (*see under* friendship)
clientage, 123
clientelism, 113
clients, 122–24
closeness, 22, 31, 112
    genealogical, 21, 22, 26
co-habitation, 92–93
Cohen, Yehudi A., 3, 14nn1,5,6, 115n1, 131n1
cohesion, 104, 106, 110–11, 113, 150, 157
    social, 13
commitment, 80, 141

with reference to friendship, 3, 24, 36, 60
with reference to kinship, 13, 135, 143
competition, 26, 27, 32, 36, 38, 44, 51, 75, 85, 94, 139, 141
comradeship (camaraderie), 7, 42–53, 76, 102, 106, 128
comrades in arms, 150, 157
commensality, 36. *See also* tea drinking
confidence, 44, 83, 112, 114, 122, 124, 125, 129
    as distinguished from trust, 131nn3–4
    See also trust
conflict, 2, 10, 26–28, 32, 36, 40n1, 41n9, 59, 65–68, 92, 98, 99, 101, 145, 151, 154, 160n8
    violent, 9, 12, 61, 153, 159–60
    See also under loyalty
consanguinity, 157, 159–60
consumption, 98, 103, 105, 171
contractual relations, 10, 104, 107
conviviality, 11, 65, 104, 107, 144n3
co-operation, 2, 26, 27, 28, 72, 111, 129, 139, 141, 172, 173
cousins, 9, 22, 23, 27, 28, 29, 41n11, 50, 147, 148
craft-workers, 59, 62, 69–71. See also *hauda*
Crete, 37
cultural neurohermeneutic system (CNHS), 164, 179n6
curse, 43, 44, 47–48, 51, 52, 68, 85

D

Dahl, Robert, 178n4
Dassanetch, 62, 63, 70–71, 73nn11,15
daughters, 7, 43, 50–53, 65
debt, 49, 84, 121–23, 125. *See also under* marriage
descent, 1, 3, 7, 21–22, 25, 39, 48–49, 52–53, 145–47, 156–59
    cognatic, 22
    matrilineal, 28

patrilineal, 8, 26, 59, 127
unilineal systems, 21, 22
See also kinship: modes of descent and friendship; kinship: and political alliance building
deindustrialization, 171–72
distance, 21, 28, 109
   social, 109, 110–12
   genealogical, 21, 26, 28
distrust, 26, 93. *See also* mistrust
diviners, 87–89, 95n20
Donahue, Sean, 173
Du Boulay, Juliet, 30
dyad, 35, 42, 163–64, 166
dyadic relations, 7, 94, 101, 108, 109, 111, 113, 134, 147
Dyson, Jane, 119
Dyula, 120, 124

E

East Africa, 9, 26, 42, 48, 130
edanda, 69. *See also* Konso
egalitarian ethos, 7, 136–38
Egypt, 119
Epstein, Arnold L., 133–34
Eisenstadt, Samuel N., 2, 3, 14nn1,6, 115n1
elderhood, 44, 46, 47, 48, 52, 134
elites, 11, 12, 23–24, 133–44, 146, 172–75, 176
   and friendship (*see under* friendship)
emotion, 21, 35, 77, 164, 179n6
emotional economy, 12, 33, 40, 161, 172, 174
endogamy, 6, 8, 37
equality, 23, 46, 69, 101, 141
equity, 101, 106
enemies, 13, 49, 50, 59–63, 65, 67, 150–56
enmity, 30, 63
Ethiopia, 9, 57–73
ethnicity, 1, 6, 20, 23, 25, 34, 58, 63, 70, 135, 136, 139, 142
Europe, 20, 22, 37, 121, 130

exchange, 4, 9, 11, 20, 23, 24, 36, 49, 51, 58, 60, 63–66, 71, 73n10, 76–79, 80, 83–84, 92, 94, 101, 106, 110, 114, 124, 155, 169, 170. *See also* gift; women: exchange of
exile, 12, 146, 147–150, 151, 152, 156, 157, 159
exogamy, 6, 7, 8, 48, 49–50, 51, 59, 61, 78
   age-set, 50, 52

F

favours, 25, 32, 83, 89, 101, 102, 109
fecundity, 86–91, 93
   problems, 8, 84, 86, 87, 89, 95n18, 96n22
femininity
   ideologies of, 5
   performances of, 37
Fischer, Claude S., 19
forces, 7, 11, 49, 50, 67, 81, 85, 93, 100, 121, 130, 133, 152, 153, 158, 161–79
   global, 10
   spiritual, 86–88 (see also *kinkirga*)
force resource, 165, 169–70
   access to, 5; with reference to friendship, 5, 161, 165–67, 169–72, 174, 176–78, 179n10; with reference to kinship, 172, 176–78, 179n10
formality, 26, 123, 124
Fortes, Meyer, 41n5, 172, 179n9
France, 119, 132n8, 145, 146, 152
friendship
   circle, 11, 134–40, 142, 143, 144n6, 175
   difficulties studying, 19, 20, 23, 30–31, 33, 34–35, 39–40
   elite, 11–12, 23–24, 133, 134–44; in the United States, 172–75
   freedom/limits of choice regarding, 5, 25, 28

girls' friendship in the Indian Himalayas, 119
ideal of, 4, 7, 15n10, 36, 112, 113, 176
institutionalized form of, 2–3, 9, 10, 14n6, 28–30, 37, 57, 60–61 (see also *abujal;* bond-friendship; *jala; miso*); best friendship, 2, 28–29, 61 (see also *baami; belayDo*)
and instrumentality, 4, 11, 24, 41n17, 84, 93–94, 106, 112, 125, 128, 129, 165–66, 175–76, 179n8
intercultural friendship in the United States, 35
interethnic, 6, 9, 30, 31–32, 34, 36, 41n15, 57, 58–59, 61–72, 76, 79, 80, 81, 83–84, 85, 86, 87, 89–90, 94, 96n22, 97, 101–116, 135, 140–141, 153–54, 159, 160, 169–70 (see also *jala*); compared to intraethnic friendships, 6, 31, 33–34, 36–37, 83–86
intraethnic, 8, 28–30, 31, 35, 36–37, 76–79, 84, 91, 141, 153, 160
and kinship, 1–2, 6–10, 11, 12, 13, 14, 19, 20–23, 24, 25–30, 31–33, 35, 36, 37–38, 39, 90, 97, 114, 119–20, 125, 129–130, 142–43, 147, 156–60, 177 (see also kinship: marriage and friendship)
and patronage, 10–11, 32, 97, 109–110, 111, 114, 122–25
and political alliance building, 147–50, 159
as source of power, 12, 37, 161–79
as survival strategy, 106
women's, 5, 8, 28–29, 30, 31, 37–38, 41nn10,18, 77 (see also *belayDo*); in Andalusia, 37–38; in Crete, 37; compared to men's friendships, 5, 8, 43, 52; decline of friendships after marriage, 37
working-class friendships, 10, 171–72; in Cairo, 120; in the United States, 171–72
Front Populaire de Libération de l'Azawad (FPLA), 152–53. *See also* rebel movement
Front Populaire de Libération du Sahara Arabe Central (FPLSAC), 149
Fulbe (Pullo), 8, 29, 31, 33–34, 36–37, 74–76, 78–96, 99, 115n13, 169–70, 178
  Mbororo, 29, 36–37, 41n11; Aku, 29
fuld'o (fund'o), 62, 70–71, 73nn7,15

G

Gaborone, 11, 136, 138–40, 143, 175, 176
Ganda Koy, 153, 156, 159
Gareis, Elisabeth, 35
Gemeinschaft, 3
gender, 1, 5, 8, 20, 25, 29, 143
genealogies, and reconstruction of, 12, 157
generosity, 48, 61, 64, 170
Ghana, 74, 99, 100, 179n9
Ghannam, Farha, 119
gift, 36, 49, 52, 59, 61, 64, 69, 71, 77, 78, 89, 103, 106, 121, 174, 177, 179n9
  exchange, 50, 58, 69, 170
Gluckman, Max, 170
godparenthood, 2, 8
gold miners, 10, 97–116, 123, 171, 178
gossip, 29, 77–78, 83–84, 133–34, 143
government, 135, 138, 172–75
  French, 127, 132n8, 148, 153
  Malian, 148, 151–53, 157–58, 167

Greece, 28, 31–32
grazing relationships, 169–70
group indulgence, 45, 47, 49
Guatemala, 35
Gulliver, Philip H., 20, 22–23, 27–28, 41n9

H
habitus, 113, 178n2
Hamar, 58, 62, 63, 65, 67, 69–71, 73n9
hauda, 59, 69–71. See also Konso
Hausa, 74, 109, 120, 124
Hayward, Richard, 57
hierarchy, 5, 12, 77, 99, 100, 114, 137, 167
history, rewriting of, 12, 156–57
Hobbes, Thomas, 178n4
homophily, 5, 6, 134
Hor (Arbore), 9, 57, 59–72, 73nn5,8–10,13
hospitality, 43, 48, 64, 65, 170
host-guest relations, 8, 10, 108–10. See also *tutorat*
host-stranger relations, 79–80, 81, 83, 143. See also host-guest relations
hostility, 12, 38, 49, 68, 85, 152, 159
Houis, Maurice, 87
hur-or, 168
hypogamy, 52

I
imidiwen, 149
immigrants, 99, 101, 107, 109, 110, 111
    clusters of, 101, 107–8, 111
incest, 7, 50–52
India, 119
Indians (Guatemala), 35
industrialization, 3
inheritance, 7, 21, 25, 26, 39, 73, 163, 177
    impartible or partible, 25
    See also kinship: patterns of inheritance and friendship

in-law relations, symbolic, 78, 86, 90–92
institutions, 7, 9, 10, 11, 42, 57–58, 72, 74–76, 101, 107, 109, 114, 121, 129–30, 131n3, 136, 138, 144n5, 163, 167, 168, 170–75, 177
    banking, 125, 129
    modern, 167, 171, 172, 174, 176
    nonmodern, 167
integration, 3, 9, 32, 34, 79, 81, 91–94, 98, 105, 108–10, 158
    differentiated, 110
intimacy, 11, 31, 41n13, 46, 50, 85, 111, 112, 115n13, 139, 147
instrumentality. See *under* friendship
Islam, 89, 95n18, 122, 124–25, 128, 132n5
    sharia law, 158
Islamic Legion, 149, 151, 154, 156, 157
Ivory Coast, 28, 82, 99, 121

J
Jacobson, David, 23, 41n15
jala, 61–69, 70, 73nn5,13
joking relations, joking relationships, 9, 15n12, 79, 80–81, 92, 94n7, 147

K
Kabre, 36, 37, 78
Kalanga, 136–37, 138–42, 175
kapam, 165
Kenya, 26, 42–53, 63, 70, 169
Kennedy, Robinette, 37
kin-friends, 21–23, 30
kinkirga, 86, 88, 95nn14,16. See also forces: spiritual
kinship, 1–14, 19–24, 27–34, 38, 39–40, 41nn5,11, 48, 64, 76–78, 81, 85, 90, 91, 97, 101, 103, 104, 113–14, 115n8, 119–32, 135, 142–43, 145–60, 161, 165, 167, 172, 176–78
    as idiom applied to friendship, 6–7, 12, 23, 60, 114, 147, 149

friendship; compared to, 6, 9, 19, 30, 143, 177; overlap with, 6, 19-20, 21–23, 26–28, 29, 34, 39, 97
milk kinship, 7–8, 15n10
modes of descent and friendship, 21, 25, 39
patterns of inheritance and friendship, 7, 23, 25, 39
patterns of postnuptial residence and friendship, 7, 25, 37–38, 39
and political alliance building, 151, 156–59
spiritual, 8, 92
transformation of friendship into, 7–9, 11, 36–37, 108, 120, 125, 129, 130 (see also marriage: and friendship)
See also godparenthood; pseudo-kinship; spiritual parenthood
Konso, 57–59, 62, 63, 67, 69–72, 73nn5,7,8,14,15

L

labour, 10, 82, 83–84, 124, 127, 141, 163, 166, 168–69, 171, 172, 176, 177, 178, 179n9
  migration, 23, 97–116
Ladinos, 35
leadership, 13, 72, 137, 155, 159
Lévi-Strauss, Claude, 7, 15n11, 49–51, 52
Libya, 145–9, 150–51, 154, 156, 157
Liebow, Elliott, 24, 179n10
life style, 92, 104–6, 111, 114, 116nn17,22
liminal space of migration, 110
liminality, 10, 91
lineage, 2, 28, 48, 50, 52, 78, 160n2
loan, 69, 122–23, 129, 131n4, 172
loyalty, 6, 21, 68
  conflicts of, 3, 28, 30
  peer-group, 42–53
Luning, Sabine, 81, 115n5

M

Maasai, 7, 10, 42–53, 169, 178
Maison des Anciens Combattants (MAC), 126, 128
Mali, 12–13, 99, 119–32, 145–60
Manchester School, 133, 144n2
manyata, 44–49
market economy, 9
markets, 4, 63, 99, 101, 120, 121, 141
marriage, 7–8, 11–12, 15n11, 21, 27, 36, 38, 39, 43–45, 48–52, 61, 65, 75, 76, 77, 78, 81, 84, 90, 95nn18,21, 125, 154, 156–58
  'marriage debt', 49
  and friendship, 7–8, 12, 15n10, 36, 37, 38, 39, 43, 86, 90, 91, 96n28, 142
  See also alliance; kinship: transformation of friendship into
Martinelli, Bruno, 77, 79, 80, 91
Marx, Karl, 162
masculinity
  ideologies of, 5
  representations of, 106
matrilocality. See under postnuptial residence: matrilocal
Mauss, Marcel, 15n12, 49–50, 106, 113
mediator, 10, 95n20, 109, 110, 152
merchants, 11, 119, 120–125, 128, 129, 131nn2–3
  aspiring, 121–23, 125
  See also traders
Merker, Moritz, 48–49
migrants, 10, 12, 98–100, 102–3, 106, 108–10, 113–14, 115n4, 145–51, 159
migration, 10–13, 23, 25, 76, 82, 84, 95n12, 99, 103–4, 108, 110, 147, 150. See also under labour
milk kinship. See under kinship
militia, 152, 153, 155–56, 158, 159
mining team, 100, 102–4, 107, 111, 114. See also working team

miso, 60, 72n2
mistrust, 106. *See also* distrust
modernity, 20, 129, 131n3, 171, 172
modernization, 130
Moors, 152, 154
Moose (Moaga, Mossi), 8, 74–96, 109, 169–70, 178
money, 77, 84, 100, 103, 104, 105, 108, 109, 112, 121, 122–23, 127, 130, 141, 166, 172–73
moral economy, 107
morality, moralities, 50, 52, 102–29
moran, 44–47, 49, 51, 52
*moran*hood, 44–46
Morewagae, Isaia, 140, 141
Mouvement National de l'Azawad (MNA), 158. *See also* rebel movement
Mouvement National pour la Libération de l'Azawad (MNLA), 158, 160. *See also* rebel movement
Mouvement Patriotique Ganda Koy (MPGK). *See* Ganda Koy
Mouvement Populaire de l'Azawad (MPA), 154–56, 158, 160n10. *See also* rebel movement
Muammar Gaddafi, 149
Muslims, 89, 95n18, 124, 132n5
    Sunna, 132n5
    Wahhabi, 124–25, 132n5

N

Ndendeuli, 22–23, 27–28, 41n9
neighbourliness, 39, 82, 111
neolocality. *See* postnuptial residence: neolocal
networking, 110–11
networks, 4, 22, 26, 41n9, 76, 92, 110, 111, 113, 114, 119, 120, 127–28, 129, 133, 136–37, 140, 142, 164, 173, 179n6
    friendship, 4, 9, 12, 22, 24, 37–38, 52, 57–73, 84–85, 103, 110, 115n4, 127, 130–31, 142, 167
    kinship, 85, 113, 120, 130–31, 142
    trade/trading, 71, 72, 76, 100 (see also *fuld'o (fuln'o)*; *hauda*)
nicknames, 105, 137
Niger, 145, 146, 147, 148, 149, 150, 152, 156, 159
Nigeria, 168–69
nongovernmental organization (NGO), 9, 66, 69
Nietzsche, Friedrich, 161–62, 164, 175
nobles, noble tribe, 12–13, 149, 154–57, 159

O

obligation, 2, 13, 28, 48, 60, 62, 109, 110, 131n3, 170
    moral, 79, 81, 106, 112, 129
    with reference to age-set membership, 47–48
    with reference to friendship, 60, 83, 84, 86, 90, 142, 177
    with reference to kinship, 26, 27, 30, 33, 142, 143
ol-chore, 49, 169
otherness, 6, 34, 75, 79

P

partnership
    business, 134, 175
    trading, 2, 71, 141
patrilocality. *See* postnuptial residence: patrilocal
patron-client relations, 35–36, 101, 107, 111, 131n4. *See also* friendship: and patronage
patronage, 11, 31–32, 97, 103, 109, 113–14, 123. *See also under* friendship
patrons, 121, 125
Paine, Robert, 14n5, 40n3, 115n1
peace agreement/treaty, 66, 151, 156, 160n10
    National Pact (*Pacte National*, Mali), 153, 154, 156

peer group, 47, 102, 105, 107. *See also under* loyalty
perceptual culture, 163, 179n6
Perinbaum, B. Marie, 124
Piot, Charles D., 36, 37, 78
Pitt-Rivers, Julian, 23, 24, 25
pogroms, 152–54
polyadic relations, 101
polygyny, 43
postnuptial residence, 7, 25, 37–38, 39
    matrilocal, 38
    patrilocal, 28, 29, 38, 127
    neolocal, 38
    uxorilocal, 38
    virilocal, 28, 29, 38
    See also kinship: patterns of postnuptial residence and friendship
poverty, 75, 172, 176, 179n10
    and friendship, 5, 24, 64, 93, 165, 171–72, 176, 178
power, 4, 5, 12, 13, 25, 30, 32, 33, 37, 38–39, 40, 44, 47, 51, 52, 59, 62, 64, 74, 75, 85, 87, 88, 119, 123, 133, 134–35, 137, 143, 148, 156, 160n7, 161–79
procedural culture, 163–64, 166, 171, 174, 176, 177–78, 179nn6,10
processual approach, to friendship, 36, 114
property, 25, 66, 68, 71–72, 82, 100
protection
    of friends (during visits), 64, 66–68
    of the weak, 155
pseudo-kinship, 8. *See also* godparenthood; kinship: spiritual; spiritual parenthood
Putnam, Robert, 132n10

Q
qawot, 59, 62, 67, 68, 69

R
rafiq, 165, 166–67

rebel movement, 12, 146–47, 150, 152–54, 156, 159, 160n2
rebellion, 12, 13, 51, 146, 148, 151–53, 156, 159, 160. *See also* upheaval
reciprocity, 8, 69, 77, 78, 101–4, 106, 116n6, 165, 166
    balanced, 77
    delayed, 103, 113
    generalized, 113, 168, 170, 172, 174
reconciliation, 13, 68, 156–57, 159
reegdo, 85
reementaaga, 76–77
Reina, Rubin E., 35–36, 41n17
reintegration, 156, 157
risk-minimization, 25, 98, 168–69
ritual leader, 59, 62, 67. See also *qawot*
rivalry, 26, 32, 38, 43, 51, 52, 77, 84, 141

S
Sarakatsani, 28, 31–32
Schlee, Günther, 26, 160n8
secrecy, 28, 32–33, 82
segre, 86, 88
Seligman, Adam, 131n3
Senufo, 28–29
sentiment, 148, 156, 174, 179n8
sharing
    ethic, 102, 104, 179n8
    ethos of, 10, 45
    rules, 102
shoreisho, 49
siblings, 25, 26, 127
siiga, 86, 88
Silver, Allan, 2, 4, 112, 165–66, 175–76, 179n8
slaves (former), 155
Sikasso, 11, 119, 120–25, 128, 130, 131n3
Simmel, Georg, 42–43
Sobania, Neal W., 57, 58, 73n8
sociability, 31, 81, 109, 113, 114, 142

sociality, 143
social capital, 4, 161
social change, 13, 129
solidarity, 9, 13, 34, 52, 107, 127–29, 158
   diffuse, 2–3
Songhay, 152, 153, 156, 159
sons, 10, 43, 44, 46, 50, 86, 109, 122, 127, 143
Spain, 37–38
spheres of exchange, 36, 78
spiritual parenthood, 74, 76, 86–94. *See also* kinship: spiritual; pseudo-kinship
Stack, Carol B., 5, 24, 179n10
stock-friends/stock-partnership/stock-partners, 26
Stone, Linda, 22
strangerhood, 78, 79, 91
stratum, strata (social), 12, 148, 149, 155, 160
string, 162–64, 166, 167, 168, 172, 178, 179n7
'string being theory' (SBT), 5, 161–64, 166, 168–70, 172, 174–76, 178n2, 179n8
Susser, Ida, 171–72

T
Tallensi, 174, 179n9
Tanzania, 22–23, 27–28, 41n9, 42–53, 169
tea drinking, 123–24
Tiv, 168–69, 174, 178
theory of size, 6, 20
Tirailleurs sénégalais, 11, 119–20, 125–26, 132n6
Tönnies, Ferdinand, 3, 120
Togo, 36, 37, 78, 100
total social institution, 113
trade, 58, 62, 69, 71, 73n8, 108, 115n8, 120–21, 124, 129, 131n1, 141. *See also fuld'o (fund'o)*; networks: trade/trading; partnership: trading

traders, 58, 59, 62, 67, 69–71, 74, 100, 107, 110, 111, 116n14, 120, 122, 170. *See also hauda*; merchants
trading partnership. *See under* partnership
transhumance, 79–80, 83, 92, 169
triad, 42
triadic relations, 101
tribal affiliation, 150, 160
trust, 3, 6, 11, 21, 25, 31, 38, 41n13, 44, 48, 58, 61, 78, 82, 83, 86, 98, 101, 106, 111, 112, 121, 131n3, 134, 140–42, 144n5, 166. *See also* confidence
Tuareg, 12, 145–60
Tuareg nation, 145, 146, 150, 151, 159
tudentaaga, 76–77
tutorat, 108–10. *See also* host-guest relations
Tswana, 136, 140–41
Tylor, Edward B., 50, 51

U
Uganda, 23, 51
Uhl, Sarah, 37
United States, 5, 20, 22, 24, 35, 132n10, 161, 168, 171–74, 179n10. *See also* America
unity, 45, 46, 47, 49, 59, 146, 157, 159
upheaval, 12, 145–60. *See also* rebellion
urbanization, 3–4, 129–30, 143
utility. *See* friendship: and instrumentality
uxorilocality. *See* postnuptial residence: uxorilocal

V
vassals, vassal tribe, 12–13, 149, 154–57
Veblen, Thorstein, 139
veiling, 30–40, 161, 172, 174

veterans, 11, 119–20, 125–32
veterans' association, 127–29
violence, 115n3, 126, 145–60, 163
virilocality. *See* postnuptial residence: virilocal
voluntary associations, 120, 141

W

Waller, Richard, 47, 73n8
war, 12–13, 59, 61, 127, 130, 146–47, 148, 152, 154, 155, 156, 157, 159
    World War I, World War II, 126
warriorhood, 43
Wata, 62, 67
wealth, 3, 5, 23, 25, 36, 46, 58, 82, 84, 85, 93, 119, 121, 137, 173, 176
Weber, Max, 120, 131
West Africa, 9, 10, 79, 80, 97–116, 120, 124, 127

wife-givers, 26
wife-receivers, 50
women
    exchange of, 7, 50, 78, 91
    women's friendships (*see under* friendship)
working class. *See under* class
working team, 10, 101, 102–4, 113. *See also* mining team
Wright, Paul H., 5

Y

yiggiraagu, 78
youth culture, 98

Z

Zambia, 168, 170
zoodo, 77
zoadamba, 77